Delinquent

Delinquent

INSIDE AMERICA'S DEBT MACHINE

Elena Botella

UNIVERSITY OF CALIFORNIA PRESS

University of California Press
Oakland, California

© 2022 by Elena Botella

Library of Congress Cataloging-in-Publication Data

Names: Botella, Elena, 1991- author.
Title: Delinquent : inside America's debt machine / Elena Botella.
Description: Oakland,California : University of California Press, [2022] |
    Includes bibliographical references and index.
Identifiers: LCCN 2021055861 (print) | LCCN 2021055862 (ebook) |
    ISBN 9780520380356 (cloth) | ISBN 9780520380363 (ebook)
Subjects: LCSH: Consumer credit—United States—History. | Banks and
    banking—United States.
Classification: LCC HG3756.U54 B68 2022 (print) | LCC HG3756.U54
    (ebook) | DDC 332.7/43—dc23/eng/20211227
LC record available at https://lccn.loc.gov/2021055861
LC ebook record available at https://lccn.loc.gov/2021055862

Manufactured in the United States of America

31 30 29 28 27 26 25 24 23 22
10 9 8 7 6 5 4 3 2 1

Contents

Illustrations

TABLES

Preface

ELENA: Has there ever been a time when you weren't sure how you were going to pay your credit card bill?

JOE: No. I think I've gotten right up against the edge of that.

   The closest I've gotten is like, having to really not eat for two days, you know, to pay this bill because I know I'm gonna get paid Friday.

   So, it's always been something where the problem will alleviate itself within the next seventy-two hours. But I've gotten that close.

.   .   .   .   .

When things go wrong in America, we are often on our own.

At the time I'm writing this sentence, the wait list for one night in a bed in a San Francisco homeless shelter hasn't dipped below one thousand people in over a year.[1]

And although by law you'll get medical care at the emergency room even if you don't have enough money, that assurance doesn't apply to the rest of the hospital. If you get cancer or diabetes and you don't have insurance, or can't afford to meet your deductible, nothing in America guarantees a doctor will see you, or that you'll get your prescriptions filled.

Nothing in America guarantees that you'll have the cash you need to get your car out of the impound lot if it gets towed, or that you'll be able to pay your rent if your boss stiffs you on your paycheck.

This is the world in which America's lenders operate—both the Fortune 100 companies like JPMorgan Chase and Citi, and the more fragmented family of "specialty" lenders like Ace Cash Express, OneMain Financial, Credit One, Merrick Bank, and CashCall.

These companies say, "We'll help you . . . for a price," when nobody else offers help at all. Every action these lenders take is seemingly justified by their borrowers' lack of alternatives: after all, what's worse—to gouge the needy or to ignore their needs completely? High-interest debt is accrued by the unemployed, and by the working poor, desperate to avoid material hardship. But high-interest debt is also accrued by middle-income and high-earning people, sometimes accrued on wants, and sometimes on needs, sometimes after great deliberation and planning, sometimes impulsively, and sometimes by people struggling with addiction. I've talked to people around the country about their debt, and sometimes they are glad they borrowed money, sometimes they aren't, and often, they're not sure.

The price charged for all these loans is substantial. In 2018, more than 100 million Americans paid a total of $143 billion in interest and fees on credit cards, payday loans, title loans, and pawn shop interest, a cost of $1,184 per borrower per year.[2] The vast majority of this interest—88%— was paid to credit card companies. Credit card borrowing is not a small part of the American economy; it is central to the economic lives of roughly half of American adults.

I worked at one of the country's biggest consumer lenders, Capital One, for five years, eventually taking charge of the company's "revolver proactive credit limit increase program." That means I managed the analysts who, by algorithm, decided which already-indebted people would get the chance to take on more debt. I saw the inner workings of the industry's well-oiled debt machine: a system of experimentation, product design, marketing, and underwriting practices engineered to push those Americans who could be pushed into as much debt as they could be pushed into, without, ideally, pushing them over the edge into default. And, as I'll explain, this industry's machine doesn't require the existence of corporate tycoons who wear Monopoly Man hats while they grind the faces of the poor into the dirt. The story of consumer debt in America isn't about a few bad people breaking laws and telling blatant lies, but, rather, about the market, political, and social forces that allow the machine to operate in plain sight. Those reaping the profits get the chance to sleep peacefully.

In *Delinquent: Inside America's Debt Machine*, I'll take you on a journey through the open-office floor plans of glassy skyscrapers, to the courtrooms where judges rule that lenders are free to garnish parents' paychecks, to street corners in Detroit, to kitchen tables in Sacramento, and through my own journey as a banker-turned-journalist trying to grapple with a few haunting questions. When is access to credit a good thing, something to protect and promote, and when is debt a harmful thing that sets American families back? And can we create a lending system that continues to make credit available for families that need it, without pushing people into crushing debt?

There are plenty of people who suggest a better system isn't possible. On the right, you have defenders of the financial sector, who insist that banks are barely scraping by, charging the bare minimum in interest. These voices suggest that any attempt to rein in industry excesses will just make it harder for struggling families who need loans to get them. On the left, commentators are pushing back against decades of misleading rhetoric that claims only irresponsible, or lazy, or stupid people struggle financially. To create a strong counterargument, these commentators insist we hold as given the proposition that all financial decisions made by the working class were absolutely the perfect choice given the circumstances.

But clinging too hard to this assumption leads us to a grim (and inaccurate) conclusion: Americans needed to borrow exactly the amount of money they ended up borrowing, and, therefore, the best we can hope for is a discounted price on all that crushing debt.

And across the political spectrum, advocates, everyday people, and policymakers frequently assume that access to credit, by and large, is a good thing. They push for more lending (and, therefore, more debt) to historically excluded communities, without always reckoning with what those larger debt burdens will mean for the borrowers. People who believe they are fighting the banks often, without realizing it, take as given a pro-bank precept: credit is, essentially, good.

I'll make two main arguments in *Delinquent* that together explain why a more humane lending system is possible, without ignoring the basic financial realities constraining banks and families.

The first argument I'll make is that Americans come to regret a huge proportion of the principal of the debt that they borrow. The problem isn't just that prices are too high; it's that borrowing money was never in the families' best interest in the first place. As I'll show in Part I of *Delinquent*, Americans are induced into unnecessary debt through bank marketing, product design, and "customer management strategies" that exploit common weaknesses in how we think about money. The amount of consumer debt isn't driven by the amount of money consumers need to borrow: it's driven by how much money the banks have chosen to lend. And I'll argue that effective consumer protection needs to push back against the strategies banks use to tempt American families into unproductive debt, rather than just regulating interest rates and fees. I'll call this "the principal argument," that America's debt machine leads the country to borrow too much money. Importantly, debt can be a crushing burden even at a 0% interest rate. Chapter 1 takes a look at the United States prior to the introduction of credit cards, and before most Americans held any consumer debt. Chapter 2 examines the historical conditions that gave rise to mass indebtedness in the second half of the twentieth century. Unlike some authors that attribute the rise in consumer debt to stagnant wages or a rise in the cost of living, I make the supply-driven argument that legal and economic events increased the profit margin of consumer lending, and, therefore, made banks more eager to peddle debt, irrespective of what was in the best interest of ordinary families. Chapter 3 takes a deeper look at who has credit card debt in America: disproportionately Americans between the ages of forty-six and fifty, near the peak of their income, who have had credit card debt continuously or intermittently throughout their adult lives. Credit cards, as they are most commonly used, aren't a short-term bridge out of a bad situation; they're an anchor around the ankles of families who otherwise had a fighting shot at economic stability. Chapter 4 explores the fact that credit card debt *falls* during recessions and *rises* when the economy is doing well—it fails to be a buffer against economic insecurity, and, in fact, compounds insecurity. Chapter 5 takes a closer look at the specific tactics that banks have engineered to encourage indebtedness, many of which, I'll argue, should be more tightly regulated.

The second argument I'll make is that Americans consistently overpay on their debt. As I'll show in Chapter 6, Americans, generally, aren't being charged the "competitive price" for their debt—that is, the interest rate that the lowest-bidding bank or credit union would want to offer them at an auction. The high interest rates of credit cards, payday loans, and many personal loans aren't an inevitable byproduct of the risk level of the borrowers. In fact, the debt machine prevents most borrowers from finding the lowest-price loan that they're eligible for. "Big Data" and machine learning have helped lenders lower the costs of lending and reduce their odds of lending to a customer who will immediately default, but all the gains from this innovation went into shareholder's pockets instead of bringing down consumers' borrowing costs. I'll call this "the interest argument." Chapter 7 assesses what a fair price for credit would be. While I still believe in the power of market forces, competition, and incentives, as I'll show in *Delinquent,* in the consumer debt market, competition has failed to serve American families.

Finally, in Chapter 8, I look at America's "credit invisible" population, and explore why some Americans choose to or are forced to live free of debt. In Chapter 9, I'll conclude with specific proposals for how to build a lending system that better serves the needs of low-income and middle-income Americans.

I'm writing *Delinquent* at a moment in which credit card debt and personal loans have largely disappeared as a political issue (although student loans, of course, are highly politically salient). By contrast, most Americans, including most indebted Americans, have accepted the credit card debt machine as a necessary evil, an inevitable byproduct of an economic system in which crummy jobs and high medical bills push Americans into lenders' arms. In 2010, at the apogee of the financial crisis, Congress passed a law, the CARD Act, that reined in some of the most misleading and egregious practices of the credit card industry; the remaining industry practices looked, on the surface, defensible. The credit cards issued by the biggest banks are now largely free of the most egregious pre-crisis product terms—"clean" of obvious gotchas.

I'm often asked about my time working at Capital One, by people who assume I must have hated my job. The truth is, most days, I loved my job. My coworkers, including the company's executives, were for the most part very friendly people, who earnestly shared a (self-serving) belief that providing "access to credit" was a very good thing to be doing. Without absolving myself or anyone else of moral responsibility, I came to understand something about the debt machine: it might have bad actors, but it doesn't rely on the existence of bad people. I'm writing *Delinquent* not because I have an axe to grind, but because we have a better economy to build.

Welcome inside the debt machine.

A Note

In this book, when I use the term "consumer credit," I mean all loans made to individuals or families, except student loans, home mortgages, auto loans, and loans intended for use in a small business.

Delinquent focuses on credit cards, but I'll also talk about the products that Americans sometimes use instead of credit cards, especially payday loans (a loan where payment is normally requested in full within fifteen or thirty days, typically with an interest rate above 300%), and personal loans (any loan made to an individual, typically with fixed, monthly payments, which includes loans made by some banks and credit unions, by newer "fintechs" like LendingClub and SoFi, and by storefront installment lenders like OneMain Financial), and loans made at the "point of sale" at online and physical retailers, either by the merchant itself, or by a lending partner like Affirm, Klarna, or a bank.

PART I The Principal Argument

1 The Time before the Debt Machine

We could have a country without much debt, and I know this to be true, because we once had a country without so much debt. Once you realize that Americans haven't always been as deeply indebted as they are now, it becomes easier to see that this system of debt had to be built, and hence, that our system of debt could also be torn down.

Credit cards, particularly, are a relatively recent invention. Although the first credit card, Diners Club, was invented in 1950, it took a while for credit cards to gain any traction. In 1961, while many stores had their own credit plans, only 1 percent of stores accepted general purpose credit cards issued by outside banks.[1]

Of course, while credit cards are new, credit is not.

Naomi Sizemore Trammel was born in 1887, and started working in South Carolina's textile mills at the age of ten; her father and mother had both died in quick succession—her father of a fever. While her younger siblings were taken in by uncles and aunts, she and her older sister Alma had to find jobs, so they found work spinning string and running frames of cloth. Naomi married at twenty-one to Percy Long, who worked in the weave room at Greer Mill, and who pitched for Greer Mill's baseball team, the Spinners. During the Great Depression, the mills laid off workers and cut back on hours.

"We couldn't even find a job nowhere, everybody else was laid off around. That was a bad time. We got in debt, but nobody didn't refuse us. And when we all went back to work, we soon paid it off. It just come around so good," said Sizemore Trammel. "Well, we was out of work a pretty good while. And there was a man, Frank Howard, we were trading with him, out there at the crossing, getting groceries and things from him, before that happened. And we always paid our debts. And we's getting milk from another man. And so we got in debt with that, and they wouldn't cut us off. So when we went to work, we'd pay our bills. We can pay a little bit, you know, add on to our bills. First thing you know, we come out on top. It wasn't near hard's it seem. But we didn't know what in world we's gon' do."[2]

That's what American debt looked like for much of the 1800s and 1900s. If you weren't a farmer, or a small business owner borrowing money for your company, typically, any money you borrowed was lent from whatever store sold the thing you needed to buy. Stores lent people like Naomi money to earn a profit on the goods they were selling, and occasionally, as a social courtesy, not necessarily to make a profit from the loan interest itself. These storekeeper-customer relationships were sometimes friendly, and sometimes predatory. Sometimes, like with Naomi, these relationships were personal, while for shoppers using installment credit at larger department stores during the same decade, the exchanges were at arm's length: credit, there, was provided after the submission of a formal application, with the merchant usually reviewing data from by a locally run credit bureau before making the lending decision.[3] But by most accounts, the customers who purchased goods on credit in the late 1800s and early 1900s were *less* profitable for shopkeepers and department stores than those who purchased with cash.[4] Credit was a means for retailers to drive sales, not its own center of profit; the costs of extending the credit and the interest collected generally canceled one another out.

It should be noted that the book you are holding is just one of many written throughout American history with complaints about household debt. Benjamin Franklin's *Poor Richard's Almanac,* dating back to 1732, but widely quoted throughout the Victorian Era, was littered with adages like "The second vice is Lying, the first is running into Debt."[5] The moral panic around consumer debt continued into the 1800s with Mark Twain's *The Gilded Age: A Tale of Today,* into the 1900s with Upton Sinclair's *The*

Jungle, which described in great detail the Rudkus family's installment debt, and once the credit card arrived, in books like Hillel Black's 1961 *Buy Now, Pay Later*.[6] But while there have always been some Americans in debt, and some who worried about the Americans in debt, the fact is our current moment *is* distinctive in two important ways. The first is that, by every conceivable measure—in absolute terms, per capita, adjusted for inflation, and as a percentage of household income or household assets— the amount of consumer debt is higher in the twenty-first century than it was at any point in the twentieth century, with the precise amount of credit card debt since roughly the year 2000 mostly ebbing and flowing in the opposite direction as what you might expect: more debt when the economy is doing well, and less debt when the economy is doing poorly.

What is less commonly discussed, though, is the second key distinguishing factor about American debt today relative to any other point in the past: the prices paid for credit card debt have risen substantially. The average credit card interest rate, 17.14 percent, reached a twenty-five-year high in May 2019, a fact that isn't explained by Federal Reserve interest rates, loan default rates, or any other cost of doing business.[7] Sitting with these two facts together begs the question, why exactly are Americans saddled with more debt, and more expensive debt, than ever before?

While the rest of the book will take you on a tour of the United States as it sits today, introducing you to Americans in debt, and to the managers, investors, and machines that control that debt, I want to share with you a bit more about how Americans managed their budgets prior to the introduction of the credit card, because the more I came to understand about the history of debt in the United States the less certain I was that our status quo was defensible.

WHEN ALL CREDIT WAS "BUSINESS" CREDIT

Until the 1910s and 1920s, most states capped maximum interest rates on loans as low as 6 percent or 8 percent per year. It was rare for a chartered bank to make a loan directly to an individual if that person wasn't a businessman.[8] Although banks didn't lend directly to families, there were still a few (legal) options for cash loans, mostly pawn shops, and companies that issued installment loans, who were often at the time called "industrial lenders" because they focused on serving wage workers with industrial jobs in big cities. The largest of these industrial lenders, Household Finance Corporation, was founded in 1878, acquired by HSBC in 2003, and then sold off to Capital One and Springleaf Financial during the 2010s.[9] As late as the 1910s, though, wealthy individuals were one of the most important forms of credit: in 1910, 33 percent of home loans came directly from another individual person, rather than a financial institution.[10] When the first income tax was created by Congress in 1913, all forms of loan interest were tax-deductible, reflecting members of Congress' assumption that people only borrowed money if they were entrepreneurs, not to cover normal household emergencies or buy household goods. With that assumption, all loans were assumed to be business expenses, so of course all loan interest would need to be deducted against business revenues to calculate taxable business profits.[11]

Until the introduction of the credit card, most working-class Americans had *no* non-mortgage debt at any given point in time, and in fact, that situation persisted until 1983: until that point, most Americans in the bottom half of the income distribution didn't have a single dollar of installment loan debt, auto loan debt, credit card debt, student loan debt, or retail debt. When working-class Americans did borrow money, to buy a car, or a dishwasher, or, less commonly, to deal with an emergency, the amounts borrowed were comparatively low. Non-"retail" credit, by which I mean, credit that was not tied to a specific purchase, was even less common than retail credit. In 1950, families in the bottom half of income distribution had an average of twenty-seven cents worth of non-housing debt for every dollar of income. By 2016, that number had tripled: seventy-seven cents worth of non-housing debt for every dollar of income. For families in the top half of the income distribution, retail borrowing was already common by 1950, as postwar families outfitted their new homes with appliances and furniture purchased on credit, but their own levels of debt also tripled over the same period: these families had 10 cents worth of non-housing debt for every dollar of income in 1950, and thirty-seven cents in 2016.[12]

I don't mean to paint a utopian picture of life before credit cards. Life, clearly, was not perfect, and even if Congress assumed that all household borrowing was for business purposes, the questions of who received credit, and on what terms, were absolutely urgent.

It may have been the case that debt in the late 1800s and early 1900s wasn't a major part of life for Americans who weren't farmers or small business owners, but of course, for much of American history, most people *were* farmers or worked on farms. According to the 1860 census, of the 8.3 million Americans who were considered to have an "occupation"—free, adult men, mostly—3.2 million, or nearly 40 percent, were counted as farmers or farm laborers.[13] An additional 4 million Black Americans lived in slavery, the vast majority of whom were forced to work in agriculture.[14] These enslaved people made up roughly 15 percent of the country's population.[15] All-in, roughly half of American adults spent their days farming, some in enslavement, and others who kept fruits of their labor.

Our highly unequal system of banking has its roots in this era. Before the Civil War, enslaved people were a valuable form of collateral that made it easier for White enslavers to get loans: lenders considered enslaved Black people to be even better collateral than land, because people can easily move or be moved, while land is fixed in place. And as a result, credit was more accessible to slaveholders than it was to free farmers in the North or West.[16] JPMorgan Chase, Bank of America, Wells Fargo, and U.S. Bancorp are all known to have accepted enslaved people as loan collateral.[17]

Contemporaries who lived through the Civil War might have initially assumed that the Confederacy's defeat would ruin White enslavers financially, but these enslavers became the major beneficiaries of the National Bankruptcy Act passed in 1867. The founding fathers had planned for a federal bankruptcy law, even giving Congress the power to legislate bankruptcy in the Constitution, but Congress had a hard time reconciling the competing interests of creditors and debtors, farmers and merchants. Earlier attempts at writing bankruptcy legislation, in 1800 and in 1841, were both repealed within three years of their passage.[18]

The 1867 law, passed just one year after the Civil War ended, was considerably friendlier to debtors than the 1841 law. According to historian Rowena Olegario, although Southerners made up only a quarter of the population, they held most the debt in 1867, and accounted for 36 percent of all bankruptcy filings under the 1867 law. The new law gave Southern enslavers a chance to protect their land and other assets: former

Confederates were given a fresh start, and the children and grandchildren of former enslavers remained at the top of social and economic life in the South through the 1940s.[19]

The average interest rate for farm mortgages in the South after the Civil War was around 8 percent, but other types of debt relationships emerged as well: sharecropping and tenant farming.[20] As Mehsra Baradaran writes in *The Color of Money: Black Banks and The Racial Wealth Gap*, under a sharecropping arrangement, "Sharecroppers paid for the land, supplies, and tools using credit, and they paid back their debts with their crop yields, typically with nothing left to spare. Usually the landlord did the calculations himself, and the illiterate debtor would have to trust that he had made no surplus year after year."[21] Persistent indebtedness, clearly, was not invented in the twentieth century.

Sharecroppers' debt could be said to be a close cousin of the institution of slavery, and a distant cousin of the types of debt Americans hold today. Black southerners could be arrested and jailed under vagrancy laws if they didn't show a work certificate from a White employer, and even if Black southerners saved enough cash, laws often stopped Black people from buying land owned by White people.[22] It's easy to look at the situation of most Black southerners in the late 1800s and early 1900s, and identify that their sharecropping debt wasn't a voluntary arrangement: White political elites had foreclosed on the alternative ways that Black southerners could have made a living. The question of whether Americans today have freely chosen their debts is much thornier.

While their position may have been enviable compared to Black sharecroppers, the burdens of debt nevertheless weighed on White farmers in the South and West, and many ordinary White farmers demanded looser credit at lower interest rates. When William Jennings Bryan gave the famous "cross of gold" speech at the Democratic National Convention in 1896, arguing that the gold standard helped wealthy bankers at the expense of farmers, who paid higher loan interest rates as a result, it helped him leave the convention with the Democratic nomination for the White House.[23] For American farmers, the terms and availability of credit could make the difference between destitution and sufficiency.

The case of home mortgage credit in the twentieth century follows a similar arc: who received credit, and on what terms, determined who would become rich, and who would remain poor. Black families in the 1920s through the 1950s were forbidden, even in most northern cities, from receiving mortgages to buy houses in White neighborhoods, and were charged high markups to receive mortgages in Black neighborhoods, if they qualified at all. No individual choices a Black American could make would override their race in the eyes of lenders, or in the eyes of the Federal Housing Administration, who set the rules under which most mortgage lenders operated.[24] Millions of White working-class families received a massive handout in the form of access to federally guaranteed, low-interest rate mortgage loans, a subsidy worth about $200,000 per White family that was denied to Black families.[25] As with the case of farm credit, the fights over mortgage credit were about the opportunities for Americans to build wealth and to have one's hard work translate into a decent living and a safe home.

. . . . .

WHAT ABOUT LOAN SHARKS?

Today, any attempt to reign in the excesses of the credit card industry is met with the charge that it would merely push borrowers into the hands of payday lenders, or worse, loan sharks. It is helpful to consider, then, how Americans used to handle things like the loss of a job, a broken window, or an unexpected hospital bill, in the era when interest rates were capped at 8 percent per year, a price that meant most Americans had limited or no access to legally provided, small-dollar, short-term loans.

For much of the late 1800s and early 1900s, loan sharks operated in larger towns and cities, charging interest rates from 60 percent to 480 percent per year. Notably, the loan shark interest rates of the early 1900s aren't so different from payday loan industry of the 2020s—today, the customary rate charged by payday lenders is $15 per $100 borrowed for a two-week period, or 360 percent per year. The term "loan shark" first became popular in the 1890s, to refer to any lenders whose interest rates or repayment terms ended up trapping the borrower in debt; these business practices were illegal and widely believed to be unethical.[26]

The industrial lenders like Household, mentioned earlier in the chapter, didn't become legal and popular borrowing options until the 1920s, when states began to loosen their interest rate caps for some small dollar loans to rates as high as 24 percent or 36 percent per year, and occasionally as high as 42 percent per year. These first "Uniform Small Loan Laws," gave reprieves for non-bank lenders, but not banks themselves, and only lifted the interest rate caps for small loans; larger loans still fell under the 6 percent or 8 percent caps. The theory pushed by social reformers at the time was that if the government allowed legal loans with interest rates of 30–40 percent, it would push the loan sharks out of business.

It should be noted that before the Great Depression, when organized crime began to take over the loan shark business, Americans viewed loan sharks as rapacious but not bloody—a hybrid, perhaps, between how people today view unsavory landlords and how they view those who engage in insider trading, not as violent thugs, but as greedy businesspeople. By the time mafiosos entered the game, in the 1930s, the old school of unlicensed lenders had mostly either fled the market, or, like Household, lowered their interest rates and applied for licenses to operate legally. When Prohibition ended in 1933, organized crime syndicates could no longer make money selling bootleg liquor; high-interest rate lending was an attractive alternative. While the pre-Depression loan sharks lent directly to families, the mob-backed juice lenders gave out much larger loans to three main groups: business owners, gambling debtors, and operators of illegal rackets like gambling or drug dealing.[27] Black entrepreneurs were especially likely to turn to loan sharks, because they were generally denied business credit from White-owned banks, regardless of the strength of their business plan or profit statements; one estimate from 1972 suggested that as many as one in four Black-owned businesses were funded by the Mafia.[28]

The earlier generation of loan sharks, when legal interest rates were capped at 6 percent or 8 percent, didn't hire enforcers to break borrowers' kneecaps; most of their collection officers were women, under the assumption you'd be less likely to turn away a woman from your front door. These "bawlers-out," as they were called, would also frequently show up to your office, to loudly give a speech in front of your coworkers, embarrassing you into repaying your debt. The loan sharks' target customer was a salaried employee of the government or the railroad, someone with family ties and a steady income, who wouldn't skip town if they ran into financial trouble, and who would be willing to pay a high price to avoid public humiliation.[29]

What is most striking about the loan sharks of the early twentieth century is how tame their criminal actions seem in comparison to the actions legally taken by payday lenders today, even as newspapers and nonprofits of the early twentieth century decried the loan sharks as one of the country's greatest economic ills.

Enforcement of anti-usury laws ebbed and flowed in the late nineteenth and early twentieth centuries. At times, unlicensed loan sharks even felt emboldened enough to run ads in newspapers.[30] But campaigns in the 1910s led to organized national crackdowns. One notorious high-interest lender, Daniel Tolman, who operated at least sixty loan sharking offices in the United States and Canada, was sentenced to prison by a judge who declared at his sentencing, "Men of your type are a curse to the community and the money they gain is blood money."[31]

The loan sharking industry was always highly contentious, and mainstream newspapers frequently covered the industry, offering lurid details to eager middle-class readers. But in absolute terms, the loan shark industry never lent out very much money: it was tiny compared to today's credit card industry, and even compared to today's payday loan industry. Rolf Nugent, director of the Department of Credit Studies at the Russell Sage Foundation estimated that in 1939, the loan shark industry had about $72 million in outstanding loans. Adjusting for inflation, $72 million works out to $1.3 billion in 2020 dollars—roughly half the size of today's payday loan industry per capita.[32]

The pawnshop industry attracted even more interest from middle-class readers and observers than did the loan sharks: mainstream newspapers treated pawnshop borrowers with prurient contempt. One New York Times article from 1932 with the headline "His $100 Teeth In Pawn, Negro Cheers Rise In Cotton," offered a paragraph describing the plight of Joe Milligen, a Black man who "had to pawn his thousand-dollar set of gold teeth for $55 to get something to eat." Another article was written in 1933 to inform readers that historians had discovered that late President Ulysses S. Grant had pawned a watch seventy-six years earlier—noteworthy, ostensibly, because such an action would strike readers as a huge embarrassment.[33] Pawnshops were legal in many states, and were sometimes operated on a nonprofit basis by charities. Pawn operators could easily evade anti-usury laws by only giving borrowers loan amounts that were fraction of their belongings' auction values, generally, one-fifth to one-third the auction value for clothing, or up to two-thirds the value for bigger-ticket items like jewelry.[34]

The cost of all types of material goods were much higher during the Gilded Age than they are today: before the era of Walmart, fast fashion, or mass manufacturing, nearly any physical object a working-class family owned was valuable enough to serve as collateral. Even underwear had a high enough resale value to pawn—clothing as an overall category was the most commonly pawned item. The pawn industry appears prominently in novels and magazine articles of the era, but it was even smaller than the illegal personal loan market.[35] In *Harper's Magazine,* writer William Stoddard, former assistant secretary to Abraham Lincoln, estimated that pawn lenders did at most half the amount of business as New York City's unlicensed lenders.[36]

The biggest difference between the loan sharks of the early twentieth century, and the payday lenders of today, is the fact that we legalized what was once illegal. Today's payday lenders require borrowers to provide a checking account number; if the borrower doesn't pay on time, the lender will attempt to pull money from the borrower's checking account, two or three times a day. Any money a borrower receives effectively gets routed directly to the lender, before children are fed, diapers bought, or rent is paid. If the automated withdrawals don't work, the payday lender can take the borrower to court, and sue them to win a civil judgment, allowing the lender to garnish the borrower's paycheck. Purposefully evade a civil judgment, and the borrower winds up in jail. All in all, today's system is considerably more violent: the "enforcers" aren't private associates of the loan sharks, but police officers, bailiffs, and sheriffs who ultimately make sure payday lenders don't get stiffed.

Two Ways of Life

The basic nature of Americans' financial lives has completely changed over the last seventy years: on average, we each have a lot more debt, but we also each own more in assets. In 1950, just over half of working-class families owned a home, roughly the same proportion of working-class families that own homes today (51 percent versus 47 percent). But in other respects, lower-income families owned a lot less than they own today: In 1950, only 41 percent of lower-income families owned a car. By 2016, 77 percent would own a car. In 1950, adjusted for inflation, lower-income families had an average $45,000 in physical assets, including the value of their home if they owned it, and $13,000 in other savings. By 2016, lower-income families had an average of $121,000 in physical assets, and $49,000 in savings. Although assets have risen, debts have risen much more quickly. While assets rose threefold, debts rose fivefold.[37] Credit is more widely available in the twenty-first century than it ever was before, but a higher proportion of each American's paycheck is sent directly to lenders.[38]

How did Americans deal with emergencies before? Partially, through setting aside more of their paychecks. For every year between 1959 and 1984, the personal savings rate was over 10 percent; by comparison, in 2019, it was 7.5 percent, although even this figure is misleading, because in our era of acute inequality, the ability to save is itself unequally distributed. Economists Atif Mian, Ludwig Straub, and Amir Sufi have shown that that in the 1960s and 1970s, the bottom 90 percent of income earners had a positive savings rate, but since the 1980s, their savings rate has been *negative* each year, meaning, they spent, on average, more than they earned.[39] Importantly, as we'll discuss in chapter 2, 1977 is the beginning of what I call the First Debt Boom—the moment when credit cards, two decades after their invention, first became commonly used. Before the 1970s, when working-class Americans didn't have any open credit lines, and had limited access to cash loans, particularly any type of cash loan that would be available quickly, setting aside money for a rainy day was a practical necessity.

Amid our country's present economic despair, it might seem naïve to even point to a higher savings rate as a possibility for ordinary people. And yet, we must grapple with the fact that many Americans can't afford to save *because* of the proportion of their income that is given to lenders in the form of interest. The fact that Americans, in general, *do ultimately pay the interest* is the very proof that over their lifetimes, they could have afforded to save, and summed across borrowers' lifetimes, the majority of items purchased on credit are ultimately paid for, with interest added. As we'll discuss in chapter 3, it would be a mistake to chalk this just up to timing issues, a mismatch between when people earn money and when they have to buy things.

And more importantly, it would be a mistake to attribute the tripling in debt to a belief that life was simply easier during the 1950s and 1960s.

We seem to have forgotten how hard life has always been for most people in America, imagining a utopia of white picket fences, and union jobs, when purportedly any able-bodied man could walk into a factory and leave with a job that could support a family. The men and women wearing red hats reading "Make America Great Again," and the people who show up to Bernie Sanders' town halls on the "40-year decline of the middle class,"[40] often share the assumption that life during and before the 1970s was easier for ordinary people than life is today.

But of course, there has never been a time in the United States without a substantial proportion of the public struggling economically. The rise of consumer debt from the 1950s until the 2000s can't be explained purely by things like wage trends or health-care costs, because many Americans during the middle of the twentieth century struggled to afford health care and other basic needs. But they rarely used loans to cover the gaps. Michael Harrington's 1962 book *The Other America: Poverty in the United States* documents the nation as the 1950s turned into the 1960s, before Lyndon B. Johnson's War on Poverty, prior to the introduction of Medicaid, Medicare, the Food Stamp Act, and Head Start. Harrington described bedridden seniors fit to leave their homes, except for the fact that they couldn't afford wheelchairs; Chicago families without proper food or clothing during harsh winters; and many sorts of workers, including day laborers, laundry workers, dishwashers, and people working in retail stores, who were exempt from the minimum wage, who were rarely unionized, and who lacked any workplace benefits. While the media often discusses the fact that the federal minimum wage has not kept up with inflation, it should be noted that the minimum wage was established in 1938, but until amendments were passed to the Fair Labor Standards Act in 1961 and 1968, the federal minimum wage only applied to "employees engaged in interstate commerce or in the production of goods for interstate commerce," which excluded roughly half of all working adults.[41]

Getting a union job often helped, but was no guarantee; as Harrington described, corrupt unions would occasionally arrange deals with management for a kickback, and organized labor's "no poaching" agreements meant the corrupt unions stopped workers from finding more effective union representation. By Harrington's estimations, at least 50 million Americans were poor in 1962, over a quarter of the population.[42] Some were disabled or otherwise unable to work, but many had jobs. In the decade that followed Harrington's book, poverty fell substantially, both according to formulas that ignore the impact of government transfers, and according to formulas that take government transfers into account.[43]

The 1970s hardly seem like an economic fairy-tale either. A nationwide shortage of oil helped to trigger inflation that made groceries and gas unaffordable for many. Housewives staged protests around the country about the high price of food, and Seattle erected an anti-suicide net around the Space Needle for the first time, reportedly in response to city's widespread joblessness after Boeing scaled down production.[44] In 1979, Jimmy Carter told the nation in a televised speech that the American public was "losing" the faith that "the days of our children would be better than our own." He explained that "10 years of inflation began to shrink our dollar and our savings." In addition to announcing measures to conserve electricity and increase domestic energy production, the President asked that the public "start praying."[45]

Empiricists may disagree about whether life in 2019 was harder or easier for the working and middle class than it was in 1979, 1969, or 1959— according to official government statistics, the median American was doing better in the latter half of the 2010s than at any point in the past, although this doesn't match everyone's experience, and some researchers disagree with the government's conclusion.[46]

As we will see, the amount of consumer debt is driven mostly by how eager the banks are to lend, not by how much families want or need to borrow. No matter how one slices the numbers, it is hard to argue that the explosion in consumer debt since the 1970s is directly attributable to rising economic difficulty, because the many struggling families during the 1950s, 1960s, and 1970s generally held very little debt. As we'll discuss in chapter 4, when you look year by year, the relationship between the strength of the economy and how much people borrow is the *opposite* of what you would expect; they borrow more when the economy is doing well. This should make us suspicious of any claims that the rise in consumer debt over the last century is driven mostly by a rise in the consumers need to borrow. And as we'll discuss in chapter 3, higher-income Americans are more likely to carry credit card debt than lower-income Americans, providing a point-in-time counterargument to the idea that debt arises only out of financial difficulty.

On the surface, it's not completely obvious which of the two ways of life is better: is it better to own little, but to have it be yours, free and clear, knowing it can't be taken from you unless you choose to sell it? Or is it better to own a bit more, but know that every paycheck that comes in is already spoken for by your lenders? Did workers benefit from America's new system of debt? Was the opportunity to be in debt helpful, or did it create more problems for workers than it solved?

None of these questions have simple answers. As hard as I have tried, I have not reached a satisfactory conclusion myself, so rather than explaining in this book whether, in aggregate, the construction of a system of debt has been good or bad for ordinary people, I'll instead articulate how we might build a system that combines some of best attributes of both systems, the easy access to credit of the 2000s, combined with the lower debt burdens of the mid-twentieth century.

What is most obvious is this: some people did benefit from the construction of a system in which hundreds of millions of Americans are chronically in high-interest debt. The beneficiaries were bank managers, bank shareholders, and the even wealthier-than-average Americans who were only able to earn 2 percent on their savings during the 2010s because banks wanted more cash to hand out in the form of credit card debt. This system is the set of laws, market conditions, ideologies, and assumptions that lead American families to, on average, turn over $1,023 in credit card interest and fees each year as payments to the wealthy.[47] This system is the debt machine.

2 How the Machine Was Built

I should take a detour to better explain my own insignificant role in the debt machine. I was not a major player, but I was given a closer-than-average vantage point.

I was twenty, a rising college senior, when I took an internship at Capital One, and I started working there full time the day before my twenty-second birthday in July of 2013. I gave my two weeks' notice shortly after I'd worked at the company for five years, an event that my coworkers celebrated by presenting me with a combination birthday and anniversary cake.

I mention this to acknowledge that I am writing about the debt machine as one of its beneficiaries: as one of the people that some of the money of the debt machine was funneled toward.

There were two reasons I decided to quit working at Capital One, a company that by every conceivable measure was more than fair *to me*, and was more than kind *to me*, a place that generally was a very pleasant place to work (indeed, the overwhelming pleasantness of work there, the friendly colleagues, supportive managers, and generally healthy culture is why I stayed so long).

The first reason I quit was that I was working very long hours. This, on its own, would not have really bothered me, if not for the second reason, which is that I'd stopped believing that the work I did was also good for the world.

My belief that the work I did might be good for the world rested on two assumptions: the first was that "access to credit" was a good thing, and the second that, as someone with a middling amount of influence within the company, I could tilt the company in a direction that was better for consumers. After all, I reasoned, would it be good for America if the financial sector was abandoned by everyone with a shred of conscience, left entirely for the wolves?

The idea that I might be a wolf myself never crossed my mind.

The day I decided I would be quitting Capital One, I was in a half-day meeting with my boss, and about ten other people who worked for him or worked closely with him. My boss had just moved across the country and transferred from another division of the company a few weeks earlier. I didn't know him very well, and neither did anybody else in the room. He oversaw the subprime credit card division, euphemistically named "Mainstreet Card," and the rest of us who worked for him were accountable for some chunk of this debt machine.

We had just winnowed down the division's list of "key initiatives"—the specific projects we'd concluded were most important. Next, we would choose the division's goals, or, more precisely, decide what real or fictitious goals we would write on a PowerPoint slide that could be circulated to everybody in the division. These goals were aspirational, or, some would say, delusional, such as "radically improve customers' lives." The goals, we were all to understand, were the reason we were completing the key initiatives that had already been chosen.

Some possible goals had been brainstormed. Coming up with a handful of goals wasn't difficult, as most of these were loosely recycled quarter-to quarter and year-to-year across all the divisions, except when a critical mass of executives had all read the same *Harvard Business Review* article illustrating the need for a new corporate mandate. When maybe five or six possible goals had been written on Post-it notes, and we had not yet begun the process of winnowing down, a director named Mike asked, "Should we have some sort of revenue or a growth goal?"

Capital One cared deeply about making money. And yet, to have a specific dollar goal for how much money we planned on making, particularly a goal that every associate in the division would know about, was considered uncouth. Mike, a former Accenture tech manager oversaw our division's technology. At Capital One we would have said, "he didn't grow up in the business," which made him unpredictable, not inculcated into the same ways of thinking and manners of speaking as the many former Capital One analysts, those hired right out of college or grad school, who made up most of the company's management.

"I don't think we really need that," my boss said. "If we accomplish all the other goals, great financials will come naturally."

And yet, one of the "key initiatives" still listed on the board was to finish a project about raising customers' interest rates. The division had recently raised the interest rate on most of its newly issued subprime credit cards from 24.9 percent to 26.9 percent. Just minutes ago, the people in the room agreed it was a key initiative to figure out whether some or all customers should get an even higher interest rate than that.

I asked, "If we don't actually have a revenue goal, what's the point of the pricing project? It obviously doesn't fit into any of the other goals we've listed."

I knew I was being difficult by asking the question, intentionally pushing buttons. Of course, the point of the pricing project was purely to make money. I knew that no good answer was coming. That said, I didn't realize how nonsensical the actual answer would be.

"Isn't it actually good for customers to raise interest rates? It discourages them from borrowing too much. Also, they don't seem to care," my boss said.

I wasn't sure if this was an off-color joke, or the utterances of a mind that no longer could distinguish between what it wished was true, and what it knew to actually be true. Charitably, maybe the question just caught him off guard.

When the meeting ended, my boss's words bounced around in my head. *"Isn't it actually good for customers to raise interest rates?"*

The magazines I read, the podcasts I listened to, the conferences I attended, and the meetings I participated in were full of people who believed in the religion of Doing Well by Doing Good. The religion's central dogma says that, over the long run, only ethical business practices will make money, that your business would be more profitable if you constantly "erred" on the side of what was best for society. According to the theory of Doing Well by Doing Good, helping customers "succeed" wasn't just the right thing to do, it was a good business strategy. Believers in Doing Well by Doing Good considered themselves to have already displaced the earlier, more vicious form of capitalism of Gordon Gekko and Milton Friedman. They were not rapacious, and their wealth was basically a happy accident.

According to this theory's internal logic, the best way to serve shareholders' interests was in fact to spend less time thinking about the shareholders' interests: with the right time-horizon chosen, there was no trade-off. Anyone who did not attempt to "do the right thing" was only selfish, but also a less savvy businessperson, a stooge whose greed would ultimately lead to his own stock price's demise.

Did my boss really believe charging our customers a higher interest rate was somehow good for them?

In the moment, I understood that he had just taken the ideology to its natural conclusion: if, over the long run, doing the right thing for customers is always the best business strategy, and if the "raising interest rates strategy" was, over the long run, making money, it must be better for customers than the alternative of not charging them so much interest.

"Increase our quarterly profit by a billion dollars" did not need to go on a separate Post-it note as "radically improve lives," and there was no longer a need to evaluate things on multiple dimensions: If ethics were profitable, then profit was also ethics.

"Also, they don't seem to care."

My boss was speaking to a point that we all understood. Raising the interest rate on a credit card didn't seem to cause fewer customers to apply for the product, or cause people to borrow less, or to pay down their debt any more quickly; in the words of economics, consumers were not very "price sensitive." To my boss, this was evidence that the price we charged customers was not important to them. If customers "cared" that we were raising interest rates, they wouldn't apply for our product, or they would choose to borrow less money once they were approved for the card, or we would at least see their disapproval in customer satisfaction surveys. If we could not observe their reaction to the fact that we were charging each of them more money every year, it must be true that raising prices was good for us, but of no real consequences to them. I'm sure there are people out there who truly don't care or notice when they are $50 or $100 or $500 poorer—indeed, many top managers at Fortune 500 companies, people like my boss, would likely fall into this category—but, by definition, people in credit card debt are strapped for cash.

My boss was, in a sense, echoing what Ralph Spurgin, the head of JCPenney's credit division told the company's management council two decades earlier, explaining his decision to raise the company's interest rates for the first time, from 18 percent to 21 percent: "In the past, consumers have generally not been rate-sensitive. Our surveys have consistently shown that they are more concerned about annual card fees than finance charge rates."[1]

Of course, this isn't a legitimate trade-off; the only reason you'd care about one fee over another fee is if you aren't able to calculate the total cost easily.

I objected to my boss's statement, but I couldn't identify a tactful way of asking the question on my mind: "Are you stupid enough to believe in the words you just said, or was this your idea of being funny?" At this stage in my career, few things mattered more to me than being polite.

I first tried to quit in my one-on-one meeting with my boss later that afternoon, but as I started to articulate my reasoning—that we did not view the "customer agenda" in the same way—he began to monologue and before I knew it, our thirty minutes together were up. The next week, I wouldn't make the same mistake, so I printed out two copies of a resignation letter that I could hand to him during our meeting. Our one-on-one meeting was canceled at the last minute (admittedly, for a very good reason, but one that I can't state here), so I gave the letter to his assistant, finished up some work, and left at nine that night.

MORAL REASONING AT WORK

I just told you the story of the moment things shifted in my own mind, the moment I went from thinking "It is a good use of my time for me to work at Capital One," to "It is not a good use of my time to work at Capital One."

I didn't yet think it was *bad* for me to work at Capital One.

That's why I said yes, when, two or three days later, one of my old bosses asked if I would be open to consulting for Capital One part time.

Everyone who works for a living must grapple with the consequences of their work: Are the consequences of my work good, bad, neutral, or unknowable? If I didn't do my job, would someone else do it, and what would the consequences of that be? Is there anything I can do to make the consequences of my work better? Can a company itself be said to be good or bad? Can a good person work for a bad company? Does it matter what their role is, whether they are there to sweep the floors, flip burgers in the cafeteria, schedule meetings, enter data into spreadsheets, be a manager who makes the smallest decisions, or act as an executive who can make some bigger choices but is nevertheless bound by the imperatives of their corporate machine?

.   .   .   .   .

This book is about the structural forces that drive the debt machine, but it is also about the human beings who operate that machine, about the assumptions they make and the ideologies that shape their decisions. I believe those assumptions and ideologies are important, and I'll use an example from another industry, retail fashion, to prove my point.

In April 2020, the COVID-19 recession triggered 30 million lost jobs, and Americans sharply curtailed their spending, including on clothing. Clothing brands were stuck with excess inventory and offered big discounts to customers. Many brands also canceled orders with their suppliers. According to the Worker Rights Consortium, brands like ASOS, Gap, and Urban Outfitters/Anthropologie canceled their orders without paying garment workers for work already completed, effectively stealing from some of the poorest people in the world. In contrast, H&M, Target, Uniqlo, and Inditex/Zara committed to paying workers for all orders they'd already started.[2] What determined which list a company would fall on, whether it would behave ethically or unethically, when every company knew that workers in the developing world had little leverage that they could use to hold them to account?

These are all publicly traded corporations. If "capitalism" was just a single, immutable force guaranteeing maximal exploitation, none of the companies would have paid their garment workers, knowing there would be minimal consequences. Their actions may have been shaped by incentives and data, but people ultimately made these decisions.

.   .   .   .   .

At Capital One, there were two types of decisions: credit decisions, and noncredit decision. A credit decision was something that would obviously impact the company's default rate, or the total amount of loans we'd give out: the number of credit card solicitations to send in the mail; the amount to bid to get the top placements on "affiliate" sites that recommended credit cards, like Credit Karma or CreditCards.com; the policies that would determine which credit card applicants would get approved; the credit limits and interest rates each customer would receive; and the set of customers who would receive credit limit increases or balance transfer offers. Everything else was a noncredit decision.

Capital One had a small number of "judgmental underwriters," employees who would individually look at applicants' and customers' credit files to make decisions if they fell into special categories, such as being exceptionally wealthy. But "credit decisions," the creation of the rules that would impact thousands or often millions of customers, were never made by a single person. An analyst, or, more often, a team of analysts, would make a recommendation; depending on how many dollars were at stake, a set of formal rules determined whether one, two, three, or four sign-offs were necessary. A level two sign-off could come from my boss; a level three or level four sign-off came from a separate department, Credit Risk Management.

If we revisit the two lists of clothing retailers, ASOS, Gap, and other shirkers on one side, and H&M, Zara, and other (relatively) upstanding corporate citizens on the other, it is hard to imagine that the decision to steal or not to steal wages from garment workers was not related to choices made by individual people who consulted or failed to consult varying moral codes.

There was a specific business decision that caused me to turn in my contractor badge and laptop and conclude, with great certainty, that I would never go back to Capital One. That story will appear in the next chapter. Shamefully, when I decided to stop consulting for Capital One, I didn't explain my reasoning to any of my former peers, saying only that I needed to dedicate more time toward exploring other professional interests.

It's not easy from the outside to answer why Gap screwed workers over, but Target didn't. These aren't small decisions.

THE DEFINITION OF THE DEBT MACHINE

The definition of a machine, in general, is "an assemblage of parts that transmits forces, motion, and energy one to another in a predetermined matter."[3]

The credit card debt machine, then, is the system of parts that transmits wealth from ordinary American families to bank shareholders, bank managers, and to a lesser extent, any American who has saved a significant amount of money. Later, we will talk about the extent to which ordinary bank savers are also implicated in the debt machine. For now, though, we'll look at the *system of parts,* paying special attention to the four most important of those parts:

Part 1: A market equilibrium where the most common consumer lending product—the credit card—has a set of product terms that are hard to understand, but that are on the surface, appealing;

Part 2: The widespread belief that "access to credit" is a good thing; that it would be a policy failure if fewer people were able to get a loan;

Part 3. A prevailing sense that not having a credit card is low status and a form of social exclusion; and

Part 4. An asymmetry of information between the banks and their borrowers, derived from the ability of banks to freely run experiments on their borrowers without disclosing the results.

Let's explore each of these moving parts in turn.

The First Moving Part: The Product Terms of the Dominant Type of Loan

To really internalize the complexity of the credit card, it's helpful to compare it to another type of common financial product: the home mortgage.

When Americans buy a house, they typically make several decisions in quick succession, usually considering a range of possibilities jointly across each decision: Should I buy a house at all, or should I rent? How expensive of a house should I buy—how big will it be, what will it look like, and where will it be located? And what loan should I use to borrow the money to pay for the house?

Under 10 percent of home buyers will choose an adjustable-rate mortgage: most home buyers will have a fixed monthly payment. If they're buying their first house, they likely have some idea of what it would cost to rent a similar property. Most Americans know how to add, subtract, multiply, and divide; while math skills are somewhat lower in the United States than in other wealthy countries, 90 percent of adults can do arithmetic, and 70 percent of adults can do multistep math problems with decimals.[4] Understanding an installment loan, like a fixed-rate home loan or an auto loan, uses the type of math proficiency that most Americans possess. Most Americans can see a payment amount and compare it to the amount of money they earn every month. They can look at a billing statement that comes from a lender and see the amount of each payment going toward interest and going toward principal. They can multiply a monthly payment amount by the number of payments they must make, and compare it to the purchase price, and observe the difference. There are a few ways home mortgages or auto loans can be made complicated by lenders—through "points," or complex insurance products, or fees—but a basic mortgage isn't hard for most people to wrap their heads around.

The simplest credit card, by comparison, is quite a bit more complicated that the simplest home mortgage. Credit cards are so commonplace that their complexity seems to disappear into the background. It seems odd to define a credit card in a book, like explaining what a carrot is, or a paper clip. Nevertheless, I must draw all this complexity into the light so we can examine it together. A credit card is a financial account that a person or business opens with a lender. Typically, the lender establishes a maximum amount of money they're willing to lend to that person—the "credit limit"—and usually that credit limit is disclosed to the customer, although often the lender allows some transactions that exceed that credit limit, and sometimes the credit limit is not disclosed to the customer (if the credit limit isn't disclosed to the customer, it is typically more than

$5,000). The credit limit can be changed at any time without the consumer's permission. The "credit card" comes with one or more ways that the customer can borrow against their credit limit: by presenting a physical "card" indicating the account details to a merchant; by providing those account details online or over the phone; or by withdrawing cash at a bank or ATM. A network—usually either Visa, Mastercard, American Express, or Discover—transmits data back and forth between the lender and the merchant to determine whether the transaction is permitted, charging a transaction fee called "interchange" to the merchant. The network keeps a small portion of that fee and gives the rest to the lender (American Express and Discover operate both as a network and as a lender, while Visa and Mastercard are only networks, and Chase, Citi, and Capital One are only lenders). The lender issues a credit card statement once per month and sets a due date that is between 21 and 30 days after the statement is issued. Most but not all credit cards include a grace period: If the bill is always paid in full before the grace period has elapsed, no interest accrues. Typically, once a consumer "loses grace," any new purchases that consumer makes on the card start immediately accruing interest, until grace is "regained." If the card has a grace period, it is almost always the same length of time as the period between statement date and the bill's due date. Otherwise, interest accrues daily, and that interest is added to the balance. The lender sets a formula for calculating the minimum payment, which by law must be large enough that the debt is eventually paid off if no new purchases are made, but often is just barely large enough. For example, a balance of $10,000 on an interest rate of 24 percent takes more than 25 years to repay using the basic formula employed by both Citi and Capital One, by which time the customer will have repaid $28,886.[5] When Americans makes purchases on credit cards, it usually is hard for them to figure out how much they'll eventually owe, or when they'll be done making payments. Those mental projects are made more complicated if, for example, the borrower has multiple balances on different interest rates (a balance transfer on a credit card is often subject to a lower rate, purchases to a second rate, and cash advances to a third higher rate). To figure out how long they'll be in debt, they'd have to look up the specific "payment allocation" rules for their credit card: if the card is a Citi card or a Capital One card, typically the minimum payments are allocated to the lowest interest rate balance first, while any payment amount that exceeds the minimum, by law, must be applied to the highest interest rate balance first. Obviously, it would be less complicated for banks to always apply payments to the highest interest rate balances first, but because that would result in less money being transferred from consumers' pockets onto banks' balance sheets, they don't do it that way.

I'll now define two terms that will be useful to us: a "revolving" account is any loan, like a credit card, or a home equity line of credit, where the borrower can make any number of purchases against a credit limit. In a revolving account, every payment made by the borrower "frees up" more credit for the borrower to use again. An "installment" account is any loan, like most car loans, student loans, and mortgages, where the borrower is told in advance how many payments they'll need to make, normally equally sized, and their balance goes down every month if they make at least the required payment.

In February 2017, economist Mary Zaki conducted an experiment. For about twenty minutes' worth of work, every participant in her experiment would earn $65, to be paid out in increments of $5 per month over the course of thirteen months. Zaki let her participants use that income to buy discounted Amazon gift cards: every participant could choose to take their monthly five-dollar salary without buying a gift card; they could receive a discounted gift card once they'd saved up enough of their salary; or they could buy a discounted gift card immediately on a credit plan that Zaki offered. Participants were randomly divided into a few groups; the credit plan was either presented as an *installment loan,* appearing in much the same way that Sears and JCPenney used to advertise their installment loan plans to their department store customers, or as a *revolving loan*, expressed with a monthly or annual compounding interest rate on the declining balance (if that sounds confusing, remember, that's how credit cards work and millions of people use them!). The interest rate that participants were offered was either 0 percent (e.g., a free loan), 18 percent (around what you'd expect on a credit card), or 42 percent (randomly determined). Everyone in the study was asked to calculate how long the loan they'd been offered would take to repay with five-dollar payments—the repayment schedule, five dollars per month, was fixed across all the loans.

Participants were about four times as likely to correctly calculate how long repayment would take when they were offered credit as an installment loan, rather than as a revolving loan. Around 60 percent of people correctly understood the cost of credit for installment loans, while only about 15 percent of people correctly understood the cost of credit for revolving loans. And the errors were nearly always in the same direction: participants were seven times as likely to underestimate how expensive the revolving loans were than they were to overestimate. When participants were in the revolving loan group, more than a third of the time, the actual costs of the loan were greater than twice as high as what the participants calculated.

At an 18 percent interest rate, participants were slightly more likely to borrow on an installment loan than they were to borrow if offered the revolving loan, presumably because some people were deterred because they couldn't compute the cost of the revolving loan, even though they would have chosen to borrow if they could've seen it was an OK deal. But when Zaki raised interest rates from 18 percent to 42 percent, people offered installment loans were quickly scared off: about four in ten people offered an installment loan at 18 percent decided to take it, while only about two in ten people decided to take the installment loan at a 42 percent rate. But when the loan was a revolving loan, raising the interest rate from 18 percent to 42 percent didn't scare away anybody: about one in four people borrowed under both conditions. In other words, if you have no way of translating APRs into actual borrowing costs, 18 percent and 42 percent are either both equally good or equally bad.[6]

What's more, it took people nearly twice as long to calculate their incorrect answer for revolving loans as it did for people to calculate the correct answer for installment loans: about two minutes, compared to about one minute. Consider the implications. Only about one in five people can figure out how much they'll pay in interest on a revolving loan, with no restrictions on using calculators, the Internet, or any other resource, even though half of Americans currently *are* paying interest on a revolving loan. The product simply doesn't operate on the same level as human brains operate.

Revolving credit was first offered by a handful of department stores in the 1930s. The biggest department stores, Sears and JCPenney, began offering revolving credit in the 1950s, around the same time banks launched their revolving credit accounts. As Harvard political scientist Gunnar Trumbull has written, we're all so familiar with revolving credit now that it is "difficult to capture the novelty and uncertainty that surrounded this new financial instrument when it was first introduced."[7] But now, "revolving credit" in the form of credit cards, completely dominates over installment loans: at the start of 2020, 75 percent of all consumer debt was in the form of revolving credit.[8] Although the media sometimes talks about the resurgence of installment loans, the market has changed only modestly: at the peak of credit card dominance, from 2009 to 2013, revolving credit made up 80 percent of all consumer debt.

Obviously, there are a few reasons a person might want a credit card instead of an installment loan. Even if a person aspires to repay their credit card debt in one year or two years or four, it's nice to have the flexibility to make very small payments if there is a month when their finances are especially tight. And although it wasn't at all unusual during the first half of the twentieth century for a person to have a bunch of small installment loans—one that they'd used to buy a vacuum cleaner, and another that they'd used to buy a winter coat—the idea of having multiple installment loans strikes a lot of people today as inconvenient relative compared to one credit card that can accommodate many purchases. (It's not so clear that Americans are necessarily opposed to juggling multiple accounts, given that those with at least one credit card have an average of four credit cards each).[9]

But what is so important about Zaki's research is that her study strips away the ancillary benefits of revolving credit compared to installment credit: when Zaki's participants chose to borrow money from the study, the payments were five dollars per month, regardless of whether they'd been randomly assigned to see the loan presented as an installment loan or presented as a revolving loan. It became obvious how much extra borrowing happened simply because of the participants' confusion around borrowing costs. In real life, we can't separate the popularity of revolving loans from the fact that Americans are woefully ill-equipped to understand their cost in real-time.

You would think shopping for a credit card would be a little bit like shopping for gas to fill up your car. Gas is a commodity. Most people don't care if they buy their gas from BP or from 7–11, and, as a result, when you drive past a gas station, you see the huge sign out front where they tell you the price, so you can comparison shop from one thousand feet away. Gas stations managers know that if they don't make their prices obvious, you'll pick another gas station. And that's largely what the market for mortgages and other installment loans is like. These lenders know that when you're shopping for an installment loan, you just care about the interest rate. But its unbelievably rare to see a TV ad for a credit card that mentions the interest rates the lender charges. Zaki observes that the only way to make it clear to shoppers that your credit card is meaningfully cheaper than other credit cards is to draw attention to the dollar cost of borrowing with a few illustrative examples. But any credit card issuer who tries to make it obvious how much a borrower could save, for example, runs a huge risk: by pointing out the price savings of the 15 percent APR you offer, say, instead of a 20 percent APR offered by a competitor, you could just as easily scare the borrower away from using a credit card at all. In Zaki's words, "revelations of true costs can lead consumers to avoid credit purchases altogether rather than borrow from the most competitive creditor."[10]

Joe, who I interviewed in Washington, DC, was twenty years old when he got his first credit card, but he told me it was more than five years later that he first started to think about the total amount of interest he was paying on his credit card debt. And what triggered the epiphany about credit card interest? It was buying his first car. "Having financed the car was like a whole new education in credit really [. . .] I looked at the interest and the charges that I was going to pay over the length of the financed term, and I was like, 'oh, this is such an exorbitant amount of money.'" The car loan was concrete, while the credit cards were abstract, and, he pointed out, the fact that he was putting any extra money he had toward his higher-interest credit card debt meant there would be no way to pay the car loan off early. Because the car was financed using an installment loan, he got to see how much money was paid in interest; it was only then that he internalized how much he had also been paying in credit card interest.

For profit-seeking Silicon Valley idealists who worship at the altar of disruption, the differences between revolving and installment credit pose a hard-to-dismantle barrier to "fixing things." Installment loans, in their relative clarity, trigger the feeling of "this loan is too expensive for me; it's better for me to not borrow," while the complexity of credit cards prevents that realization.

Perhaps not surprisingly, the installment loan market today is largely geared toward people who want to refinance existing credit card debt. At LendingClub, the largest and best-known fintech installment lender, four out of every five borrowers use their loans to pay off other loans—often, credit cards.[11] Once an American has already realized that credit card payments are swallowing up most of their paycheck, there are many start-ups they can turn to find a lower interest rate, at least if they have a relatively good credit score. But so far, no start-up seems to have made a dent in addressing the high cost of credit *when Americans initially need to borrow money*, ostensibly, because at the time Americans choose their credit cards, they often haven't yet realized that they're about to get fleeced, that they're making a decision or a set of decisions that will end up being extremely costly. Unless you're already in credit card debt, the interest rate number that appears in a credit card solicitation doesn't really mean anything. Few Americans, at the outset of their experiences with credit cards, can look at those numbers and figure out they are especially high, or especially low, or whether they might find a better deal elsewhere, and the interest rate certainly can't be translated into a dollar cost of borrowing. As a result, the problem of people accumulating unnecessary debt because the prices are unclear isn't easily solved by competition: the high cost of borrowing doesn't emerge when the initial "purchase" is made. More recently, a new breed of lenders has emerged, companies like Affirm, Klarna, and Afterpay: if you shop online, you may have noticed during checkout the option to pay with a loan from one of these companies, sometimes with no interest or fees. A major advantage of these companies is that they clearly state their costs: shoppers can see the dollar amount and number of fixed monthly payments they'll need to make. But so far, it is unclear whether these companies have caused people to divert any meaningful amount of credit card debt, or merely go into debt for purchases that they otherwise would have paid for immediately. Although Affirm has more than 6,500 merchant partners, almost one-third of its total revenue comes from a single merchant, Peloton, the purveyor of $1,895 stationary bicycles.[12] Through a partnership with Affirm, the Peloton is available is available for thirty-nine payments of $49 each, at a

0 percent APR (Peloton pays Affirm money for this arrangement). This variety of free loan is only possible because the customers are low risk (or are assumed to be low risk), and the Peloton is sold at a substantial profit margin.

Until the mid-1950s, retailers, mostly department stores, issued more than half of all consumer credit. Zaki traced the loans that the five largest department stores, Sears, JCPenney, Spiegel, Montgomery Ward, and Aldens, offered from the 1950s until the 1990s. JCPenney came late to the credit game because its founder, James Cash Penney, was deeply opposed to debt, but the other four stores offered both charge plans, where shoppers could make a lump-sum payment in full each month, along with installment plans, throughout the twentieth century. Spiegel was the first to offer revolving credit by catalog in 1958: within three years, the other four largest department stores would follow suit.[13] In the 1950s, the department stores could borrow the money cheaply, with a "cost of funds" usually under 5 percent: in the decades that followed, with inflation skyrocketing, their costs of funds rose quickly, peaking north of 12 percent around 1981, before falling back under 5 percent by 1991. You would expect these changes in the department stores' cost of funds to be reflected in what interest rates they charged their customers, in the same way that if the cost of grain rises, you'd expect bread rises to go up, and if the cost of grain falls, bread prices should go down. That's what happened with department stores' installment loans: when the store's cost to borrow rose and fell, the interest rates they charged customers rose and fell too. But with the store-issued revolving credit plans, the prices only ever went one way: up. The same thing happened with bank-issued credit cards: between 1989 and 1991, the prime rate fell from around 12 percent to around 8 percent, but virtually every major bank kept their credit card interest rates fixed between 18 percent and 20 percent, even as the interest rates on mortgages and other installment loans fell.[14] Lower lending costs and increased competition don't drive down the price of credit cards or revolving loans, because consumers simply aren't attuned to when they're getting ripped off.

The invention of revolving credit stopped lenders from trying to compete on price: prices had become totally inscrutable. The debt machine couldn't function in a market where installment loans were the dominant product: when installment loans dominate the marketplace, consumers are much more hesitant to borrow (especially when the cost of borrowing is high), and consumers are less likely to be overcharged, because they can comparison shop easily.

The Second Moving Part: The Belief That Access to Credit Is a "Good" Thing

In 1973, the world of lending could be divided into three clean spheres: very good loans that came from banks with rates usually under 10 percent; OK loans that came from department stores and other national blue-chip retailers, whose rates were often 18 percent; and a small sphere of very bad loans from mob-backed loan sharks.

Sears and JCPenney, the two largest issuers of retail credit, weren't especially restrictive in who they offered credit to, and everyone who was approved for the credit plan got the same interest rate as others living in their state. Half of Americans had a Sears card, and one-third had a JCPenney card.[15] Still, not everyone qualified, and in lower-income neighborhoods, especially immigrant neighborhoods and Black neighborhoods, retailers sold expensive goods like televisions and furniture at a huge markup, while advertising "easy credit" plans.[16] Their outrageously high prices gave them the wiggle room to stay within the low maximum interest rates set by law. Inflation, meanwhile, was high, around 9 percent, which made bank loans and department store loans an especially good deal: saving up to make big-ticket purchases wasn't especially attractive, when you thought the price tomorrow would surely be higher than the price today. The effective interest rate on all types of formal loans, after subtracting inflation, was nearly always under 10 percent. Fewer people could get loans, but the loans that people got were much cheaper than loans are now.

Lending discrimination against women and people of color was blatant and egregious. Mortgage lenders would only consider a woman's income if they were convinced she wouldn't get pregnant: the lenders asked for "baby letters" from women's doctors explaining what type of birth control she used, and at least some banks also demanded affidavits from both husband and wife promising to get an abortion if an unplanned pregnancy did occur.[17] Banks weren't shy about declining Black applicants for loans under thinly veiled racism, officially offering reasons like the applicant lacked a "harmonious home life" or a "good reputation."[18]

It was in this context that 1970s civil rights groups campaigned for access to credit. The National Welfare Rights Organization lobbied retailers like JCPenney and Lane Bryant to offer loans to welfare recipients and the National Organization for Women formed their Credit Task Force.[19] In 1974, Congress passed the Equal Credit Opportunity Act, which said lenders couldn't discriminate on the basis of race, national origin, gender, or marital status, and in 1977 they passed the Community Reinvestment Act, which required banks to issue loans to low-income and middle-income people, and people living in low-income neighborhoods. It made sense to fight for equal access to credit, because the credit that banks and retailers offered was cheap and inflation was high. Bank credit was a good deal, and anyone in their right mind could see it.

White moderates eagerly embraced the idea that expanding access to private bank loans could be a cornerstone of the civil rights movement. A popular theory at the time was that the urban race riots of the 1960s were primarily "consumer revolts," driven by anger toward the retailers selling televisions and sewing machines at high markups under less-favorable credit terms.[20] Expanding access to consumer credit was billed as an inexpensive way to right historic wrongs; certainly, it was less costly than spending government money to directly improve living standards, or to compensate people through the wealth lost because of racist government policies.

But as soon women and Black Americans gained access to credit, credit itself got worse. In a 1978 decision, *Marquette National Bank of Minneapolis v. First of Omaha Service Corp*, the Supreme Court ruled that loans only had to comply with the laws of the state where the bank was chartered, not the laws of the borrower's state. In an instant, all the consumer protections that states had painstakingly written, the ones that made sure that when credit was offered, it was good credit, became functionally irrelevant. Credit card companies could set up shop wherever they wanted—often they would pick South Dakota, which wrote permissive laws for the explicit purpose of luring banks into the states—and still mail high-interest rate credit cards all over the country. State level usury caps would continue to apply for lenders operating storefronts—for example, payday lenders, and some auto lenders—but not for any type of loan that could be offered by mail, or later, over the Internet. Within three years, forty-five states that had previously capped interest rates had either raised their caps or eliminated them altogether.[21]

The language of civil rights that had been applied to loans with interest rates just 2 or 3 percentage points above inflation would now get applied to loans with interest rates that were more than 20 percentage points above inflation. At Capital One, under the auspices of the Community Reinvestment Act (CRA), I oversaw a program to extend $100 credit limit increases on our credit cards to people who wouldn't ordinarily qualify for credit limit increases, but who lived in low-to-middle income neighborhoods.

Consider, for a moment, who didn't already qualify for these credit limit increases, on credit cards whose interest rate often topped 24 percent.

The economics of credit card lending are intuitive, but nevertheless, I'll spell them out. When interest rates are high—for example, 24 percent— there are only two reasons it wouldn't be profitable to raise somebody's credit limit: either you think they're unlikely to use the extra credit, or you think they're *particularly* likely to default on the loan and never pay you back.

In the first category, you have people who haven't used their card in years, or people who already have high credit limits they're barely using: they've paid down their debt and now they're just charging their Hulu subscription to their Capital One card to make sure the company doesn't close their account. In the second category, the very-likely-to-default, you have people who already have $15,000 or $20,000 worth of credit card debt, or who are behind on their auto loan, or who have had their credit card open for many years without ever making more than the minimum payment.

What this meant was that these $100 credit limit increases, wrapped up in the gauzy glow of civil rights, would be sent to people who were either already struggling to repay their existing debts, or who had a significant amount of unused credit open on their Capital One credit card. Each of these tiny credit limit increases, the very smallest amount we thought wouldn't be blatantly offensive, counted as a distinct loan to a low- or moderate- income family: in the eyes of the law, there was no apparent difference between a $100 limit increase on an existing unused credit card with a $5,000 credit limit and an interest rate of 24 percent, versus a $3,000 loan at a low interest rate that might help a homeless parent with a job put down the security deposit for a new apartment. It wasn't until May 2020 that the Office of the Comptroller of the Currency officially told banks that issuing credit cards to the poor would no longer count toward CRA requirements, admitting that credit cards had a "potential negative impact on borrowers if those products were not offered with affordable rates and terms."

People fought for the CRA because it was obvious to those living in cities like Chicago and Baltimore that, in the 1970s, banks accepted the deposits of people in poor neighborhoods but wouldn't lend to them. Affluent liberals who couldn't see what was happening with their naked eyes were convinced by the data released by the 1975 Home Mortgage Disclosure Act, which required banks to document the number of loans granted in each neighborhood. The evidence of credit deserts bolstered the case for the passage of the CRA two years later.[22]

Now, in effect, the exact opposite problem occurs: banks send credit card solicitations to poor people, but they don't want to take their deposits. Issues of racial animus aside, the economic logic is obvious: when inflation was high, deposits were valuable for banks, worth collecting even in small quantities from people living paycheck-to-paycheck. There are some fixed costs for a bank to maintain a checking or savings account—things like sending statements, issuing a debit card, or answering phone calls, so taking deposits from someone living paycheck-to-paycheck is only attractive if they plan to squeeze the person with overdraft fees. Conversely, once states eliminated or substantially raised their interest rate caps, dragging poor people into debt became enticing. The environment has reversed itself—getting into debt is now easier than finding an affordable checking account that is not riddled with a high minimum balance requirement or punitive overdraft fees—but the law still says that more debt would be a good thing. Banks dissuade poor people from saving at their institution by avoiding entire metropolitan areas that are lower income, imposing high minimum balances that customers need to have if they want to avoid monthly maintenance fees, and by closing bank branches in poorer parts of town.[23]

Of course, the Community Reinvestment Act isn't to blame for the vast bulk of subprime credit card lending, nor was it to blame for the vast bulk of subprime mortgage lending a decade earlier. Nearly all subprime loans are originated to make money, not because of any government mandate. And yet, those $100 credit limit increases at Capital One were a byproduct of a system that views the extension of credit as an intrinsically good thing.

The prevailing attitude of American legislators is that credit cards are more like automobiles than they are like cigarettes: useful tools that require some minimum quality standards. The goal has been to make credit cards safer, not to abolish credit cards, or to make them unappealing, and not to make them hard to get. Former New York City Mayor Michael Bloomberg pushed legislation to have retailers store their cigarettes out of sight for shoppers, available only on request, and the FDA moved to cover cigarette packages with miserable images of emaciated cancer patients and gangrenous toes. Both initiatives were derailed at least once by legal challenges (as of May 2020, the FDA initiative is expected to be revisited), but the goal of these policies was clear: getting people to stop smoking.

Of course, people smoke for a reason. Smoking feels good. Cigarettes are relaxing. But you'll never hear a politician talk about protecting or expanding access to cigarettes. Few people criticized CVS for making the decision to stop selling cigarettes. Presumably, the only reason Bloomberg never tried to ban cigarettes altogether is that he knew banning such an addictive substance would cause the illegal market for cigarettes to explode in volume: politicians aren't typically shy about going "too far" in their campaigns against smoking, only about triggering secondary negative consequences.

By contrast, America can't make up its mind about whether it should be trying to expand access to credit or protect itself from debt.

In 2009, when Senator Mark Udall (D-CO) introduced the Credit Cardholders' Bill of Rights, he said, "I hear often from hard-working, honest Coloradans who are asking only to be treated fairly by the credit card industry, whose deceptive practices have plagued consumers for years," but he added that Coloradans "benefit from the widespread availability of consumer credit, and their use of that credit has been important to our economy. In fact, for many Americans, consumer credit is more than a convenience. It is something that many people need to use to pay for their everyday needs. For them, it is a necessity." While tobacco is regulated because it is dangerous, credit cards are regulated, in Udall's words, because they are necessary, a framework that presupposes that a successful regulatory regime would improve the terms under which money is borrowed but wouldn't change the overall level of borrowing.

The early 2000s saw two influential documentaries about the credit card sector: PBS Frontline's 2004 "The Secret History of the Credit Card," and "Maxed Out: Hard Times, Easy Credit and the Era of Predatory Lenders," a 2006 film that won the Special Jury Prize at South by Southwest and was screened across the country. When President Barack Obama signed Udall's bill (which was renamed the Credit Card Accountability Responsibility and Disclosure Act of 2009, or the CARD Act for short), on May 22, 2009, it would end nearly every specific business practice described as unfair by the two films. The CARD Act effectively ended over-limit fees and stopped issuers from raising borrowers' interest rates on their existing balances. It cracked down on marketing credit cards to college students, and banks could only lend to people under the age of twenty-one if the bank assessed their ability to repay based on only their own income, not their household income, a reaction to frequent media accounts about exploitation of assumed-to-be-vulnerable college students. And it ended double-cycle billing, a practice where credit card companies would inflate how much interest they charged customers, by looking at the average balance a customer held over the last two months, instead of only at the last month.

Perhaps nothing sums up this era better than the Pew Charitable Trust's "Safe Credit Cards Project," launched in 2007 with support from the Sandler Foundation, and input from Elizabeth Warren.[24] Its mandate was to "research perceived dangers associated with consumer credit cards"; the goal was to improve cards, not to end them.[25] In their March 2009 report, they suggested seven specific standards for a safe credit card,[26] all but one of which, an end to binding arbitration agreements, were a part of the law Barack Obama signed.

All of this would imply that credit cards are now safe; we stripped out most of the unpredictable fees, and the sudden changes in interest rates. With few exceptions, consumers are getting the products that they signed up for, if you believe in the "safe credit cards" framework.

The "hidden" costs of credit declined sharply post-CARD Act. Before the CARD Act passed, 48 percent of cardholders paid an over-limit fee.

After it passed, only 3 percent did. Before the CARD Act passed, average late fees per late payment were $33: after it passed, average late fees dropped to $23, and the late fee incidence rate dropped from 26 percent to 20 percent. To make up for their lost ability to charge gotcha fees and suddenly change interest rates, issuers raised the average initial interest rates and annual fees, but all in all, research by the Consumer Financial Protection Bureau (CFPB) indicates that the CARD Act likely lowered the combined cost of credit for consumers by about 2 percentage points, from around 16 percent to around 14 percent. And even if interest rates went up, most people would agree it is better for the prices to be in the form of "known" terms, like the annual membership fee and basic interest rate, than in hidden terms and in unpredictable surprise fees.[27]

Yet, the reforms left basic mechanics of credit cards unchallenged. In the immediate aftermath of the Great Recession, banks, afraid of rising default rates, and hesitant to carry big marketing budgets that would result in them posting a quarterly loss, made some pullbacks in their lending practices and marketing budgets (as we'll later discuss, in the United States, how hard or easy it is to get a credit card is intimately connected to the size of credit card marketing budgets). But by 2015, per capita credit card debt levels started rising again, and by the end of 2019, per capita, inflation-adjusted credit card debt levels rose to 80 percent of their pre–Great Recession peak.[28] Some excesses were reined in by regulation, but, for the most part, the industry returned to business as usual.

Every two years, as a part of a requirement of the CARD Act, the CFPB measures whether the CARD Act has had any negative consequences on the "availability of credit." They ascertain this by counting the number of new credit card solicitations sent in the mail, the volume of new credit cards booked each year, approval rates on credit cards, average credit lines for new customers, and how frequently banks raised credit limits. In other words, by the regulation's very design, if banks became less eager to push families into debt, it was measured as an unintended consequence, not as a desired outcome.[29]

The assumption that most debt is good debt, unless it is somehow poisoned by outrageously deceptive terms, keeps the debt machine spinning: it gives the banker social and psychological cover for their actions, and it sharply limits the actions the government is willing to take in response to

American's debt burdens. My argument isn't that loans are never helpful; instead, I'll challenge the assumption that credit "availability" is an intrinsically good thing.

The Third Moving Part: The Sense That Credit Is "Inclusion"

In the book *The Innovator's Dilemma*, Harvard Business School professor Clayton Christensen examined industries like pharmaceuticals, construction equipment, and computer parts to argue that most product innovation follows a familiar path: a new company develops a technique that makes it cheaper and easier to manufacture something people need. Initially, the quality is inferior to the "mainstream" version of that product, but the new version is attractive to some customers who care a lot about price, and the new company gains market share starting with the lowest end of the market. They manage to improve their product over time, such that it eventually is both better and cheaper than what previously existed, and the original market leader goes out of business.

Credit cards followed the exact opposite path: they started as a luxury good, and only decades later became widely available.

The initial version of the Diners Club credit card was free for the customer, paid for entirely by a 6 percent transaction fee charged to the merchant.[30] Diners Club founder Frank X. McNamara understood the product's potential utility for business travelers—they'd have a single record of their transactions for work reimbursement or tax purposes; they wouldn't have to carry as much cash; and they'd pay for everything with a single monthly check—but, in his words (as relayed by his first head of marketing, Matty Simmons), "most importantly, it's prestige. It's having a good enough credit rating to own one of these cards so restaurants will treat you like somebody who's somebody. If you're a businessman and you're entertaining clients or working on a deal, the people with you will be impressed."[31]

Diners Club, said Simmons, "was a card for people who could afford to carry what amounted to a blank check."[32]

And so, from the beginning, this loan was barely a loan at all—it was a sense of belonging. The first Diners Club applicants were marketed a "charge card" that they were supposed to pay in full each month; they were nominally borrowing money, but only for a month, and the assumption was that they were good for it. An advertisement celebrating the Diners Club's ten-year anniversary declared, "To charge is to attain a status and this has been an age of status. The businessman is striving for success and to have automatic credit wherever one goes has become a symbol of success."[33]

When journalist Hillel Black wrote *Buy Now, Pay Later* in 1961, by which time Diners Club had allegedly already loosened their credit standards, the minimum income for approval was still $5,000 a year (roughly $43,0000 in today's dollars). American Express and the Hilton Hotels-owned Carte Blanche were the other two of the "big-three" card issuers: their minimum incomes, likewise, were $5,000 and $7,500 per year ($65,000), respectively.[34]

Nearly seventy years later, credit card usage is still associated with prestige, not penury. Pulling out a metal credit card can trigger "oohs" and "ahhs," or, more intimately, a request to pick up or hold the card. The cost of manufacturing these metal credit cards, like the Chase Sapphire Reserve Card, the Capital One Venture Card, or Wells Fargo Propel American Express card is around $40 per card, between ten and twenty times more than the cost to manufacture a standard plastic credit card. Most of these cards come with relatively high annual fees, but some, like the Wells Fargo Propel, or the Amazon Prime Rewards Visa Signature Card (issued by Chase) do not.

Of course, you could argue that every visible possession of a status-oriented person is a status symbol: their clothes, their phone, their shoes, their watch, their wallet, or their purse. Even ostensibly non-ornamental items can become status symbols, like certain blenders, high-end children's strollers, or water bottles. Why then would we expect credit cards to be different than these other physical objects, to somehow not be used as a signifier of class or taste? Well, because this special item, the credit card, represents wealth, but unlike all the other objects mentioned, it has *no* asset value on its own. The object gives no indication of whether its owner is very wealthy, or very much in debt—shall we say, anti-wealthy. It is a symbol of its own meaning as well as of its opposite. What a feat the credit card marketers have achieved: each swipe of the credit card could mean you have no idea how you'll pay for rent this month, or the reverse!

None of the earliest crop of Diners Club competitors, founded over the next five years, would survive the decade as a standalone company.[35] But American Express, which until that point had focused on selling traveler's cheques and money orders, launched their charge card in 1958,[36] and in the same year, Bank of America became the first bank to offer a credit card that didn't require monthly payments in full, two developments cementing the importance of credit cards.[37] As late as 1970, you could use a credit card at Michelin-starred restaurants, and at high-end hotels, but not at a typical American grocery store, and not at department stores, which still insisted that the only credit you could use was the credit they offered.

The sixties and early seventies saw hundreds of banks copying Bank of America to offer credit cards, most using either the processing systems pioneered by Bank of America (the processing system became known as Visa, and spun off from Bank of America), or the Interbank Card Association, which would become Mastercard. But credit limits in this era were low, card acceptance was limited, and credit card lending rarely turned a profit.

After the 1978 Marquette Supreme Court decision, interest rates rose from around 12 percent to a standard of 20 percent. Credit card companies were hungry for more balances at these higher interest rates, prompting them to lower the processing fees they charged to merchants from 4 percent to 2 percent. Soon, nearly every store in the country accepted these bank-issued general purpose credit cards.

And so, the First Debt Boom began, a boom that would hit families that were better-off-than-average, but still middle class, between the 50th and 90th percentile of income. Between 1977 and 1989, these families nearly tripled their amount of inflation-adjusted credit card debt, from an average of $706 each to an average of $1,932.[38]

In 1989, credit cards were a little like AirPods—a status symbol, not of the "one percent," but of the top half: 56 percent of Americans had a credit card, compared to 83 percent today.[39]

When Nigel Morris and his coworker Rich Fairbank kicked off the Second Debt Boom, they were young consultants at Strategic Planning Associates, commuting together from Northern Virginia to New York to advise banks about how to increase their profitability. "Basically, the idea was busting a bank up to its constituent parts, you allocated equity, and you figured out where the bank was making money and where it wasn't," Morris said.[40]

"And we found time after time doing this for the big banks that there was this business called the credit card business that was growing 20 or 30 percent a year, it was making 30 percent or 40 percent return on equity and candidly it wasn't being managed by the superstars of the bank. The superstars were in the investment banking area, the superstars were doing FX trading. We would go to the banks and say, 'let's talk more about the credit card business, look at how much money you make' and the banks would say, 'well, yeah, yeah, yeah, but let's talk about other business.'"[41]

Most bank-issued credit cards shared the same interest rate, 19.8 percent, and they were only issued to people with "high credit standing."[42]

Morris and Fairbank became increasingly convinced they had a better idea: to adopt the "actuarial" practices of the insurance industry to calculate the specific risk level of each American and offer them prices accordingly. Higher risk Americans would get credit cards, but at rates above 20 percent, and the least risky Americans would get interest rates under 15 percent. Fairbank and Morris shopped their idea around to anyone who would listen, hearing rejections from fourteen of the twenty biggest banks in the country, before Signet Bank in Richmond, Virginia, agreed to let them test out their ideas.[43] The credit card division of Signet Bank became Capital One in 1994.

In 2005, Capital One executive vice president Marge Connelly told the US Senate that "the resulting reductions in price and expansion of credit [from Capital One's market entry] into traditionally underserved markets sparked a consumer revolution that can fairly be called the 'democratization of credit.'" To prove her point, she shared some of the low interest rates that credit card companies offered in 2005: Capital One as low as 4.99; Chase as low as 7.99; and Bank of America as low as 5.25.[44] A key point that she neglected to mention was how easily Americans could lose those low interest rates on a whim. In effect, the credit card companies could change customers' interest rates at any time, for nearly any reason, until that practice was outlawed by Congress a few years later.

In 1989, the average credit card holder had an income of $43,000; in just six years, the average income dropped to $38,000.[45] Over the same period, the proportion of credit card borrowers that were executives or managers fell by 6 percentage points, and the percent working retail or in manual labor rose by 7 percentage points. An April 1993 *American Banker* article describing the rapid growth of Signet Bank's credit card division pointed out that Signet had both the best credit card and the worst credit card of all the offers surveyed in the marketplace.[46]

Fairbank and Morris shouldn't get all the credit for this purported democratization. Just as Isaac Newton and Gottfried Leibniz both discovered calculus simultaneously, and two centuries later, Louis Daguerre and Henry Fox Talbot independently invented photography, at the end of the 1980s, Shailesh Mehta and Andrew Kahr stepped onto the scene to invent the low-end credit card roughly in sync with Morris and Fairbank.

At First Deposit, Kahr and Mehta discovered the same tricks as their Signet Bank counterparts. They figured out how to mine Americans' credit bureau data to determine who should be sent credit card offers and at what interest rates (other banks created their marketing lists by buying datasets like who subscribed to the *Wall Street Journal* or *Golf* Magazine), and they learned how to devise experiments to determine the most lucrative offer to send each person. Fairbank, Morris, Mehta, and Kahr reframed banking forever, by creating models that could answer the question, what is the *worst* product that this particular American would still accept? Kahr, like Fairbank and Morris, concluded that the business of credit cards wasn't a sleepy operation to be overseen by those of middling talent, but rather, a scientific machine best put in the hands of presumed quantitative savants. Kahr himself earned his PhD in mathematics from MIT. Mehta, Kahr's most important hire, joined First Deposit in 1986. The *New York Times* called Mehta a "charismatic Bombay-born mathematical genius."[47] Two years later, Kahr moved to the south of France, sold his shares of First Deposit, and turn over the company's reigns to Mehta.[48]

The pioneers of the First Debt Boom, from 1977 until 1989, set their price for credit, and then figured out which Americans were profitable to approve within that price. The pioneers of the Second Debt Boom, from 1989 until 1998, concluded that nearly every American could be offered credit if the price was set high enough. The sleepier banks that housed these explosive credit card businesses spun them off. In 1994, Signet Bank spun off their credit card business, with Fairbank and Morris at the head, with the new name Capital One. First Deposit took on a new name, Providian, in

1994; and in 1997, Mehta would spin off Providian's credit card business into a separate company, leaving behind First Deposit's much older insurance company. To dive deeper into subprime lending, Providian would roll out a credit card that charged a mandatory $156 "credit protection fee" on a credit limit of just $500, and products where interest would begin accruing the day you made purchases (unlike conventional credit cards, where, if you're not already carrying a balance, you have an interest-free "grace period"). A Providian executive would assert that they were finding "the best of the bad."[49] In their annual reports for the year 2000, Providian and Capital One boasted that each had more than 16 million accounts, and more than $25 billion worth of credit card debt on their balance sheets.[50]

But Capital One and Providian, and their more upmarket competitors like Citi and Chase, all continued to operate under the halo effect of credit cards as a luxury good. Paying with a credit card was completely free of stigma—not a signal that you were broke, but an indicator that somebody believed you weren't. In 2018, Capital One spent more than $2 billion on advertisements, or roughly $16 for every family in America. While the direct mail they'd send to people with subprime credit scores might loosely allude to the concept of borrowing money, in their TV and online advertisements, they'd never mention the premise that a credit card might be useful if you weren't making ends meet.

Sell to the rich, the thinking went, and the poor will come along too, but if you talk directly to the poor about their actual financial problems, you will scare the rich away.

Over the course of the Second Debt Boom, from 1989 to 1998, the amount of debt held by working-class families (those at or below the median income) would roughly triple from just $653 per household in 2016 dollars, to $1,638 in 2016 dollars. In 1999, the New York Federal Reserve would publish a report called "Meet the New Borrowers," in which they'd explain that credit card companies had started to write off bad loans at a much higher rate. "Credit card carriers in the 1980s seemed like an elite club," they wrote. "Now it seems that anyone can join," adding that, based on their analysis, the new borrowers were "more willing to borrow, and to borrow for seemingly riskier purposes, such as vacation, [. . .] owe substantially more relative to their income" and were "more likely to work in relatively unskilled blue-collar jobs."[51]

The same basic product is held by a subset of people getting a wonderful deal, people earning hundreds or thousands of dollars annually in credit card rewards, without paying any interest, and a second, disjoint subset of people for whom the products are tremendously expensive. The latter, though, get to belong to the same club as the former. When a twenty- or twenty-five-year-old gets her first credit card, it's not an admission of financial vulnerability; it's an admission into the financial mainstream.

When I talked to people around the country who ended up struggling with credit card debt, it was striking to me how often the initial choice to get a credit card was, effectively, a non-decision. Tasha, a thirty-three-year-old White mother and grad student in Milwaukee, got her first credit card when she was in college.

"I realized I needed a bank closer to where I was going to school. So I go into M&I Bank to open a checking account. The banker asked if I would like a credit card. And I hadn't planned on it. But I was like, I don't know, maybe. And so he's like, 'Well, let me go get something figured out.' So, he comes back with this piece of paper, and basically tells me all I have to do is sign it. And I will get a credit card with a $2,500 limit. And I am 18 or 19 at this point. Yeah. And so, I hadn't intended to and then I did."

Alisha, a twenty-nine-year-old Black small business owner, was twenty-three years old and working at a bank in Georgia when she got her first three credit cards in the same month. "My first real credit card was a Discover card with a $6,000 limit. There was no reason *why* I got the credit card. I was basically encouraged by a, then friend, that I could get approved for a credit card due to my great credit and she applied for me and I was approved."

Kathryn R., White, thirty-four years old, and living in Washington, DC, was twenty-three and in grad school when she got her first credit card. "One of my fellow classmates in the program was shocked that I didn't have any" credit cards, she said. "For the first few months, I would use it if I was going to Target or the grocery store, I'd use it for one or two purchases, and then, you know, pay the exact amount back, just so that I was using it, but not accruing debt. And then eventually, it would occasionally cover a bar tab, and I would not pay the whole balance back."

Tasha ended up defaulting on her credit card. Alisha dug herself into what she called a "black hole" of debt. Kathryn's total credit card debt would swell to $28,000, which ten years later she would still be struggling to repay. Neither Tasha, nor Alisha, nor Kathryn, expected that the decision to get a credit card would be a life-changing one. All three women had the sense that obtaining a credit card was a basic rite of passage.

Getting a credit card doesn't feel like you're falling behind financially, and neither does using a credit card to buy something. It is only when the bill is due, and you compare that bill to the amount of money you have in your checking account, and you remember that the money in your checking account will be needed to cover your rent, that you realize that you became a debtor.

The Fourth Moving Part: An Asymmetry of Information between Banks and Borrowers

Morris and Fairbank saw the credit card industry as a "giant laboratory."[52] They would build a credit card business rooted in the idea of mass experimentation. Every American with a credit report became a test subject: then, as is the case now, banks could pull credit report data on nearly every American in the United States, as long as they then proceeded to offer the person a "firm offer of credit."

"Information-based strategy," as they would dub it, was a regime of experimentation somewhat more advanced than the A/B testing you might have in mind. When you imagine a company running an experiment, you might be thinking of them sending half their customers mail in a blue envelope, and the other half mail in a red envelope, and then deciding whether blue envelopes or red envelopes are better. But "sophisticated" companies like Capital One don't just randomize a single variable at once in order to figure out a single answer to apply to every customer. They'd randomize interest rates *at the same time* as late fees, *at the same time* as annual membership fees, and many other attributes, to figure out uniquely profitable combinations. One key hire, Tom Kirchoff, had been a statistics professor at the University of Missouri-Rolla; at Capital One, he would introduce the use of D-optimal test design, a method for building these multivariable tests.[53] A typical credit card solicitation has more than twenty different price points—either distinct interest rates or fees a customer can trigger depending on their actions.[54] Testing even five or six of these price points at once would seem impossible, especially, for example, if you wanted to test interest rates as low as 3 percent and as high as 29 percent. D-optimal test design was an algorithm that would help Capital One decide which specific combinations of product terms to test that would give them the clearest picture of all tens of thousands of possible combinations. And the goal of this testing wouldn't be to figure out the single most profitable strategy to apply to all customers. The vision, even if it was never fully realized, would be to figure out the *specific* strategy that Capital One should use to earn money from each individual American.

"The second piece of it," *it* being the idea behind Capital One, said Morris, "was using net present value as the currency with which you compare ideas."[55] Net present value, or NPV, is an expression of profitability: to compare the NPV of every idea in a lending business means you'll need to forecast the profitability of every loan you could give to every person as well as how that profitability would change as your "ideas" were implemented. The difficulty, of course, with credit cards, is that when somebody opens a credit card, you don't know how long they'll have it: some people keep the same credit card for decades, and others will default on their loan within the first year. Every action a customer can take needs to be translated into dollars the company will earn and dollars the company will lose. When those forecasts are extended out into perpetuity, you create a "cash-flow," a projection of how much money will be transferred from the customer's wallet to the company in the first month, the second month, and then every month after that. Finally, you choose a discount rate, a number that reflects how much less excited you are about money you'll earn in a year, compared to money you could have right now. That discount rate translates the possible future earnings into a single number: the net present value.

There is no way to calculate the NPV of a credit card without having a prediction for how likely a customer is to end up in collections, the total amount of fees you expect to collect from them, and the total amount of interest—a forecast for everything they could do with the card that would earn money or lose money, today, tomorrow, and for every month in the future.

Capital One, therefore, knows that when Jenny applies for a credit card, they expect her to borrow $3,000, but ultimately have to repay

$7,000, and they know her odds of eventually defaulting are one in four, and in fact, they know her odds of defaulting in March of 2022.

And if Capital One shortens the number of days that customers have to make their payments, as they did while I was a contractor, that means they know how many people can pay their bills on time if they're given twenty-eight days to make their payments, and how many people can pay their bills on time if they're given twenty-five days to make their payments.

Although Nigel left Capital One in 2004, his idea of comparing every idea using NPV never went away. When I left the company in 2018, nearly every proposal still came attached to an NPV estimate.

No important decision would get implemented without a specific prediction of NPV: it wasn't enough to just say, "I think this will make money," because everybody thought their ideas would make money. If all the managers and directors put their ideas for making money on a PowerPoint slide with an NPV number attached, it was easier for executives to decide which ideas to pursue and which to put "on the backlog."

Consider, then, a decision like the one Capital One made while I was a contractor, the decision to shorten the "grace period" for existing customers (this was the aforementioned decision that led me to turn in my contractor badge and conclude with great certainty that I would not return). The grace period is the number of days a customer has in between the date the statement is mailed and the due date. To figure out the NPV of this type of choice—whether to either keep the grace period the same, shorten it, or perhaps lengthen it—you have to calculate all costs and all the revenue streams of each possibility. If you're not sure if something will be "material" to the decision—for example, sway the calculation by more than $5 million or so—you check just to be safe. Therefore, to calculate the NPV of shortening a grace period from twenty-eight days to twenty-five days, you calculate how much you'll earn in extra late fees, from the people who aren't able to make their payment in 25 days but could have done in it 28 days, and how much less you'll earn in finance charges (after all, if people are asked to pay you faster, they'll borrow the money for less time), and subtract from that your extra losses: if people miss more payments, then some people will default, because the extra $30 late fee tips them over the edge. Your NPV, therefore, is your new late fees, minus your lost finance charges, minus your extra dollars of lost principal that never gets repaid. Get a little bit more out of each customer, and suddenly you're sitting on several hundred extra million dollars in cold hard cash. In theory, you'd also have to subtract your lower cost of funds—the fact that the bank doesn't have to itself borrow the money for quite as long if the grace period is twenty-eight days versus twenty-five days—but for this type of decision, it isn't a material component of profitability. The customer might notice that before their due date always was on the 17th and now it's always on the 13th, but they aren't told why the change was made, and they're certainly not told that you made the decision knowing that it made them more likely that one day they'd get a letter in the mail summoning them to court to put a lien on their paycheck.

Using net present value, you could "fully optimize the whole laboratory," said Morris. Meanwhile, most Americans don't even know how to calculate how much interest they'll be charged on their credit cards.

For years, Capital One would brag to the media about how many experiments they ran. A glowing 1999 profile of Capital One in *Fast Company* claimed the company ran twenty-eight thousand experiments per year. Jim Donehey, then the chief information officer told *Fast Company,* "For every action we've taken, we know what the reaction has been. If we sent out a blue envelope and a white envelope, we know which envelope went to which customer—and we've recorded what the reaction was in each case."[56] By the time I joined the company thirteen years later, it would have decided that bragging about treating customers like guinea pigs was no longer in its best interest; the media strategy may have changed, but the business strategy had not.

Shortening customers grace periods, while doing as little as possible to notify the customer that the change had been made, felt like an obvious lie by omission, but it was completely legal. By law, credit card companies can't change the terms of a credit card without giving customers forty-five days' notice and giving them a chance to close their account before the change takes effect. But the length of the grace period isn't formally considered a "term," so those "change in terms" rules didn't even apply. Changing the grace period with the intention of extracting more late fees implied that we didn't think we were taking enough of each customer's money. We would take more, as unobtrusively as possible.

For middle managers at Capital One, the mood ebbed and flowed with what we all called "investor pressure": our perceptions, based on the rumor mill, about what Fairbank was hearing from major shareholders—something tied to the stock price, but not on a one-to-one basis. By that measure of perceived "investor pressure," the last months of 2018 and the first months of 2019 were not a happy time for the bank. Although revenue was rising, costs had risen even more quickly.[57] Over the summer, in the week between when I'd given my two weeks' notice and when I left, we'd moved into the new shiny headquarters building, the tallest in the Washington DC, area, replete with high-end modern art by the same guy who made the colorful string sculpture in the Hirshhorn. More construction was underway, which was expensive, although probably not as expensive as the company's initiative to move all its customer data from on-premise data centers to the cloud.

If Capital One's investors weren't feeling so antsy, or if the new executive in charge of Mainstreet Card, Mr. "Customers don't care when you raise their interest rates," had figured already figured out another "victory" to show he was worth his position, perhaps Capital One wouldn't have chosen to shrink the grace period.

After all, after much handwringing, Capital One had come to opposite conclusions just a few years earlier: the company chose to make payment-due reminders opt-out, instead of opt-in, for their whole credit card customer base. In 2016, describing the change, Jennifer Jackson, then a managing vice president in the subprime credit card division, told the *Christian Science Monitor,* "We're designing products and services to help our customers succeed. We're measuring the impact, and we know that it's impacting customer behavior."[58] When Capital One rolled out the payment due alerts, they did so knowing it reduced the likelihood a customer would fall behind; when they shortened the grace period, they did so knowing it would increase the likelihood. The forces of capitalism might be immutable, and yet, different groups of Capital One executives gathered in different conference rooms would reach more and less evil decisions, depending on how their own personal ethics, how afraid they were that the company would experience a hostile takeover, and how confident they were about their own position in the corporate hierarchy. Chapter 4 will elaborate in more detail the tactics issuers have developed to increase consumer indebtedness.

To me, the grace period decision felt like a sea change. In other ways, the choice to shorten the grace period was no different than every decision that Rich Fairbank or Nigel Morris or their well-compensated deputies had ever made, from the original decision to offer a historically underserved population a credit product with a pricing structure too complicated for most of their prospects to understand. Every choice was justified with information that was hidden from the customer. The core premise of value creation was to know things competitors didn't know—to have better data, better statistical models, and more finely tuned experiments—which would, of course, mean this information would have to be hidden from our customers too.

The story of credit cards would ultimately be different from most stories about corporate malfeasance: the central innovation of Capital One would be to kill the "designer," the person who in an earlier era would have written memos suggesting various dastardly schemes the corporation might attempt. The history of the credit card industry would render as irrelevant the question of whether credit cards were *designed* to trap people into debt. Were rewards added to trick people into spending more money than they had in their checking account? Were zero-interest rates teasers added to cause people who would have ordinarily stuck to a budget to charge big items on credit? Were minimum payments lowered from 5 percent to 2 percent to extract more interest from each borrower? Nobody would need to say. If there was a plausible reason a customer might prefer a term, it could be tested: for example, giving someone the freedom to make a lower minimum payment would clearly be helpful some of the time, and customers could always choose to make bigger payments if they wanted to. Once it was tested, if it were a more powerful way of getting any specific type of person to part with their money, it would be adopted.

Of course, not everyone can be tempted into debt. At my starting salary, it took me no effort, no discipline, and no budget, to spend less than I earned. If the credit card I used (a standard Capital One Journey card, which I applied for in my first week of work, which, though marketed as a student card, didn't penalize you for not being a student) convinced me to spend 5 percent or 10 percent more than I would have otherwise, it wouldn't have been enough to dip me into the debtor class. But plenty of people my age, even with college degrees, earned half my salary, and some less than half. If they were going to have an emergency fund, or save for a house, or for a retirement, they'd need either family wealth, or good luck and constant vigilance. Using a debit card instead of a credit card made their daily mental calculus one step easier—they could look at one number, their checking account balance, and have some idea of what they could safely spend until their next paycheck arrived. Those that avoided credit were told in no uncertain terms that they'd screwed up adulting. A 2017 CNN Money headline read, "Millennials Aren't Opening Credit Cards. That's a mistake." A September 2014 CBS News article on "Why Many Millennials Don't Have Credit Cards," would quote three people, two women in their twenties who insisted it was easier to not worry about missing a credit card bill, and that they didn't want to put down money that that they didn't have, and one ostensible expert, Jeanine Skowronski, a credit card analyst at Bankrate.com, who said, "Millennials may think they're staying out of financial trouble by forgoing credit cards, but they're actually doing a disservice to themselves and their credit scores."[59] *Bankrate.com*, like NerdWallet, WalletHub, and Credit Karma, is a company whose business model is to refer Americans to banks and credit card companies, earning referral fees when new accounts are opened.

I'll discuss Skowronski's claim about credit scores later, but for a moment, let's pause to summarize and consider the combined implications of what we've talked about. In the midst of a social context where consumer credit was fairly scarce, but incredibly cheap, and doled out in a discriminatory fashion, Americans developed an understanding that access to credit was always a good thing. Nearly all loans were installment loans with fixed monthly payments, and easy-to-understand terms. Credit cards, initially, were only offered to the wealthiest Americans, and could only be used in high-end restaurants, hotels, and luxury establishments, and at first required monthly payment in full. Courts then offered lenders the legal grounds to more than double their interest rates. Credit cards, as a result, gradually trickled down to the middle class, and then to people in poverty, but the original cultural understanding persisted, that having a credit card was a signifier of social inclusion, rather than an entry point into penury. Only a small minority of Americans would be able to figure out in dollar terms how much it would cost them to borrow money on these credit cards. Although there has never been a time in American history when people in the middle of the income and wealth distribution weren't economically stressed, two important things would change. The first thing that changed was that, when revolving credit was introduced, with its heavily obscured prices, getting into debt started to feel like a reasonable response to that economic stress, when it hadn't before. The second thing that changed was that, with no legal caps on interest rates, plenty of banks became happy to profitably bury American families. Credit cards would become the first financial product that banks would learn to finely tune to extract maximum profit from each consumer, pushing whichever of a person's buttons that would lead them to borrow the greatest amount of money.

3 The Debtor Class

Doreen and her two sons were living in a park in Fresno, California, in February of 2017, when the skies burst open.

Homeless, they'd often pitched their tents in a spot within the park that Doreen had assumed might've been the bottom of a riverbed a century or so ago, based on the smooth, round rocks. When it started to pour, Doreen realized that maybe that valley where she'd been living had only dried up during the current five-year drought. Her backup campsite, under a bridge, where she normally pitched her tent during storms, was already a few feet under water.

Doreen, a fifty-five-year-old White woman, had heard that the worst of the storm was yet to come, and she didn't know how she'd be able to keep her computer dry in all the rain. Her cystic fibrosis, a diagnosis she received late in life, made it hard for her to work full time, but she didn't qualify for federal disability insurance payments, so her laptop was her connection to the gig work and freelance writing that she used to make money. Doreen took out a payday loan and booked three nights at the cheapest hotel she could find.

She and her sons took showers, relaxed, watched TV, and waited for the storm to pass. But she also worried that maybe the hotel room had been unnecessary, a waste of money.

When she returned to her old campsite, it was clear she'd made the right decision. "It looked like a war zone," she told me. "There were downed tree limbs, and every tree had been stripped to their leaves." Even the park's bathroom, a place where other homeless people sometimes slept the night, was flooded with water. In the week ahead, she read the news and found out people had died in the storm.

Although Doreen wishes she'd been charged less interest for the payday loan, she also says she's never regretted borrowing the money. A few months later, she asked her credit card company for a credit limit increase and was approved. It was an almost unthinkable amount of money. Initially, she was only hoping for a few hundred dollars, enough to buy food that month. Instead, the limit increase was for several thousand dollars, enough for Doreen to change her life. She paid off the outstanding balance on the payday loan, bought train tickets to Washington State, and put down a security deposit on one of the cheapest single room occupancy apartments on the West Coast. Doreen has been living there ever since, paying down her credit card debt gradually. She is adamant that financial regulators shouldn't do anything that would take away access to credit: "People decry the products that are available to the underclass as predatory, and then they want to put a stop to that, rather than offer them an alternative. You have to have that alternative." Although she doesn't think payday loans or credit cards are right for everyone, she doesn't know how she would have left homelessness without them.

But for every Doreen, there's a Michael.

Michael, a forty-year-old White driver and dispatch manager, got his first credit card at twenty-two, and for the first two years, he used it for regular bills and paid it off every month, without accruing interest. But eventually, he says, "I started using it for less necessary expenses: eating out, books, records, and CDs. And then my credit limit got raised once I started carrying more than a zero balance every month. Hot damn! More records, more books. I thought I'd pay it back easily, but a $1,500 limit gains quite a bit of interest when you don't pay it. All of a sudden, I owed around $2,000. I stopped even trying to pay it." Nowhere in his story can one hear a conscious choice to become a debtor, so much as a gradual slide into debt, driven by a set of asynchronous decisions, whose consequences were multiplied by the bank's decision to extend his credit limit. Eventually, he would pay back $2,500 more to the collection agency the debt was sold to (and would show up in court to defend himself against an entirely separate collection agency suing him for the full amount of that debt, a case which he won).

When I started my journey to understand credit cards, I wanted to add up all the Michaels and all the Doreens and figure out whether credit cards, in aggregate, had been good or bad for working-class and middle-class people in this country.

I still believe that Doreen's and Michael's stories are important, but, of course, adding up stories, in some ways, is a fruitless task. Stories, while valuable, can easily be weaponized: the more people I asked about their debt, the more convinced I was that stories, on their own, had the potential to both confuse and to clarify. When you talk to ten, or fifty, or one hundred, or two hundred people, you risk focusing on the conversations that were the most remarkable, rather than the stories that are the most typical. And how easy it can be to remember most closely the stories that confirm the story you had in your head, rather than the stories that didn't neatly fit into the narrative you'd imagined.

Approximately 91 million American adults currently have unpaid, interest-bearing credit card debt, and another 24 million adults have had unpaid, interest-bearing credit card debt at some point in the last year. To put this into perspective, for every one person with student loan debt, there are two people paying interest on their credit card debt.

While there is more in total student loan debt outstanding than there is in credit card debt outstanding, the much higher interest rates on credit cards mean that more credit card interest is paid each year than student loan interest.[1]

The adults with credit card debt are paying a total of $121 billion in credit card interest annually, a bit more than $1,050 each in interest on average, usually to finance the ordinary expenses of daily life. In many cases, this credit card interest sits on top of other forms of consumer debt. Americans, in total, pay approximately $25 billion in overdraft fees, $7 billion in short-term installment loan interest, $6 billion in payday loan interest and fees, and $4 billion in title loan interest each year: more than $155 billion total in interest and fees to help Americans finance things that aren't their biggest-ticket items, their like houses, cars, and college educations, and, not, in most cases, things that could be reasonably categorized as "investments."[2]

There are another 86 million American adults who have credit cards but who pay those credit cards in full every month, and don't pay any interest: technically, you could say these people are in "debt" for the roughly thirty days between when they make their purchases and when they pay their bill. Many statistics about credit card debt include these soon-to-be paid balances.[3] But I don't consider them to be in debt, they don't consider themselves to be in debt, and I doubt that you consider them to be in debt either.

To return then to the 115 million debtors paying interest on their credit card debt, who together, make up almost half of American adults.

This chapter will paint the picture in broad strokes of who these Americans are and why they've borrowed money. As much as possible, I'm relying here on what can be said about the group in its totality, a group that barely resembles the most common narratives about credit card debt in America.

In the popular imagination, credit cards are used especially by people who are young, who are either broke or irresponsible. And in the popular imagination, credit cards are used by the many people with unstable incomes who must manage their expenses—a necessary evil, it could seem, in the turbulent times we live in.

Young people haven't had a long time to build up a safety net, and, hypothetically, their incomes still have time to grow, so it would make some sense for young people to be in debt. But it's not the emerging Gen Z-ers or the presumed-to-be reckless millennials who have the most credit card debt: people who are squarely middle-aged are the most under water.

As of 2018, only 10 percent of Americans aged eighteen to twenty had any unpaid, interest-bearing credit card debt. In some ways, that reflects a success of the CARD Act: Americans were outraged that credit card companies were duping college students into taking on credit card debt they couldn't afford to pay off, so the law banned most forms of marketing credit cards to people under the age of twenty-one, although these young

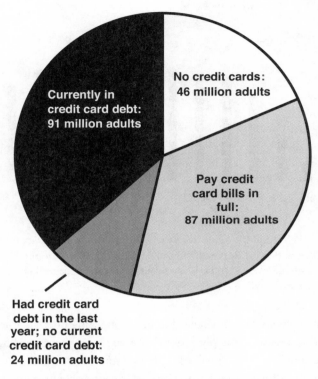

Figure 1. US Adult Credit Card Usage. Data from 2018 Federal Reserve Survey of Household Economics and Decisionmaking.

adults could still be eligible for credit if they applied, assuming their incomes were high enough.[4]

But even when folks enter their twenties, credit card debt is still uncommon: less than a quarter of Americans aged twenty-one to twenty-five have unpaid credit card debt. Nor does credit card debt peak in Americans' late twenties, when adults are most likely to be hit with the unexpected expenses of a new baby: 31 percent of those aged twenty-six to thirty have credit card debt. People are most likely to have credit card debt when they're in their late forties, at a time when their income is at their highest: 49 percent of Americans between the ages of forty-six and fifty have unpaid credit card debt.[5] The median workers' income peaks when she's

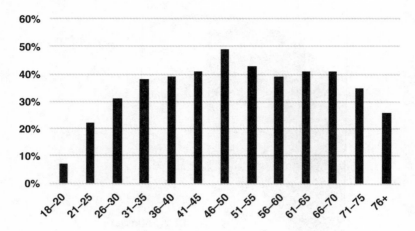

Figure 2. Percent of US Adults with Credit Card Debt by Age. Data from the 2018 Federal Reserve Survey of Household Economics Decisionmaking. Responses to question C3: "Do you currently have any outstanding unpaid credit card debt?"

forty-eight years old.[6] If credit card debt was helping people "smooth consumption," you wouldn't expect Americans to have the greatest amount of debt when they're at their peak of their income.

OK, you might be thinking, maybe this is money that people borrowed early in their lives, and they just didn't get around to paying it off until middle age.

But the typical debtor keeps adding to their credit card balance for decades: it's not until Americans are between the ages of 46 and 50 that their credit card debt load is more likely to go down in any given year than it is to go up.[7] People might start using credit cards thinking it is helping them out during a short-term crisis, but for most users, once they start borrowing money on a credit card, credit card debt will become a persistent part of their life.

Debt, once accrued, isn't so easy to get rid of. More than 60 percent of subprime credit card debt, and more than 40 percent of prime credit card debt, is held by Americans who have been in credit card debt every month for at least two years.[8] But a lifetime defined by credit card debt doesn't always look like high balances that never dwindle. Just as often, you see people who pay off all their credit card debt, get their heads above water for a moment, but never accumulate enough of a safety net, winding up in credit card debt again later that year. If you think I'm overstating how many people are either *chronically* in credit card debt (have credit card debt continuously for years) or *repeatedly* in credit card debt (get out of credit card debt but then frequently find themselves back in it), don't forget that 115 million Americans have credit card debt over the course of a year, and 91 million Americans have credit card debt at any given point in time.

It is easy to imagine debt simply as a natural byproduct of financial hardship: the symptom, more so than the cause, of a country where the costs of daily life exceed the wages paid to many workers. But hardship on its own doesn't create debt: debt also requires a lender hoping to exploit that hardship for a profit, and a person who believes that debt is the best response to the hardship that they're facing. After all, a working mom who buys diapers on her credit card this month will still have to buy diapers next month, along with paying the finance charges on her credit card; the debt, over time, makes her poorer and poorer.

Doreen, for one, decided *not* to use credit many times, even when she was living on the street, because she didn't want to saddle herself with interest payments that would have only made future months on the street harder. She wrote on her blog, "it is better to go hungry for short periods than to run up new debts." And while access to credit helped Doreen exit homelessness, it did not prevent her from sliding into homelessness, an event that happened after she divorced her husband. Although she found a steady job shortly after getting divorced, she was overwhelmed with the mountain of credit card debt and student loan debt accumulated while she was married (some of which she attributes to financial decisions her husband made that she disagreed with). Eventually Doreen defaulted on many of those bills, was evicted from her apartment, and was left with nowhere to go. Her initial problems were not solved by credit cards, and it is possible that credit cards made those problems worse.

For a lower income American, credit card debt and payday loan debt sometimes just temporarily defers, rather than being able to replace, other coping mechanisms for hardship—borrowing money from a family member, showing up to a food bank, or cutting expenses to the bone and then some. For a somewhat higher earning family, the more extreme coping mechanisms may never be required, but the use of the credit card, in the

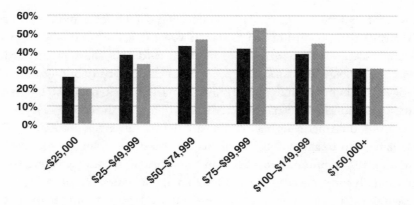

■ **Adults from all households**

■ **Adults from households with exaxtly two adults, one or more children**

Figure 3. Percent of US Adults with Credit Card Debt by Household Income.
Data from 2018 Federal Reserve Survey of Household Economics and
Decisionmaking. Unpaid credit card debt determined by responses to question
C3: "Do you currently have any outstanding unpaid credit card debt?"

absence of a sudden change in the family's income, still creates the same
basic dilemma: it can't increase a family's buying power permanently, only
temporarily, and at a high price. But once a credit card is used, not only is
it hard to pay the debt off, it's also hard to not keep using it.

Alissa Quart, author of *Squeezed: Why Our Families Can't Afford
America*, pins the blame in the rise in credit card debt in America on a
cost-of-living crisis, driven by the rising costs of college, childcare, and
health care. Quart describes a credit card "debt shadow monster" trailing
the families whose stories of unaffordable childcare, out-of-control hospital bills, and high rents she chronicles. Quart's hypothesis echoes what the
left-leaning think tank Demos described as the five possible factors driving the rise in credit card debt since 1989: stagnant incomes, job displace-
ment, underemployment, health-care costs, and housing costs.[9]

On some level, of course, Quart and Demos are right, but if the "squeezed"
hypothesis were the only explanation of why credit card debt has been rising, you'd expect poor families, facing the greatest financial burdens, to
carry the most credit card debt. But families in the top half of American

incomes are more likely to be in credit card debt than those in the bottom half, although the folks in the middle are the most likely to be in debt.

If economic hardship was the basic cause of credit card debt, you'd expect more Americans to carry more debt when the economy is doing poorly than when the economy is doing well. As we'll explore in the next chapter, the reverse is true: when the economy craters, credit card debt falls.

Part of this inverse relationship, between need and debt, can be explained by regulation: the poorest Americans are forbidden by law from accessing credit. Since 2010, the CARD Act has stopped banks from lending money to people who are unemployed or otherwise have very low incomes: these rules, often called "ability to pay" rules, were intended to stop banks from lending to people who wouldn't be able to afford to repay their debts. These rules use an almost laughably relaxed definition of who has enough income to service their debts. They require only that banks guess whether a potential borrower has enough income to cover the *minimum* payment of their credit card after deducting housing expenses and other debt payments. What that means is someone making $25,000 a year, spending $800 a month on rent, with no other debt, could be approved by a bank for a credit limit as high as $42,000.[10] In practice, the ability to pay credit card rules prevent lending to people who are unemployed, and restrict the credit limits of those who have less-than-full-time low-wage work (or receive social security as their main form of income), but do little else to make sure debtors can "afford" their debt.

But it's not exactly the case that middle-earning and higher-earning families have more debt than low-income families simply because lenders are less able (or less willing) to lend to poor people. At every level of income, nearly two-thirds of people who don't currently have credit card debt had neither applied for any type of credit in the last year nor indicated that they wanted credit but chose not to apply (for example, chose not to apply for credit because they thought they would be declined). Many people, even faced with extreme material hardship, avoid credit because they don't see how borrowing money could make them any less broke. This data makes it clear that the reason slightly higher earning families have more debt than working-class families isn't purely because they're deemed more creditworthy; it is also because they are more likely to believe that debt makes sense in their situation.

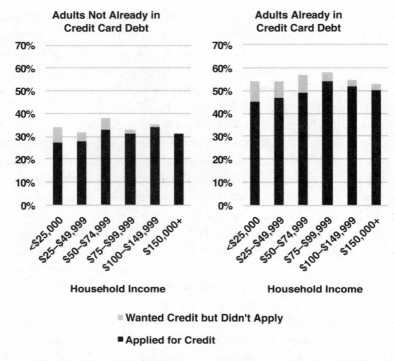

**Adults Not Already in
Credit Card Debt**

70%
60%
50%
40%
30%
20%
10%
0%

Household Income

**Adults Already in
Credit Card Debt**

70%
60%
50%
40%
30%
20%
10%
0%

Household Income

<$25,000
$25–$49,999
$50–$74,999
$75–$99,999
$100–$149,999
$150,000+

▨ Wanted Credit but Didn't Apply

■ Applied for Credit

Figure 4. Percent of US Adults Who Self-Reported a Desire for Additional
Credit in the Last Twelve Months. Data from the 2018 Federal Reserve
Survey of Household Economics and Decisionmaking.
   Percent of Adults who applied for credit is A0: ("In the past 12 months,
have you applied for any credit?")
Percent of adults who desired credit, but chose not to submit a credit
application is A0B: ("Was there a time in the past 12 months that you [or
your spouse/or your partner] desired credit but chose not to submit a credit
application?")

It's easy to chalk up credit card debt to low financial literacy, but people
with credit card debt and without credit card debt have the same basic
grasp of financial fundamentals. For example, at every level of income, data
from the Federal Reserve Survey of Household Economics and Decision-
Making shows that people with and without credit card debt are equally
likely to be able to calculate how interest accrues on savings or on debt.

·   ·   ·   ·   ·

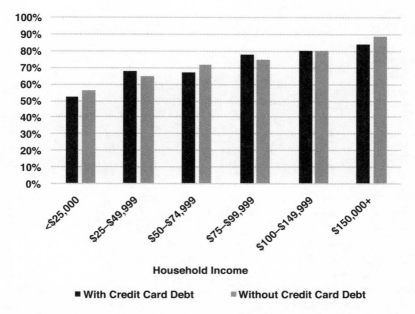

Figure 5. Percent of US Adults Able to Correctly Answer Question about Interest Rates. Data from the 2018 Federal Reserve Survey of Household Economics and Decisionmaking. "Able to correctly answer question about interest rates" based on the percentage answering question FL5 correctly: "Suppose you had $100 in a savings account and the interest rate was 2% per year. After 5 years, how much do you think you would have in the account if you left the money to grow?"

Knowing what you should do isn't the same thing as *doing* what you should do. Take nutrition as an example: many Americans (including myself) are overweight, even though they realize that "all they would have to do" to lose weight is take in fewer calories than they expend.

Credit card debtors are disproportionately married, middle-aged adults, who aren't at the bottom (or the top) of the income distribution, and, on average, these adults do understand the basics of compound interest, at a rate that resembles the rest of the population.

In other words, these are people who, in another type of economy, you might assume would stand a fighting chance of achieving financial stability. Often, the debt is a slow and steady drain from the net worth of middle-class families, not a short-term, easy fix for a one-time crisis or a

Table 1   Demographics of Americans with and without Credit Card Debt

	Currently in Credit Card Debt (37% of adults)	Have a Credit Card, Not Currently in Credit Card Debt (45% of adults)	No Credit Card (18% of adults)	Overall Adult Population
Percent with a household income <$60K	38%	31%	70%	41%
Percent with a household income between $60K and $125K	40%	35%	22%	34%
Percent with a household income over $125K	23%	34%	8%	25%
Percent who are married	60%	62%	30%	55%
Percent with any college or post-secondary education	66%	73%	42%	65%
Percent with at least a bachelor's degree	31%	46%	10%	34%
Percent ages 18–20	1%	2%	10%	3%
Percent ages 21–30	14%	19%	27%	19%
Percent ages 31–40	18%	15%	20%	17%
Percent ages 41–55	28%	20%	21%	23%
Percent ages 56–75	35%	35%	20%	32%
Percent ages 75+	4%	8%	2%	6%

NOTE: Data from the 2018 Federal Reserve Survey of Household Economics and Decisionmaking

bridge to steady footing for young adults. Although we've been dividing the population into two, those with credit card debt and those without credit card debt, to understand who is in credit card debt, it might be helpful to zoom out again into three groups: those who have credit card debt, those who have credit cards that they're paying in full (or not using), and those without credit cards at all. The people who have credit cards they've been paying in full are quite a bit wealthier, and those without credit cards at all tend to be the poorest.

Credit cards are an easy game to win if you're rich. I can't tell you how many people I've talked to, who, in hushed tones, tell me how they just use credit cards to earn points, as if they're the first people to figure this secret out. In some cases, the deal may not be as great as it appears. Credit cards defer the psychological pain of spending; some research shows this encourages people to spend more.[11] There's probably some people who spend more on their credit cards than they would if they had to pay with a debit card or cash; even if these people don't end up in debt, they might still have been better off having more money to put into savings. But, for the most part, credit cards are a windfall for the wealthy. Merchants generally pay a 1 percent to 4 percent fee to accept credit cards, a fee called "interchange," a small sliver of which is retained by the network (Visa, Mastercard, Discover, or American Express), and most of which is sent to the bank that issued the credit card. Credit card rewards are often between 1.5 percent or 2 percent cash back, because that's roughly the same amount the banks are getting in interchange fees. Effectively, 100 percent of people pay higher prices at grocery stores to cover these credit card processing fees, even though the rewards get siphoned to the minority of people who have a credit card but pay it in full every month. Economist Scott Schuh and colleagues estimate that this redistribution, from credit card processing fees into rewards and cash back, cost every low-income adult $21, and is a windfall to every rich adult of $750.[12]

If you're poor though, with far less wiggle room in your budget for indulgences, credit cards are a hard game to win. If you're tracking each penny that comes in and out, it's often easier to reference a single number, the amount of money in your checking account (or the amount of cash in your wallet), than it is to bounce back and forth between a credit card balance and a checking account balance, mentally accounting for what transactions have or haven't posted yet.

THE DECISIONS OF DEBT

Payday loans get a bad rap, but they have one thing going for them: everyone who uses them *realizes* they're borrowing money, and typically understands that they'll be expensive, even if they end up underestimating the costs. As a result, people almost never regret the "principal" of their payday loan debt, only the interest; they would make the same purchases again if they could've found a less expensive way to borrow the money.

When I spoke to Peggy, a baker in St. Charles, Missouri, she put it this way: Payday loans "were horrible, because it's like, you really need money and you have no alternatives. You know, it's like, 'What are you gonna do?' So, you get a payday loan. So, you have to go and make almost that same amount in payment every week, and it takes forever to pay them off. And it's like every week, another hundred dollars, hundred dollars, hundred dollars, and it's like a thirty-year payoff, it seems like." The first time Peggy, a fifty-seven-year-old White woman, took out a payday loan, it was to cover the cost of her family's utility bills after her husband had lost his job. "I think we would have tried other things if I had known how hard it was. I didn't realize—I mean, it just seemed like endless. It's like, every week, there we were, again. And you're using up so much of your pay every time." If she had lived in a state where payday loans were illegal, she says she would have tried to borrow money from family members, or sold household goods, both of which she says would have been better.

To get into credit card debt, by contrast, is often a series of decisions that feel like non-decisions.

At the time that this book is being written, it would hypothetically be possible, for people to wait until the day an emergency comes up to apply for credit. American Express, for example, gives most of their cardholders a credit card number they day of their application, which they can add to a mobile wallet, or use to make purchases online. Jud Linville, the CEO of Citi Cards, told investors in 2014 that "if a customer goes to buy something and does not have enough open to buy, we can ask if they would like to raise their credit limit. Without leaving the checkout process we can collect information we need, process the line increase if appropriate, and notify the customer and process the transaction all in real time without them leaving the checkout page." And it's not just credit limit increases that can be extended instantaneously; it's also new credit cards. As Linville said, "We've created the ability for customers to not only apply for the card in one of our 1,700 branches, but to obtain a functioning card they can use within 15 minutes."[13] Many personal loan companies advertise that they transfer money into the borrower's checking account on the same day as the application.[14] Americans may not feel comfortable waiting until an emergency strikes to apply for credit, and they have good reasons to be hesitant, but the limitation isn't the technology itself.

But the credit card product encourages a person to apply for the product well before he expects to need it, and to seek a high credit limit just in case. Three separate decisions get spread out in time: the decision to apply for a credit card, the decision to make a purchase on a credit card, and the decision of how large of a payment to make on the credit card bill—all three choices made in the face of an uncertain future. The imperative to shop around to find a good interest rate on a credit card is suppressed by the fact that many consumers aren't exactly sure if they'll use the card to borrow money at the time that they submit their applications.

None of those three decisions feel exactly the way taking out a loan does: a conscious choice to borrow a fixed amount of money, knowing the payments you'll be asked to make, and the total cost over the life of the loan. It might feel crazy to go down the street to apply for a loan to buy plane tickets for your cousin's wedding, but it doesn't feel crazy to buy plane tickets on your credit card, without being completely clear if you can afford it or not.

Credit cards are sometimes used for nondiscretionary purchases, but often they're used for the extras that give us joy, at least until the interest comes due. A 2019 survey of twenty-two hundred adults by CNBC and Morning Consult found that for Americans with credit card debt, 32 percent attributed their debt mostly to "discretionary spending like clothing and entertainment," and another 9 percent attributed their debt to travel.[15] In total, a similar number of people as the 37 percent of American debtors who attributed their debt primarily to nondiscretionary spending, like childcare, rent, utilities, food, and medical bills.

I think it's important to acknowledge that credit cards are very often used to finance splurges, about as often as they're used to pay for necessities. A survey conducted in 2019 found that Americans with credit card debt spent more on dining outside the home and takeout ($2,186 annually); more on clothing, shoes, and accessories ($1,892 annually); more on subscription services ($1,198 annually); and more on out-of-home entertainment ($1,538 annually); than those without credit card debt.[16]

My goal is not to shame a single person in America about their debt. We must acknowledge, however, that not all debt is strictly essential. This acknowledgment is necessary to dismantle the debt machine. If we insist that all debt was strictly necessary, it means Americans need the debt machine, operating at roughly its current size, if not necessarily at its existing cost. It works in the interest of big banks for the public narrative to insist that all borrowing was strictly unavoidable. To acknowledge that some, but certainly not all, debt is discretionary, means that it is possible that some debt is effectively coerced by products that are unusually effective at getting people to spend more than they earn. Saying this out loud, that some people borrow when they'd be better off spending less, can feel forbidden in a political culture where the left doesn't want to seem like they're criticizing the middle class, and the right doesn't want to undermine the premise of the rational consumer. This acknowledgment is nevertheless necessary to dismantle the apparatuses that banks use to tempt and coerce people into unnecessary debt, the debt from which banks derive so much profit, at such a high cost to working families. The point isn't that working-class and middle-class families shouldn't occasionally treat themselves to a restaurant meal on their credit cards because they don't deserve nice things; the point is that credit cards, by their very nature, compound economic distress. Our current system is very punitive to those who spend more than they earn, and this is true even when the "extra" purchases are things that the borrower, and I mean this sincerely, *deserve* to own or to have.

The reality is that all of us have many desires at once, desires that are often contradictory, desires that push and shove each other for our attention until we act on some and ignore others, sometimes with great deliberation and sometimes impulsively. A person's desire to relax in an Uber when his shift ends at 10 p.m. instead of taking a long bus ride home might conflict with his desire to build up enough of an emergency fund so he doesn't get evicted if his chronic illness acts up, forcing him to take unpaid time off. Roughly 40 percent of workers make under $15 per hour, a level of wages at which very ordinary things can be financially out of reach: meeting friends out for drinks once a month or buying your daughter the new pair of sneakers she asked for. The nature of economic deprivation is the fact you have to constantly deprive yourself of small, ordinary indulgences, over, and over, and over again.

Credit cards don't cause the debtor to invent desires out of whole cloth. Instead, they cause the debtor to prioritize her specific desires benefitting the credit card company, at the expense of her desire for stability and a better future.

Tasha, who we met in the previous chapter, knew it was irresponsible to borrow money if it wasn't an emergency, such as using a credit card for anything but the essentials. Her solution as a twenty-year-old to this conundrum, she told me, was to spend all the money in her checking account on the things she wanted: "I would use my real money for fun stuff, and then tell myself I have to have groceries, so I have to use my credit card."

At a middle-class income, you hardly have to be a reckless spender to spend a few thousand dollars more than you earn annually. When you have a credit card, it is not at all hard to unintentionally spend $65,000 per year when you only make $60,000, or to spend $32,000 per year when you only make $30,000, doing things that feel completely normal: it is often not clear to borrowers when they make the purchases whether they'll be able to pay them off that month or not.

After a while, a balance on a credit card starts to feel like an amorphous number, a bill to be paid like the phone bill, reflecting not the cost of some specific set of purchases, but a tax on being alive. This sense of detachment from one's debt is particularly strong for borrowers with the common experience of having zigzagging debt: a balance that grows and shrinks as they try to pay off the debt, don't fully succeed, deplete all the cash from their checking account with their card payments, and then having a growing card credit card balance the next time they're hit with an unexpected expense. In those circumstances, it is nearly impossible to say exactly where a person's debt comes from, because the total amount they've made in payments now far exceeds the amount of money they originally spent, but they still have debt remaining. Which purchases, they might ask themselves, have been paid off, and which purchases are they still paying for?

Most borrowers I talked to said they used their credit cards on essentials at least some of the time, but simultaneously they said, they wish they had made different decisions, to use their credit cards less.

Naomi, a graphic designer and Black creative in Washington, DC, defaulted on their first credit card before their twenty-second birthday. "It was a messy cycle," they told me, "of me telling myself I had everything under control, that I would pay them off next paycheck, and then after paying them off with my new money I had no money left, so I had to use them again. The cycle happened for a whole year until eventually I just ignored paying off the cards completely." It wasn't the case that Naomi had no idea what a credit card was before applying. Nevertheless, for a young person with a credit card, but without family wealth or a high income, the credit card proved to be an elusive trap.

"Sadly enough," Naomi told me, "all the lessons I've learned are warnings everyone hears when getting credit cards. 'Make sure you pay it off! Make sure you have the money to pay it off! Or perhaps don't even get one at all.'" They added, "I'm pretty hedonistic, but the truth is you don't always have to treat yourself."

Often, credit card debt feels like something that snuck up on the debtor, not something that was pursued, chosen, or wanted. In effect, if you have a credit card and already have at least some interest-bearing credit card debt, each time you swipe your credit card, you are effectively taking out a *new loan* at a 24 percent interest rate, but it doesn't feel that way at all—at least, it doesn't feel the same as walking down the street to talk to a payday lender or banker and saying, "I'd like a loan."

And once consumers have a significant chunk of debt, they become less sensitive to taking on more. Aimee Chabot from Duke University's Fuqua School of Business ran four experiments that prove exactly this point. Participants were asked to imagine they had either a small or a large amount of student loan debt, and then to consider borrowing more money, either borrowing money for something like a coding bootcamp or GRE prep class that offered the possibility of better career prospects, or borrowing to have $30 more per week to spend socializing with friends. Participants who were asked to assume they had $45,000 in student loan debt already (the high-debt condition) were 21 percent more likely to borrow money for the career-prospect-purchase than the participants who were asked to assume they had just $4,500 in student loan debt (the low-debt condition) and 24 percent more likely to borrow money for social events. For somebody with no debt, the first time they borrow money on a credit card feels consequential, but once a consumer has already racked up credit card debt, adding to it doesn't feel like a tremendously important decision, at least until they've had the experience of struggling to make even the minimum payment on a credit card.

Millennials have fewer credit cards and less credit card debt (but quite a bit more student loan debt) than Gen Xers had at our age, reflecting both the fact that we were the first generation directly impacted by the CARD Act rules limiting on-campus credit card marketing, and, reportedly, the fact that we have greater cultural aversion to debt.[17] The fact that this generational difference exists is among the clues that credit card debt does not rise organically from material hardship.

Two people, faced with the same material circumstances, will often reach different conclusions about whether borrowing makes sense. It's not unusual to turn to a calculator or Excel to plot a course to get out of debt, but the initial decision to borrow money is rarely made in such an algorithmic fashion. Talking to borrowers, it became obvious to me that people in debt carry around radically different scripts: For some, credit card debt is deeply normal, an inevitable byproduct of being American, regardless of one's level of income, and a natural part of our country's way of life. Other debtors view credit card debt as an intrinsic failure, whether that failure was, for them, avoidable or unavoidable.

In Charleston, South Carolina, a bartender's bicycle was stolen, the bike she used to commute to work. It took her a few months to save up the money to buy a new bike, a goal made more difficult by the fact that without the bike, she spent money on the occasional Uber or Lyft ride, when hitching a ride with a friend had failed. It's a situation where borrowing might have made sense: those Uber and Lyft rides were their own form of interest. But she didn't have a credit card, nor did she want one.

Hypothetically, the choice to apply for a credit card is mostly free of consequence: if a credit card doesn't have an annual fee, then getting a credit card costs nothing, and comes with no real obligation. And yet, the choice to apply for a credit card turns out to be an incredibly important one, because while the choice to apply for a credit card is generally made in a moment of low stress, once that credit card is around, debt becomes much harder to avoid, even if the applicant imagined that they would only use the credit card in an emergency.

THE PORTION SIZE EFFECT

I started working at Capital One the week of my twenty-second birthday. I was an analyst for a year on the Decision Sciences team, which built statistical models for the credit card division. While most analysts at Capital One would make recommendations about whether to change a business strategy, my recommendations were a step removed—should Capital One modify a statistical model, and if so, in what way? That work felt peacefully divorced from any larger questions about debt. All the new analysts "rotated" teams after one year; my rotation was onto a team called Customer Engagement. I thought I'd like it—after all, the team had "customer" in the name, and I knew already that I was hungry to better understand why our customers were borrowing money, and how our credit cards fit into their lives. But the company's assumption seemed to be that customers mostly cared about how well our mobile app worked, and whether or not we sent them too many emails, and how quickly we resolved fraud incidents. The customer engagement team was organized around a framework called "moments that matter," but the lingering, gnawing feeling of being in debt over time, or paying interest, was not one of these moments. I was convinced that what mattered most to customers was how much credit we offered them, and on what terms. After talking to a handful of executives, I decided I wanted to join what was called the CLIP team: the Credit Limit Increase Program. Normally, I wouldn't have been allowed to switch teams again so quickly, but luckily, the CLIP team always needed more people.

CLIP was every part of speech. You could pCLIP a customer, a verb: to raise their credit limit without having first asked their permission. You could rCLIP a customer: to approve an existing customer's request for a higher credit limit. CLIP was also a noun: a PowerPoint slide would list how many CLIPs we'd given out. And CLIP was an adjective: CLIP losses, CLIP team, CLIP outstandings (a term which refers to the total balances that customers owe, inclusive of both principal and interest).

The team had a reputation for being the most stressful place to work at the company. A few months after I'd joined CLIP, I saw a vice president, Ani, who'd previously been in charge of CLIP, give a talk on stage about career transitions. In the talk, he told the story about how he'd ended up leading a technology division: *"Eventually, I told my boss that if I had to lead one more CLIP campaign I would jump out a window."*

Capital One had millions of subprime customers, whose starting credit limits were often as low as $300 or $500. In a strategy described by the media as "low and grow," the only way to make any money off these subprime and new-to-credit customers would be to wait for the riskiest customers to default, and then raise the credit limits of the people who were making their payments on time.[18] With such low starting credit limits, the decision of who to approve and who to decline was almost irrelevant, compared to the decision about whose credit limits to raise. In the words of CEO Rich Fairbank, "The real exposure comes on the credit line side, not really the origination side."[19] The reason, in effect, to try to get more customers, was just so that you could CLIP them later.

This, to me, felt like the center of all the action, of all the power: Who would get more credit, and who would not? Would Capital One make record profits, or go bust in the next financial crisis? Would we grant more credit to people who wanted or needed some extra slack, or would we drive people into a deeper and deeper hole? So what if it would be a lot of work.

As a confused, ambitious, idealistic, center-left twenty-three-year-old of the millennial generation, it seemed deeply intuitive to me that I would have the "biggest impact" in some loosely defined, pro-social capacity, at the company's greater profit center.

A manager at Capital One once told researchers from the University of Southern California "we count everything here. There's probably a spreadsheet somewhere describing the ratio of tables to chairs in the cafeteria." And if you're going to test the optimal ratio of tables to chairs, of course you would test credit limits. Not only, as Fairbank pointed out, were credit limit increases central to the company's risk and exposure, it was also easy to observe the counterfactual of not extending a customer more credit. If you randomly chose to approve or decline a possible customer, you wouldn't be able to collect any data on the person who had been declined. But if you randomly allocated credit limit increases, you could compare exactly how profitable a customer is at a low credit line or a high credit line.

In *The Age of Surveillance Capitalism*, Harvard Business School emeritus professor Shoshanna Zuboff discusses the rise of widespread consumer testing in Silicon Valley, and the associated ethical problems.

Zuboff points out that while academics are required to get approval from ethicists on institutional review boards before they can conduct research on human subjects, who generally force them to get informed consent from their test subjects, corporations conduct research on all Americans, bound by no ethical constraints.[20] Most of us will never know that we were tested upon, and the results of these experiments are generally not released to the public to build a shared base of knowledge. Those concerns didn't trouble me, if I thought about them at all. Instead, I was attracted to the revolutionary power of these tests, for what they would teach me about the ways in which access to credit changed people's lives.

In bioethics, one principle of ethical testing is that researchers shouldn't know in advance which drug or medical intervention works better. If they already know which treatment is more effective, depriving test subjects of the better drug or treatment is unethical. If researchers gain sufficiently strong evidence mid-study about the effectiveness of the trial, they're supposed to end the study early. By at least this measure, Capital One's experiments felt not only defensible, but necessary. Wasn't it important to understand which people benefited from gaining access to credit, and under what circumstances a high credit limit would mean a person would get buried under crushing debt?

What I learned matched exactly what economists Scott Fulford and Scott Schuh documented in research published in 2015 by the Federal Reserve Bank of Boston, tracking how Americans used credit cards from 1999 to 2015, and reviewing a random sample of Americans' credit bureau data across time. Roughly half of Americans with credit cards didn't use much of their available limits on their credit cards, and rarely, if ever, used their credit cards to borrow money. For the other half of the population, every time they got a credit limit increase, their debt seemed to increase predictably. If they were using 60 percent of their credit one year, they'd use 60 percent of their credit the next year, so if their credit limit was increased by $1,000, like clockwork, they'd borrow another $600: it wasn't until Americans were in their fifties that this trend really started to slow.[21] As the authors wrote, "following a ten percent increase in credit limits, the debt of revolvers eventually increases by 9.99 percent."[22]

Capital One was no exception to the national trends Fulford and Schuh explained: typically, if we raised the credit limit of a customer who already had credit card debt, they'd use up whatever proportion of the increase—40 percent, 60 percent, or 80 percent—that they'd been using up of their initial credit limit. If customers felt like they had a say in the financial future, to decide whether or not to get into more debt, that's not the story the data told. The data showed that the draw of the additional credit was irresistibly strong.

To think about what this means, imagine you're presented with thirty fries. You might choose to eat twenty-five. Now let's say you're presented with sixty fries, and you now choose to eat fifty. On some level, this phenomenon doesn't make perfect sense—if you "wanted" fifty fries, why wouldn't you have eaten all thirty when you were given the smaller portion? As psychologists Marion Hetherington and Pam Blundell-Birtill pointed out in the British Nutrition Foundation's *Nutrition Bulletin,* the "portion size effect," where people eat more *because* more food is in front of them, outside of any impact caused by food scarcity, is "robust, reliable, and enduring;"[23] when it comes to debt, that same portion size effect is just as powerful. How much we want is a direct byproduct of what is presented to us. With food, as with credit, our "desires" and our actions are heavily shaped by context.

In effect, we had set up a restaurant where you showed up but couldn't request a "small," "medium" or "large" order of fries. You just sat down at a table, and Capital One decided how many fries to plop down, and how often to refill your plate. Asking for more credit, via a credit limit increase, or an application for a new credit card, would be like fiddling with a broken thermostat: the customer would have the illusion of some agency, but the people in the control room would be the ones to change the temperature. Credit limit increases initiated at a customer's request would often be for as little as $100, while the "proactive" credit limit increases, granted at Capital One's sole discretion, were often for $1,000 or $3,000. Why would we give up our power to set customers credit limits, by bending to customers' requests? What was even more disturbing was that those who were randomly given a small plate of fries were no more likely to request more food: they would eat if it was there but wouldn't think to request it if it wasn't there.

I have been asked by more than one economist if I think consumer credit is addictive. But most of America's credit card debt is accumulated passively after credit limit increases, not actively after applications for new credit cards. People who suffer from addiction aren't only tempted by drugs or alcohol that are freely available within their own home: once addicted, they are driven, chemically, to seek the addictive substance. That compulsive behavior, an overwhelming desire to get access to more credit, certainly describes some people, and of course, some people struggling with drug or alcohol addiction apply for loans or credit cards to finance their addiction.[24] But for most people, credit cards are more like french fries or ice cream: highly tempting when they're in arms reach, and much easier to avoid when out of sight.

People who would never go out and apply for a new loan will still choose to borrow more on the credit cards they already have, especially when they get a credit limit increase. And a sizable chunk of the adult population, about 25 percent of all credit card holders (roughly half of all credit card revolvers) will use more than half of all the credit made available to them, for almost all their adult lives.[25]

When you realize this—that most consumers who borrow money on their credit cards will use most of each extra batch of credit that banks extend to them (even if they wouldn't have otherwise applied for a new credit card or asked for a credit limit increase)—an important implication emerges. The amount of credit card debt Americans carry isn't really driven by how much they want or need to borrow. Instead, it is driven by how much banks have chosen to lend.

.   .   .   .   .

To summarize some of what we have learned so far: credit card debtors are most often middle-class families, with incomes between $50,000 and $100,000, rather than the lowest income families. This points us toward the conclusion that credit card debt isn't an inevitable byproduct of a system where lots of workers earn less than what they need to support their families: it, of course, still requires a bank interested in pushing a family into debt, and a family that believes that credit card debt makes sense in their situation. Credit cards are a drain on the finances of families who might otherwise stand a fighting chance of achieving some financial stability.

And the typical credit card debtor isn't a recent college grad in her 20s, skating between internships and temp work, but rather, a Gen Xer between the ages of 46 and 50, who should ideally already have a retirement nest egg. The fact that so much credit card debt is held not for weeks or months, but years, should point us to the conclusion that credit cards aren't being used as short-term bridges, but rather, as a type of long-term crutch that makes middle-class Americans poorer and poorer for each subsequent year they carry the debt. The typical credit card debtors are no less likely to understand the basics of finance and interest rates than their debt-free counterparts, suggesting that financial education on its own is unlikely to move any needles on American indebtedness. But the fact that credit card debt is surprisingly evenly balanced between discretionary and nondiscretionary purchases suggests that we *can* turn the tide and help Americans get out of debt, leaving the American middle class with more available cash for all the things (discretionary and nondiscretionary) that they value. The distribution of credit card debt in the United States supports the principal argument: the Americans that banks are most interested in, and the most successful at, pushing into credit card debt, are those with above average incomes, taking on additional credit card debt at the time in their lives when their income peaks.

THE LESS TYPICAL DEBTOR

We have talked a bit about the "typical" debtor, the type of person who statistically represents the *mode*, or the largest group of debtors. I want to zoom in though on a smaller, but no less important group of debtors, those whose household income is less than the US median. For simplicity, I'll refer to this group as the working class: they may experience bouts of unemployment, but the clear majority of this group works for a living (many, to use the language of the pandemic, are essential workers). Some are disabled, and some provide care work within their own homes. Although they're less likely to be in credit card debt than their middle-class counterparts, it's certainly not unusual for the working class to have credit card debt—nearly 40 percent do. Their average credit card balances tend to be much lower than middle-class credit card balances, and, as a result, the working class holds only about one quarter of all the US credit card debt.[26] Although in dollars and cents they don't pay the bulk of credit card interest, in many respects they pay the largest human toll.

Peggy met her husband, Dave, when they were both working at the same Dorado's pizza parlor in Missouri; Peggy was fifteen and her husband was seventeen. They got married, had two children, and bought their first house together seven years later. "We worked pretty hard to save our money to get a down payment," she told me. "I worked days, he worked nights." She added, "As soon as we got our house, we started getting things in the mail: we were getting credit card offers." Peggy and Dave, believing better times were ahead, applied for several. "Mostly we'd try to use our credit cards for bigger purchases, not for everyday things. Like I'd never use it at the grocery store." Peggy became pregnant with her third child: suddenly, her waterbed mattress was completely unbearable, because it was so difficult to get in and out of bed. (Younger readers should note that in the 1980s and 1990s, it was common for Americans to sleep on what were effectively giant squishy vinyl bags of water that molded to your body.) The last purchase Peggy and Dave made on their credit cards before filing for Chapter 13 bankruptcy was a $600 mattress. For a while, that was the end of their story with credit cards; a Chapter 13 bankruptcy requires filers to make monthly payments, and the $126 per month bankruptcy payment eventually itself became too much to manage.

More than a decade would pass before Peggy got her next two credit cards, in 2012, both for clothing stores. Some things were different this time: she started using a small notebook to keep track of every bill. She tries to pay more than the minimum payment when she can. The credit card bills due around the same time as her car payment get the smallest payments, to make sure her $373 car payment clears (her weekly paycheck is around $420). Each month gets a new page in her notebook, and each bill gets a check mark when it's been paid. Like before, the debt is hard to manage. She now has twelve credit cards, each with a balance, although she uses her debit card for most purchases. "I try not to use [my credit cards] at all," she told me. But the month before we spoke, her cell phone had broken, which meant she needed to catch up on her cell phone bill to get a new phone. "I always pay [the cell phone bill] a little bit behind because they let you. I needed to get a new phone, and I had to be up to date on it. So, I used one credit card, and I had enough to pay it: $170. I had enough [available credit] on one credit card to do that. I was very proud of myself."

Although every person's story is different, there are a few components of Peggy's experience that are typical for working-class debtors. They are often maxed out or nearly maxed out on their credit cards (in part because banks tend to give lower credit limits to those with lower incomes). As a result, even if they have a substantial amount of credit card debt relative to their income, most of their daily purchases are made on a debit card or with cash: they need to check their available balances on their credit card before making any credit card purchases. The total amount of debt they carry might seem low compared to middle-class debtors—generally, $5,000 or less—but those balances are usually much higher relative to their income, and often, an inconceivable amount to pay off unless they get an unexpected raise or sudden windfall. Most, like Peggy, are acutely aware of the prices of everything: they can tell you to the dollar the amount of each bill, and the typical price of all the things they buy at the grocery store, a level of financial awareness substantially less common among higher-income Americans.[27] Many, like Peggy, must pick and choose which bills get paid when, learning which utility companies or lenders will cut you more slack, and which had stricter deadlines: at Capital One, we called this "payment ordering," and we were obsessed with making sure that Capital One was paid before any other creditors or bills.

Peggy is also typical of other working-class debtors in that she uses her annual tax refund to catch up on her bills and pay off debts: "We always relied on our tax refunds. That was always something we could rely on to help us pay back," she told me. Peggy's current wage, $15.50 per hour, at a unionized grocery store, is the highest wage she's earned in her life, making the earned income tax credit a major chunk of her annual cashflow.

While the most commonly used credit scores, FICO and Vantage, don't consider income, working-class Americans are more likely to experience the type of bump in the road that makes loan repayment simply impossible—and many, like Peggy, have either declared bankruptcy or otherwise experienced a credit loss, like the repossession of car, the foreclosure of a home, or a wage garnishment lawsuit against unsecured debt. Americans who live in working-class neighborhoods have a median Equifax credit risk score of 658—this means that roughly half have "subprime" credit scores. By comparison, the median credit score of an American living in a middle-class neighborhood is 735, and the median credit score of an American living in a high-income neighborhood is 774.[28] Income and geography might not strictly determine a person's credit score (and in fact, neither income nor geography are direct inputs used to calculate these scores), but they clearly play a major role in creating the life circumstances that make somebody's credit score low or high.

A subprime credit score between 550 and 660 would usually reflect a situation a lot like Peggy's: someone who tries to pay their bills but isn't always able to. Having a subprime credit score doesn't mean you can't get credit—far from it. A number of credit card companies heavily target this exact population: Capital One, Credit One, First Premier, Celtic Bank, and Merrick Bank. Some major banks and credit card issuers, namely American Express and Chase, avoid the subprime market altogether; others, like Citi and Discover play around the edges, dipping into the top end of the subprime market, monitoring conditions, and choosing to either enter or exit the subprime market year by year.[29] If a working-class adult has never used credit before, they may not know what types of loans they qualify for, but once an adult has used credit, even if their credit score is relatively low, they're bombarded with credit card solicitations from a persistent handful of companies, even after declaring bankruptcy.[30] In that sense, it's not "hard" for the working class to find credit. It is hard for the working class to find *good* credit. As a result, they pay much higher prices: while people with high credit scores are sometimes able to bounce around their debt on credit cards running a 0 percent interest rate promotion for new customers, those sorts of "teaser rates" are almost never available to people in Peggy's situation.

THE COLOR OF DEBT

Peggy's hometown of St. Charles, Missouri, is about 15 miles west of Ferguson, Missouri, which is in turn, about 12 miles northwest of downtown St. Louis. Although St. Charles and Ferguson are bordering towns, St. Charles is 88 percent White and Ferguson is 67 percent Black. Peggy was born in St. Charles, but many White residents of St. Charles (or, often, their parents or grandparents) left Ferguson or other parts of northern St. Louis County to avoid living in integrated neighborhoods.[31]

Across a twenty-minute drive, and a centuries-old divide of racist policies, Missourians experiences of credit card debt shift dramatically. In
2013, the year before White police officer Darren Wilson shot and killed
unarmed Black teenager Michael Brown, Ferguson issued more than
thirty-two thousand arrest warrants, mostly for traffic violations, in a town
of just twenty-one thousand residents. As NPR reporter Joseph Shapiro
explained, "Data from the Missouri state attorney general's office show
that black drivers are stopped in Ferguson in disproportionate numbers,
even though Ferguson police are more likely to find contraband when they
stop white drivers."[32] Over-aggressive policing of Black Americans result
in tickets, fines, and fees, often for small offenses, where a White American
might receive a warning or not be stopped at all—like having a broken tail-
light, or coming to a rolling stop at a stop sign, or failing to use a turn signal. For a low-income American, fines can quickly escalate, especially in a
heavily policed community: an unpaid fine leads to a suspended license,
and a more serious set of fines or fees if the person is then caught driving
without a license. Of course, most Americans would have no way to pay off
the original unfair fine if they weren't able to drive to work, creating a
dilemma with no reasonable exit route. Any resulting penal debt isn't dis-
chargeable in bankruptcy.[33] Unfair policing is just one of the many factors
that put many Black Americans on a different financial trajectory than
their White counterparts, long before they've had the chance to make any
individual financial decisions, lowering their credit scores, and raising
their costs of credit. The average White American has a credit score that is
125 points higher than the average Black American.[34]

The town of Ferguson may make national headlines, but segregation in
the United States is the norm, not the exception. In the years between
2014 and 2018, the typical White American lived in a neighborhood that
was 71 percent White. Meanwhile the typical Black American lived in a
neighborhood that was 69 percent non-White, and the typical Latino or
Hispanic American lived in a neighborhood that was 68 percent non-
White.[35] In theory, geography is irrelevant to the credit card industry;
while you can apply for a credit card in a bank branch, most credit card
applications are completed online, and credit card companies send their
mail solicitations all over the country. But Black Americans receive fewer
credit card solicitations in the mail, even when controlling for income and

credit score.[36] Black Americans have fewer options for credit, and pay credit card interest rates that are on average 2 percentage points higher than White Americans.[37]

Black Americans from the most disadvantaged communities sometimes lack an entry point into the entire formal banking system altogether, including credit card access. In Hamtramck, Michigan, the poorest town in the state, I spoke to a middle-aged Black man named Benny, who summarized things this way: "They don't make it easy [to get credit]. You have to go through too many questions. You have to have a perfect this, and a perfect that."[38] His neighbor, David, agreed that the system of credit was too inaccessible. The last time he'd applied for any type of credit, he was declined, and he hadn't applied for any forms of credit since. At the time, he was trying to pull together enough money to put down a security deposit for an apartment when his girlfriend got pregnant: the denial, he says, completely changed the course of his life. Had he been approved, "I might've had a house [. . .] I might've been with my first baby's mama. I might've not had felonies on my arrest record. A lot of things could have happened [for me]."

It's also worth noting that Black adults are about 70 percent more likely than White adults to *believe* they have a low credit score when their credit score is actually average or good, a phenomenon that Black academics including Sheila Ards and William Darity Jr. have pointed out could be due to past experiences of unfair loan denials, or due the fact that those shut out from financial opportunities have less knowledge of formal financial system.[39]

The experiences of the Black middle class, men and women like Alisha, who we met in chapter 2, vary significantly from the experiences of the many Black Americans like Benny and David who live in the most marginalized communities. Credit card debt is particularly common for the Black middle class: 56 percent of Black adults with a household income above \$75,000 have credit card debt, compared to only 34 percent of White adults with the same level of income.[40]

When Alisha was a recent college grad, working at a bank in Georgia, she found that she was "young and broke with awesome credit," which meant that after applying for her first three credit cards in a month, she had \$27,000 in available credit. Americans who don't have any negative marks on their credit report and have some track record of successful loan repayment (in Alisha's case, student loans) often find that banks give out high credit limits, especially when the economy is performing well. "My credit cards covered bills when I was short," Alisha told me. "I'd never lived on my own before this time and school teaches you everything about money except how to budget it."

Although the average amount of credit card debt held by Black-headed households is lower than the average amount of credit card debt held by other households—an average of about $1,900 per year versus an average of about $2,630 per year—in many ways, Black families, who generally have less generational wealth to fall back upon when they hit a rough patch, are the hardest hit by the burden of debt.[41] Overall, 43 percent of Black adults have credit card debt, compared to 39 percent of Hispanic adults, and 35 percent of White adults.[42]

The extent to which credit card debt is a racial justice issue is often understated by economists. Some falsely suggest that because credit is generally less available in Black neighborhoods, Black families have largely avoided debt's burdens, pointing out that while 85 percent of White adults have a credit card, only 68 percent of Black adults have a credit card.[43] But while Black families are less likely to reap some of the benefits of the debt machine—having access to a payment card that gives them rewards—they are every bit as likely to be hit with the debt machine's costs.

THE WIPE OUT THEORY

Earlier in the chapter, we discussed the limits of the "squeezed" theory of credit card debt, which implies that the best way of reducing credit card debt would be to make it easier for middle-class families to afford material necessities. If Americans' credit card debt could be explained in a very one-to-one way by the amount of financial distress in the United States, it wouldn't make any sense that credit card debt tends to be at its highest when the economy is booming, and at its lowest when the economy is doing poorly. Moreover, even in Quart's own book, she talks both about New York City families like the Bellamys who are struggling to make ends meet on a household income of $160,000, and a few chapters later, about how a New York City nanny, Esther, who is making somewhere in the ballpark of $50,000 per year, sent enough money home to her country of birth, Kenya, to support eight families. The juxtaposition of Esther and the Bellamys should make it clear that the feeling of not having enough is driven by more than a purely scientific accounting of circumstances, but also by our expectations, and worldview. I don't mean to insinuate that I think it easy, financially, to raise a family in New York City, even with a six-figure income, but rather to make a few observations.

Media often flattens the experience of someone making $40,000 and someone making $160,000 under a single descriptor of the "struggling" middle class, even though their material circumstances often vary drastically. Consider, for example, the *New York Times* series on the middle class in 2019, which profiled the challenges of seven families in places like Arizona, Missouri, and Minnesota, six with six-figure incomes; the series clearly insinuated that there was little these people could do to live on less money, although, of course, millions of people *do* live on less money, even within the same cities as the profiled families. A person making $160,000 might think they're *generally speaking* in the same financial boat as someone making $40,000 per year, but the reverse is rarely true. Most Americans consider anyone making over $100,000 per year to be rich. They understand their lives would be completely different at such a high income.[44]

I'm not going to talk much in this book about what America could do to make housing more affordable, make health care more affordable (or free), make childcare more affordable (or free), or make education more affordable (or free). Undoubtedly, fixing these problems would allow some number of people to avoid turning to credit card debt. Each of these problems deserves their own book. But, just as importantly, while fixing these sorts of problems would radically improve Americans' well-being, the credit card debt machine would continue to spin, because at every level of income, and at every level of necessary expenses, some people can be induced to spend more than they earn.

A second theory for why Americans are in so much credit card debt is that they're impatient and impulsive—basically, that they're marshmallow eaters. In a famous study from the *Journal of Personality and Social Psychology* by Walter Mischel and colleagues, researchers gave children the choice of getting one marshmallow now, or two marshmallows if they could wait about fifteen minutes.[45] The study found that marshmallow "waiters" went on to be more "academically and socially competent, verbally fluent, rational, attentive, planful, and able to deal well with frustration and stress" than the marshmallow eaters. Subscribers to the marshmallow theory point to credit card debt as a moral failure of debtors, often believing either that immature Americans should be protected from their own bad decisions, or, concluding that it's a lost cause to try to help people who are so clearly deficient.

In writing about credit card debt, economists Scott Schuh and Scott Fulford have said "more than half the population must be very impatient and care little about risk to hold the amount of revolving debt we observe."[46] Economist Theresa Kuchler, now at the NYU Stern School of Business, says impatience is an important cause of credit card debt, and claims that you can "measure" how impatient someone is by comparing what percentage of their income they spend in the first few days after they get their paycheck compared to the last few days when they're waiting for their next paycheck.[47] Schuh, Fulford, and Kuchler aren't isolated examples in attributing credit card debt to "impatience": the claim that there wouldn't be much credit card debt if Americans weren't so wildly impatient is widely repeated. *Impatient* isn't necessarily meant as a slur, but the term certainly insinuates that credit card debt reflects a personal defect.

Even outside of credit card debt, the concept of impatience organizes a lot of how "elites," both liberal and conservative, think about lower- and middle-income Americans. For *New York Times* columnist David Brooks, the marshmallow experiment proves that efforts to improve schools or alleviate poverty are going to be "disappointingly modest" if we don't focus on improving Americans self-control.[48] Walter Mischel consulted PBS on how to incorporate the marshmallow study findings into *Sesame Street*, leading to the Cookie Monster singing "Me Want It (But Me Wait)" about the virtues of self-control to the tune of Icona Pop's "I Love It."[49] The cultural and political resonance of Mischel's findings have remained, even as his conclusions have been somewhat contradicted by more recent research: a 2018 study in the journal *Psychological Science* found the effect of being able to wait for two marshmallows as a child on your adolescent levels of achievement were only half as large as the original studies found. The study also showed that two-thirds of the effect of childhood impatience on adolescent success went away when socioeconomic factors were controlled for, and only the children unable to wait a mere twenty seconds, not the full fifteen minutes, differed meaningfully from their peers when they got older.[50]

I'm proposing a different explanation for credit card debt, something that I'll call the "wipe-out" theory, since I think the "squeezed" theory is strongly contradicted by data, and that the "impatience" theory is both wrong and somewhat insulting to a large proportion of Americans. To explain this theory, the "wipe-out" theory I'll start by telling you the story of Kathryn G.

Kathryn G., now sixty-five years old, worked as a nurse for thirteen years, before becoming a stay-at-home mom in a small town east of St. Paul, Minnesota, near the border with Wisconsin, about half an hour from the closest grocery store. She and her husband, both White, split up right as her youngest son was starting college. Kathryn suddenly found herself alone in an isolated home, surrounded by other people's stuff: her ex-husband took half the things they'd bought together, and the realtor staged the house with model furniture. Even though the divorce agreement said the full amount of alimony wouldn't take effect until the house sold, she went ahead and moved into her own apartment in St. Paul anyway—it was too depressing to stay in the empty home—without realizing how long it would take for the empty house to sell. The Great Recession was deepening. Kathryn racked up credit card debt between attorney's fees, her car payment, and paying rent while she waited for the full amount of alimony to kick in. She ended up with $80,000 in credit card debt. When I spoke to Kathryn in 2019, that amount was down to $60,000. While all this was happening, she also gave her college-aged kids money to help them through school.

Kathryn's ex-husband, a doctor, was considerably better off than she was. He was paying a bigger share of the kids' college costs, and the kids all took out some student loans, but Kathryn still felt obligated to chip in. My kids "knew it was hard for me," Kathryn told me, "but it was just an expectation of theirs that they weren't going to have to pay for college." You could argue it would have made more sense for her kids to take out somewhat larger student loans at a 4 percent or 5 percent interest rate than it did for Kathryn to give her kids money she could have put toward her own credit card debt, but Kathryn didn't want to tell her kids she couldn't help them. Cleary putting your children before yourself represents a clear "future orientation": it would be hard to argue that Kathryn was impatient. "Impatience" suggests a willingness to sacrifice pleasure tomorrow for pleasure today. "Impatience" isn't a particularly apt description for how hard it is to say "no" to the people close to you, or how challenging it is for all of us to admit defeats, whether our failures be material, professional, social, or ethical, to acknowledge when our life, while not necessarily bad, is not the life we had wanted for ourselves.

When we truly mine the concepts of "want" and "need," we see that these ideas have surprisingly fluid boundaries. Do you need to go to your cousin's wedding? Do you need to go to your mother's funeral? If your kid is bullied, do you need to send them to private school? Do you need to get your kid a birthday present? Do you need to pay for a uniform so your kid can play soccer? Do you need to buy a new crib, or a new car seat for your kid, or is it fine to use a hand-me-down?[51] Do you need to join your friends when they go out for drinks the night before you all graduate from college? Does your teenager need to buy a dress and a ticket to go to their high school prom? You need to eat: how much food and how high in quality? Do you need to fix the broken window in your house? Do you need to replace the moldy carpet? Can you, your husband, and two kids live in a two-bedroom, one-bathroom apartment? For how long? You clearly need at least one pair of shoes: how many pairs of shoes do you need in total? Does your cat need veterinary care, or will you let her die when she gets sick? Do you need to get an oil change every ten thousand miles? Even the things that might feel like wants over one time horizon can start to feel like a need over a longer time horizon: there's a difference between forgoing small luxuries during a rough patch versus imagining your whole life extending out in front of you with no expenses beyond what Congresswoman Alexandria Ocasio-Cortez has called "mere animalistic survival."

When I spoke recently to my two closest friends from childhood, both of whom are doing well by millennial standards, but both of whom face formidable student loan burdens, we talked about what we all thought it meant to be rich when we were teenagers versus what my friends would buy now, as adults, if they had more disposable income. As teenagers, we thought being rich meant having designer clothes, an expensive car, or maybe a chandelier in every room. As adults, my friends wished they had enough money for an in-unit washer and dryer, a dishwasher, and a kitchen large enough to even have a dishwasher. Nothing fancy. My friends are twenty-nine years old, and in many respects well off.

It is in this liminal space between want and need that credit card debt blossoms, and not, generally, a result of a failure to reign in out-of-control impulse spending. It blossoms between the quotidian purchases that are easy to justify. It stems sometimes from pure necessity, but often, from the reluctance to utilize the deeply uncomfortable coping mechanisms that are often a person's only way out of a sticky financial situation, whether that's moving to a cheaper apartment, even though it would mean ripping your kids out of a school where they're thriving, declining all social invitations, or getting another job, even though you're exhausted. My point is not that Americans should have to do these things to survive; my point is that many credit card debtors come to find that credit cards merely delay when they must take these actions, and at an exorbitant cost.

Instead of the marshmallow test, a better analogy for thinking about credit card debt is a wipe-out video game. In any wipe-out game, it makes sense to do everything you can to make it to the next level. Once you're dead, you're dead, regardless of what loot was in your backpack. The challenges come so quickly and furiously that you're too distracted to plan ahead. Saving your strength or resources for later would be not only useless, but counterproductive. Everyone has some set of things that would feel like a "wipe-out" to them, things they would do basically anything to avoid. Those wipe-outs can be material, like getting evicted or losing your car; or emotional, like not being able to hop on airplane to visit your long-distance girlfriend when she's struggling, not being able to provide your college-aged children money so they can take an unpaid internship, or needing to get roommates when you're in your 60s, after decades of sharing a middle-class life with your family. The marshmallow test is quantitative: I can have one marshmallow now or two marshmallows in fifteen minutes. The wipe-out game is qualitative: there is no moving on if I fail this round. In wipe-out thinking, everything that counts as a "catastrophe" feels roughly equivalent, so the "worst that can happen" if you borrow money to avoid a catastrophe today is that you've postponed the catastrophe until tomorrow.

Of course, not everything that we perceive will be a catastrophe is as bad as we imagine. But if you feel like your world will be over if you drop any of the balls you're juggling, borrowing to keep the balls afloat isn't exactly a byproduct of "impatience": it can also be a byproduct of failing to see all the alternatives available, or an overestimation of how catastrophic it would be if one of the balls shattered.

Consider Kate and Tom, a couple in their late forties featured in a 2018 WealthSimple Money Diary.[52] Kate and Tom both work in insurance, making a total of $160,000 per year, plus what Tom gets from moonlighting as a bartender. They have $60,000 in credit card debt, $18,000 in personal loan debt, two mortgages totaling $360,000, and more than $100,000 in student loan debt, and no particularly unusual financial sob stories laid out in their money diary: no unusual medical catastrophe, long stretch of unemployment, or real special events beyond the normal ebbs and flows of a middle-class life. On one level, it's hard to be sympathetic toward Kate and Tom, when plenty of people *do* avoid debt and save money at far lower incomes than them. That's exactly why it's helpful to plumb their example.

Where does their money go? After taxes, you might guess that Kate and Tom's take-home pay is around $114,000, or $9,500 a month. You might guess given their mortgage size ($360,000) that the housing payment should be around $2,400, maybe higher if they have a bad interest rate and live in a high-property tax area; to be safe, we could round the payment all the way up to $4,000. Using the numbers they provided, private school tuition is $15,000—$1,250 per month. Those expenses so far total $5,250 a month. Kate and Tom say they lease their cars because they wouldn't have the savings to fix anything if it broke: if we say that's two cars with a $300 payment each, plus a total of $250 for car insurance, we're now looking at $6,100 a month in expenses. They said all their student loans are in forbearance—they're not paying anything toward them. If all their credit card debt and personal loan debt is at a relatively high interest rate, like 24 percent, that would mean their loan interest is $1,200 per month, which means the expenses we've added up so far bring us to $7,300. That means after having paid for taxes, housing, cars, debt payment and school, Tom and Kate still have $27,000 a year left of wiggle room—not a luxurious amount, but a decent amount when you consider all the budget categories we've already accounted for. Many Americans have far less than $27,000 after paying for housing and transportation. So why are Kate and Tom continuing to get further into debt?

In reading Kate and Tom's description of their financial dilemma, it becomes clear there's a set of things they can't bring themselves to do. "We had every intention of sending [our kids] to public school," said Tom, and then Kate adds "last year [our daughter] got to a place where she wasn't learning, she was afraid to go to school, she got punched at one point. So we were like that's it, now she's going into private school next year." They can't afford private school, but forgoing it feels impossible. Telling their son they can't give him money for a suit for prom feels impossible. Adopting a more working-class diet feels impossible, when they're used to grabbing not only fresh produce, but also sushi and a smoothie during their trip to Whole Foods. Filing for bankruptcy feels impossible. Perhaps on one level impatience is at play here. It seems more accurate to say that Tom and Kate have a distorted understanding of what their option set is—they fail to perceive things as options that are options, like keeping their kids in public school, or asking the eighteen-year-old son to get a job. These are, of course, strategies that working-class families employ regularly. And they treat something as an option that other people might have struck from the list early on: making up the gaps in their budget with high-interest credit.

The Money Diaries doesn't discuss what will end up happening to Tom and Kate in five, ten, or twenty years, and it's very possible that Tom and Kate don't really understand what's ahead. The media often insinuates that credit card debt is *bad*, that it is reckless to live beyond your means, suggesting that credit card debt is bad maybe because it corrupts one's soul, instead of explaining how stories like Tom and Kate's often end. To exactly why debt is such a threat to American families, it's important to come to terms with the possibilities. Tom and Kate's debt might be stressing them out at the time of the diary, but they have not yet reached their story's denouement. Something will cause a radical rupture: either they'll stop being approved for new credit, or they'll lose their student loan forbearance.

At the time of their diary, Tom and Kate use new loans to finance their spending, and, it appears, to pay down their existing debts. That whole gambit could explode quickly if lenders simply stopped approving them for new loans. That could happen if Tom and Kate's minimum payments grow beyond the point they can finance: as they miss payments, their credit score will drop, and access to new credit will dry up. Or, if they can find credit, it will be at a higher interest rate, which almost always comes with a higher required minimum payment. Miss payments for nine months in a row, and the debt will "charge off." At that point, instead of just asking Tom and Kate to pay, the lenders take them to court to garnish their paychecks, in most states seizing 25 percent of their salary, an amount that for Tom and Kate would be roughly $2,400 per month, much more than their minimum required monthly payments before defaulting. And, of course, how easy or hard it is to get a new loan doesn't just depend on the person borrowing money; it also depends on the state of the economy. While 2018 Tom and Kate still found willing lenders, 2020 Tom and Kate would find banks behaving somewhat more cautiously. In 2020, during the coronavirus epidemic, the number of new credit cards issued by banks fell by 60 percent.[53]

Another shock could come if Tom and Kate lose their student loan forbearance. Tom and Kate aren't making payments on their student loans because they've applied for forbearance, which can be either "mandatory" or "discretionary." Working adults generally only qualify for mandatory forbearance if their monthly payments would be 20 percent or more of their income.[54] Tom and Kate could repay $130,000 in student loans in ten years at a 7 percent interest rate with payments of $1,509 per month: a big chunk of change, but still much less than 20 percent of their income. This strongly suggests that Tom and Kate are getting discretionary forbearance. With discretionary forbearance, it's up to the student lender or servicer to decide whether to approve or deny your request—it sounds like Tom and Kate have been getting forbearance approved for a while, but their luck could run out at any time. As Colleen Campbell, director of Postsecondary Education at the Center for American Progress explained to me by phone in 2019, "it's not possible to be in forbearance for more than three years." There is one way to "game" the system she explains—you can be in forbearance for three years, consolidate your loans, and then be in forbearance for three more years, but she adds "you do have to pay the loan eventually."

If Tom and Kate's next request for forbearance is denied, they'll have to start making student loan payments—and at their income, they're unlikely to qualify for income-based repayment plans that would lower their monthly payments, although "extended" repayment plans that stretch out the loan term may still be an option. Coming up with a $1,500 a month to put toward loan-repayment would force Tom and Kate to find ways to cut back: if they don't make the payments, they'd enter default, which, as with credit card default, leads to garnished paychecks.

In other words, unless Tom and Kate win the lottery, they won't be able to maintain their lifestyle forever. The consequences of not repaying a debt are confusing, vague, and abstract to people who've never defaulted on a loan: they are tangible to the one in ten working age adults whose wages are seized each year by debtors after a lawsuit.[55]

THE INVENTION OF OPTIONS

In July of 2018, about a week before the "leadership team" meeting from chapter 2, I was talking to my friend Sam on the phone, crying because I hated my job at Capital One. I didn't feel like I saw eye-to-eye with my new boss on what we needed to do to help customers, and I was working crazy hours after I'd taken on the responsibilities for other people who had moved roles in the company.

"What if you just quit?" he asked me. I insisted that was impossible. I had so many reasons: I was trying to shepherd some of the people on my team through the promotion process, there were people I had recruited to the company to join my team that were supposed to start in just a few weeks, and I felt like I'd be hanging them out to dry if I quit before they even arrived. I had projects to make Capital One a better place for its customers that I cared deeply about, even if I questioned whether my new boss would be willing to implement them. I also handled enough operational responsibilities that I would leave the company in a lurch if I were to quit unexpectedly.

I told him all these reasons, never acknowledging that he was right. As I've told this story since to a few other friends, I have realized that my judgment generally splits across class backgrounds: those with wealthier parents tend to side with Sam, while those without much family wealth tend to feel that quitting without having another job lined up *is not something a reasonable person would do*. But shortly after talking to Sam, I gave my two weeks' notice. Sam was right all along, of course—quitting had always been an option (and not a particularly reckless option, considering the money I'd saved up while working for Capital One, the money that gave me the financial freedom to write this book).

Options must be invented, to be born, to spring to life. We do not choose between all hypothetical possibilities: only those possibilities whose existence we acknowledge. The menus we use often miss some or many potential choices: those we have literally never heard of, those that just don't occur to us in the moment, and those that violate the constraints we've imposed upon ourselves.

Kathryn G. and Tom and Kate's stories both illustrate that a lot hinges on what things we consider imperative, off the menu, not a part of our life's system of ordinary trade-offs, whether that's not having a roommate, not living in a house that reminds you of your ex, or not sending your daughter to a school where you're afraid she'll be bullied. If you feel like there is more that is *essential* for you to spend money on than you have money available in your checking account, you'll end up borrowing money, banking on the hope that "future you" will be able to figure out how to make things work.

Often, the expectation that it's worth borrowing today because everything will be better tomorrow is a risky but not delusional bet: as Jonathan Morduch and Rachel Schneider point out in *The Financial Diaries: How Americans Cope in a World of Uncertainty,* Americans, especially low- and middle-income ones, have a huge amount of income volatility, both month-to-month and year-to-year. According to Morduch and Schneider's research, the typical poor family in the United States has 3 months per year where they bring in a lot of extra money (25 percent more than their average monthly income), and 2.7 months per year where they bring in much less than what they're used to (25 percent less than their average monthly income).[56] When household income is volatile, it's not surprising that when faced with a lot of difficulty, families will gamble on the hopes that next month will be easier.

I talked to an older White woman in a cafe in Philadelphia; she'd gotten into credit card debt late in life "bailing out" her adult sons when they'd gotten into trouble. She told me she felt like she couldn't say no to her sons, not while she was "able" to say yes—she told me she'd later come to realize that if the only way she could give them money was by borrowing money on a credit card, it meant she was never *really* able to help to begin with.

In talking about the wipe-out theory, you might have noticed I've used a lot of examples about children. That's on purpose. It's not just because having children, particularly children in day care, is tremendously expensive, although, of course, that's true. Even more important though, when it comes to credit card debt, is the fact that having children fundamentally changes how we think about spending money, above and beyond any direct costs that parenting creates. The cognitive skills it takes to avoid living beyond your means are completely different for childless adults compared to families with children: one takes discipline and creativity; the other also requires learning to say "no" in moments when all your personal values are telling you to say "yes." A person accountable only to herself can make extreme trade-offs when circumstances require. In July 2020, I talked to a Black woman laid off from her Los Angeles service sector job during the COVID crisis. She was denied unemployment insurance without knowing the reason why, so she narrowed down her belongings to what could fit in a backpack and found temporary housing in Houston where rents were cheaper. She cancelled her cell phone plan, using Wi-Fi if she needed to talk to somebody on the phone. Those drastic moves allowed her to avoid credit card debt; by the time she found a new job over the summer, she'd depleted most but not all of her savings and severance.

How many parents of children could bring themselves to take such strong steps, if borrowing money were also an option? Where the childless adult will often cut to the bone, the parent generally can't bring himself not to leave some fat: after all, we want childhood to not only be comfortable but also special for our children. No parent wants their child to watch the family struggle. It is notable that credit card debt is highest around the holidays, peaking right around or just after Christmas, illustrating how our connections to other people, rather than our own selfish wishes, often drive the most seemingly reckless of decisions.[57] Data from the Federal Reserve Survey of Household Economics and Decision Making shows that middle-class parents are the most likely to borrow to finance the holidays: more than one in four middle-income parents with children under the age of eighteen borrow money to pay for holiday presents in a given year.[58]

A Credit Karma/Qualtrics survey of one thousand parents in the United States found that 53 percent had borrowed money on things the parents had deemed were "nonessential" items for their kids.[59] When it comes to the wipe-out theory, the feeling of failure is triggered if we can't give them moments of delight, wonder, and magic, standards that far exceed what most people expect for themselves. In a study of low-income women conducted by Angela Littwin of the University of Texas School of Law, one respondent said, "you can't just take credit away from poor people. Sometimes it's the only way they can get Christmas for their kids."[60] Although this should go without saying, it bears repeating: a parent that repeatedly charges Christmas on their credit card will have less and less to spend on their children in each successive year when interest payments come due.

The wipe-out theory is ultimately all about how Americans construct their option sets—after all, we don't make choices between all the possibilities in the world, only the possibilities that occur to us.

Imagine two teenagers facing each other in a room with a facilitator. The facilitator places the ball in one of the teens' hands. The facilitator tells the other teen he has a minute to get the ball. When the Chicago non-profit Youth Guidance has tried this exercise, they find that the first thing nearly every participant tries is to try to grab the ball by force. Rarely do teenagers just ask their partner to hand over the ball, although, when asked, most participants say they would have handed the ball over on request.[61] Asking for the ball just doesn't occur to people.

In thinking about the complicated links between temporary or permanent economic hardship and Americans' propensity to take on credit card debt, it's helpful to consider a simple truth: at the upper bound, there's no level of income that can completely inoculate a person from the feeling that they don't have enough money.

A 1982 *New York* magazine article called "Downward Mobility: You Thought You'd Live Better Than Your Parents Did" is full of examples of how it is possible to feel boxed-in and limited at any level of income. In discussing how squeezed she feels economically, Marsha Rose, a twenty-nine-year-old social services administrator who grew up in Scarsdale, New York, said, "I wouldn't give up my land in the country or my cleaning lady. I'd be miserable." Joseph Benson, a professor of Sociology noted that while it took him twenty-five years to learn to appreciate fine wine, his

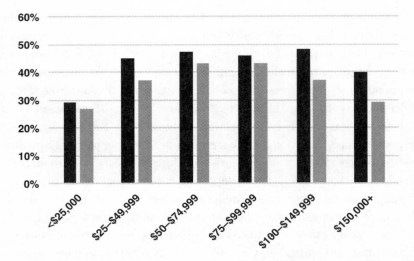

Adults who say they are worse off than their parents at the same age

Adults who say they are better off than their parents at the same age

Figure 6. Percent of US Adults with Credit Card Debt by Household Income and Economic Mobility. Data from the 2018 Federal Reserve Survey of Household Economics and Decisionmaking. Based on responses to B6: "Think of your parents when they were your age. Would you say you (and your family living with you) are better, the same, or worse off financially than they were?"

children have a "built-in cost of living" that he didn't have, since they "acquired that taste at their father's knee." A younger tenured professor, married but childless, whose name wasn't used in the piece, said it was "ridiculous" that he was "boxed into a four-room apartment" in Manhattan, while his parents had eight bedrooms.[62]

Our culture doesn't equip people to be prepared for declining living standards; our frameworks and expectations are rooted in an era in which the vast majority of people earned more money than their parents. What does this mean for the wipe-out theory? Our expectations for what we consider a "necessity" are heavily shaped by class background. Those who find themselves earning less than their parents often struggle with adapting to a lower level of material comfort than what they were raised to expect—and not surprisingly, high earners that feel "worse off" than their parents are 37 percent more likely to have credit card debt than those that feel "better off" than their parents. Although some people get into debt while making a middle-class income in order to support struggling family members, the reverse experience appears statistically more common: to get into debt to maintain the lifestyle you were used to as a child.

Feelings of deprivation or abundance are not simple byproducts of our material conditions—lots of adults my age would be thrilled to be in Marsha Rose's shoes.

When an American is faced with the dilemmas of having more defined-as-essential expenses than money, one of the biggest drivers of how things will unfold for that person is whether borrowing money is listed on his mental option set. Some families simply strike credit card borrowing from their option lists. Dave Ramsey, a personal finance guru, particularly popular in some Christian churches, whose radio show reportedly has more than 12 million weekly listeners, is one of the most famous advocates of this philosophy.[63] His rules of money are simple: in *The Money Answer Book: Quick Answers to Everyday Financial Questions,* Ramsey is unambiguous in telling readers to "say 'no' to credit cards[64]." He argues—correctly—that many people anticipate they'll pay credit card bills in full and nevertheless end up borrowing money. When callers to his show talk about payday loans, he asks them to promise to not to even consider payday loans as an option in the future: "Never set foot in one of those places again," he says, adding "If you're hungry, go see your pastor."

It's been widely reported in the press that millennials are more averse to debt than previous generations, something that's making them more likely to use a debit card instead of a credit card.[65] The media is dismissive of this choice. Credit card analyst Jeanine Skowronski told CNBC that the people picking debit over credit were "actually doing a disservice to themselves and their credit scores"; CNBC questioned why people wouldn't use a credit card and pay it off in full to earn rewards and have better fraud protection. For people committed to living within their means though, not having a credit card can be helpful in forcing you not to spend money you don't have. If I play chess against a consumer, I'll lose every time, even if I'm intelligent; deciding not to play, then, can be the "smartest" decision. It's easy to criticize strategies like Ramsey's as "suboptimal," but given how many Americans struggle with debt, maybe simple rules of thumb aren't bad.

It matters whether the cause of credit card debt is more like the marshmallow test or more like a wipe-out game. There's one set of interventions that can help make people less impatient. For example, psychologists refer to the phenomenon of the "vividness of our future self": how connected we feel to the person we will be in the future, and the extent to which we want to care for that person, and look out for what her goals and needs will be.[66] Researchers at Stanford found that showing people an age-progressed picture of themselves—think FaceApp—made them more inclined to save for retirement.[67] To combat impatience, we should make people's future selves more salient.

If we're actually facing a wipe-out game though, we should try different tactics, namely, increasing the salience of options *other* than borrowing money on a credit card—for example, by aggressively marketing to citizens all the government benefit programs for which they are eligible, and making credit card borrowing slightly less salient. Or, perhaps, by discouraging banks from offering very high credit limits except at the request of the consumer, so that people will have to proactively choose to take on more debt.

Two questions are essential for sorting through when a loan is helpful or harmful to a consumer: (1) What would you have done if the loan hadn't been available to you? And (2), looking back, do you wish you had done that instead? For the consumers I've talked to who answered "yes" to the second question, I've encountered two common answers to the first question: "I just wouldn't have bought the item at all," or "I would have borrowed money from a friend or family member."

Linda, a White, middle-aged nurse who I spoke to in New Orleans, borrowed money on her credit card when her kids were young—some months, her bills and her mortgage were more than her salary. She wishes she'd asked her parents instead and avoided all the "god damn interest." Tasha, similarly, says she wished she had asked her family for money earlier, pointing out that when she defaulted on her credit card, she'd had to ask for help anyways. Clearly, not everyone has someone in their life they can ask for money. Of the poorest Americans, those making under $20,000 per year, 46 percent of White adults, and 27 percent Black adults reported that they could find a friend or family member to lend them $3,000 if there were an emergency.[68] For those with a family member they could ask in a pinch, it's a good litmus test: Is the thing I'm considering borrowing money on important enough to me that I'd ask someone close to spot me? If it's not, paying the high credit card interest rates is probably also not worth it. Asking for money from a friend or family member has a very different "pain profile" than borrowing from a bank—when we borrow money from banks, there is no pain or stigma when we start the borrowing process, and all the pain comes when we repay. Assuming we're able to repay the loan, when we borrow from friends or family, that's reversed— we're faced with a huge burst of discomfort when we have to ask, but repaying will typically be less expensive.

Ultimately, what matters most about purchases on credit isn't whether they were truly "necessities" or mere "wants." Using high-interest credit can be counterproductive in either case, if spending money on things you "need" means you have less money available next month for the same list of needs. What matters more in assessing how credit card borrowing impacts a person's well-being is if the borrowing was driven by "usual" or "unusual" circumstances in a person's life. I talked to an analyst in Richmond who used credit cards to finance travel after grad school and paid off the debt within a few years of starting to work: he said paying 50 percent more for those experiences by using credit rather than cash was worth it to him, since it would have been much harder (and more expensive in other ways) to trek across Eastern Europe while pressed with the demands of holding down a job. Borrowing money on a credit card was in his interest because he did it at a moment in which his earnings were substantially lower (basically, zero) compared to what they would be a year later.

What is clear is this: the most common pattern of behavior we see with credit card debt, of consumers carrying high-interest debt more-or-less continuously for twenty or thirty years, is hard to explain in a way that could possibly be making American families more financially stable. Regardless of a person's circumstances, income, or expenses, holding high-interest credit card debt over years and years doesn't make sense: it's a massive drain of wealth over a person's life. A system where this is commonplace is not a good system.

4   A Broken Net

All the sins of the credit card industry could perhaps be forgiven if credit cards were effective shock absorbers in our economy. It has been estimated that, between their twenty-fifth and sixty-first birthdays, four out of ten Americans will spend at least one year in poverty, even though only about one in ten adults are in poverty at any given point in time.[1] Don't we need credit cards to help us weather these storms?

High interest debt lowers average lifetime wealth for the borrower—that much is obvious. But, of course, *averages* aren't all that matter. A person can drown trying to cross a river whose average depth is two feet if the deepest points are twenty feet. Credit cards are presumed to be necessary under the assumption that they lower average wealth for the borrower *in exchange for* helping people across the most challenging parts of the economic river.

Tragedies can strike at any time, and recessions are a special form of communal tragedy. In April of 2020, in the midst of the COVID crisis, 41 percent of mothers with children under twelve years of age reported that they didn't have enough money to buy sufficient food, a rate that had nearly tripled over the course of just a few months.[2] What role would credit cards play in helping Americans weather this economic storm—and what role had they played in prior recessions?

That same month, on April 23, 2020, Capital One hosted a quarterly earnings call with investors. One investment analyst, Don Fandetti, asked Capital One's CEO, Rich Fairbank, how he expected the crisis would impact Capital One's loan growth. In other words, would Capital One's customers end up in more debt or less debt than they were before the crisis started? Fairbank said, from his experience with other economic downturns, "a couple of things tend to naturally happen in cards. The lower purchase volume, obviously, very striking, particularly in this downturn at this point, but lower demand for credit, lower requests for credit line increases, and I want to pause on that because I think there is an intuitive logic people would think, 'Well, wait a minute. When customers feel the strain of a downturn, surely, a lot of them have to be beating a path to try to get more credit.' What I've seen in the past and what we're already seeing here is that consumer behavior tends to be in general one of battening down the hatches a bit, being more conservative, increasing their savings if they have an opportunity to do that, sometimes paying down debt."[3]

Fairbank was right: by next quarter's earnings call in July, Capital One's total credit card balances would have fallen by just over $10 billion.[4] Chase's credit card balances fell $20 billion over the same period, and Bank of America's by $8 billion, even though in other years, that time period, the second quarter of the year, was normally one of growth for the credit card industry.[5] Scott Blackley, the CFO, would attribute Capital One's falling balances to customers making bigger payments: "We've seen great credit. Part of that is high payment rates. The flip side of that is that that has a tendency to drive down outstandings."[6]

So why do people pay down their debt faster in the midst of recessions?

In the previous chapter, we looked at debt across American's lifespans, and saw that Americans were the least likely to be in credit card debt in their twenties, when their income was at its low point, and the most likely to be in credit card debt in their late forties, when income typically peaks. In this chapter, we'll look at credit card debt across the economic cycle, where the same counterintuitive trend can be found: credit card debt falls when the economy is doing poorly, when incomes are lower, and rises when the economy is doing comparatively well. Credit cards aren't smoothing the bumps in the road: they are amplifying the volatility.

In answering the Wall Street analyst's question, Fairbank wasn't trying to make an argument against credit cards, but he nevertheless exposed an important truth: Americans borrow the most when the economy is roaring, and are the least interested in borrowing money when the economy is shrinking. Fairbank acknowledged that this point was surprising, but he didn't go one step further in spelling out the implications—what it means for all of us that borrowing falls exactly when Americans are in the most need.

CREDIT CARD DEBT AND UNEMPLOYMENT

Looking across the last twenty-five years, we see an obvious trend: when unemployment falls, credit card debt rises, the exact obvious trend from what you might expect.

Zooming in just to the Great Recession, the trend is even clearer, and more puzzling. From 2007 to 2010, average credit card debt fell by nearly $1,000 per family, even as the unemployment rate roughly doubled. Where were people finding the money to pay down $1,000 worth of credit card debt in the midst of the worst job market of their lives, often while watching the value of their house and their entire net worth plummet? The same trend would occur during the coronavirus crisis: in 2020, the nation's credit card debt fell by 11 percent or $100 billion between February and June.[7]

Part of the fall in debt during the Great Recession, as well as in other recessions, was attributed to people defaulting, or "charging off," on their credit cards. When a person's balance has been unpaid for 180 days, their account is closed. The bank can still try to convince their former customer to repay, send their bill to a third-party debt collection agency, file a lawsuit to ask a judge to seize the money in their bank account, or force their employer to garnish their paycheck. Charged-off debt is still debt, but banks, the government, and consumers all think about this charged-off debt a little bit differently, although some of it will eventually be paid off, usually after legal action. Economists at the Federal Reserve Bank of New York stripped out these chargeoffs, and found that total credit card debt and auto loan debt fell by more than $50 billion in 2009 and 2010. This

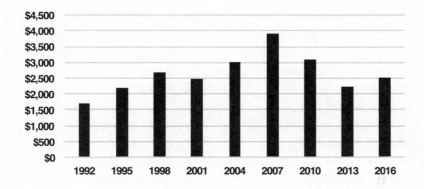

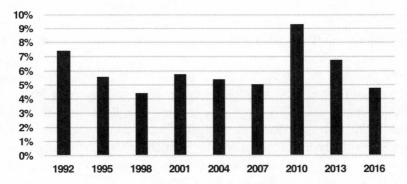

Figure 7. Mean Household Credit Card Debt in 2016 Dollars, SCF+ Data
(top), and Unemployment Rate, as of Dec. (bottom)

$50 billion was debt that had been truly paid off (or not accrued) in the
midst of a devastating recession.[8]

Of course, some people do use credit cards when they lose their jobs.
University of Chicago economists Peter Ganong and Pascal Noel studied
nearly two hundred thousand JPMorgan Chase banking customers who
received unemployment insurance payments by direct deposit at some
point between January 2014 and June 2016, 42 percent of whom had a
Chase credit card. On average, these households with Chase credit cards
had a Chase credit card balance of $2,445, and a monthly credit card
spend of $263 before someone in the household lost their job. Two months
after having lost their job, their credit card balance had increased by only
$23. And it wasn't because these out-of-work households were putting

tons of new charges on their credit cards: in fact, monthly credit card charges had decreased by $14 per month. On average, they were paying down existing debt more slowly, making smaller payments. After the first two months, every additional month of unemployment while receiving unemployment insurance was associated with a $21 increase in their Chase credit card debt. Forced with a sudden loss of income, households cut their spending much more than they turned to the credit cards to make up the difference.

For the one-in-five households who couldn't find work before exhausting their unemployment benefits, their Chase credit card balances increased again, by an average of $45 over the two months following benefit exhaustion. By comparison, those same families decreased their monthly spending when their unemployment benefits were exhausted by $190 per month.

By and large, it wasn't the case that people didn't have the ability to borrow on their credit card: the group's average Chase credit limit was $12,897 at the start of unemployment, and credit limits on average rose slightly during the period of unemployment. In other words, this population, who usually did have some credit card debt at the start of their unemployment, and who had nearly $10,000 in available credit, mostly avoided using their credit card while unemployed.

Cutting back spending was the preferred coping mechanism for these families, with monthly spending decreases exceeding new credit card debt by ten to one.[9] The households who entered their bout of unemployment with a revolving balance on their Chase card ended up making even bigger spending pullbacks than those who had a Chase card without a revolving balance: spending pullbacks of $279 per month, compared to $125 for the households that were paying their Chase bill in full. Borrowing money on a credit card in the past didn't mean that a family would willing to use their credit card to fully cushion the blow of unemployment. Other studies suggest that the percentage of people who lose their job who end up borrowing money to cushion the blow is somewhere between one-quarter and one-third: a lower fraction that you might expect, given that nearly half of adults have credit card debt in any given year, and that only 60 percent of adults say they could cover an unexpected expense of $400 in an emergency using cash or money in the bank.[10]

This all can feel deeply backwards. Isn't a job loss the perfect time, the perfect reason, to use your credit card, if you're going to use a credit card at all?

Perhaps, but in another sense, most people don't turn to credit cards because they are afraid. More often than not, people turn to credit cards because they're optimistic, for higher wages, a better job, an easier future that will make their debt dissolve away. Although unemployment, generally speaking, is temporary, the loss of a job also shatters that sense of optimism. Every $1,000 worth of credit card debt that a borrower takes on will increase their minimum payment by roughly $30; when you've suddenly lost your main or only source of income, the idea of triggering higher minimum payments feels especially fraught.

The portion size effect also appears to be at work. Fulford and Schuh, whose work we discussed in the last chapter, observed that during the Great Recession, credit limits for credit cards fell by an average of 40 percent, from around $14,000 to around $10,000 per consumer. With the portion size effect at play, it's not surprising that the fall in debt would be proportional. Consumers anchor to their credit limits when making financial decisions, even when they're not close enough to their credit limit to be strictly constrained by their amount of available credit.[11]

Of course, the Chase credit card study, along with Fulford and Schuh's research, looks at the people who have a credit card. But as Allison Cole, economist at the Federal Reserve Bank of Boston points out, younger, poorer workers are more likely to lose their jobs.[12] It's not just the case that once you lose your job, it can be hard to get credit. It's also true that the type of people who are the most likely to be fired when the economy does poorly are the least likely to have credit access to begin with. Cole found that eight in ten people who *didn't* lose their jobs between 2009 and 2014 had a credit card, compared to six in ten people who suffered a job loss. The people who lost a job were twice as likely to have a credit score under 600, and 22 percent less likely to be credit card revolvers.

It appears that recessions have the effect of scaring everyone out of their wits—lenders and borrowers alike. The decreases in debt during recessions reflect both the fact that banks are less willing to lend and that borrowers become more hesitant to take on debt, despite or because of the hardship around them. Between 2007 and 2009, the fraction of households that applied for any type of credit fell from 63 percent to 43 percent—a drop of demand, while the approval rate fell six percentage points, from 81 percent to 75 percent—a drop of supply.[13] Zachary Bethune, an economist at University of Virginia tracked what happened to two types of people: those who lost their jobs during the Great Recession and people who didn't. Everyone he tracked was employed in 2007, before the recession took hold. Both groups, those who experienced a job loss and those who did not, were less likely to apply for a credit card in 2009 than they were in 2007: the application rate fell by twenty-one percentage points for households where nobody was unemployed and by seven percentage points for the families where somebody had lost their job.[14]

Rick, a fifty-one-year-old White man, is one of the half of American adults who lost income during 2020.[15] In February of 2020, he was living with his fifteen-year-old son and many of his coworkers in a house in Bakersfield, California, that doubled as their office space. Rick's bed was in the garage. Rick was a freight broker, which means he connected truckers with companies who needed things shipped across the country. He'd worked in the industry for about fifteen years. The winter months are always lean in the freight industry, Rick told me, but the last few months of 2019 and the first few months of 2020 were especially brutal, and before California's stay-at-home order went into effect, his boss told him that they wouldn't be able to keep the office open. The company Rick worked for specialized in arranging freight for the construction industry, mostly oversized loads, and when COVID hit, new construction permits largely came to a halt. Rick was about to run out of money, and he would need to find a new place to live, all before the nationwide eviction moratorium went into effect.

Rick had two credit cards, both of which he applied for in 2015, a Capital One card, and a Credit One card. He made his payments on time, and the credit limits were raised on both cards—the Credit One card from $400 to $650, and the Capital One card from $3,000 to $4,500. Rick's boss classified him as an independent contractor, not as an employee, and his earnings varied based on how much business he brought in. Until 2017, things were pretty steady, Rick told me, and he was making around $45,000 per year, but the winters were always tighter, and his weekly paychecks were closer to $400 or $500, instead of the $800 or $1,000 that he made during the rest of the year. Rick used his credit cards during the winter when things were lean. By 2018, his business had started to slow down, and by 2019, his annual income had fallen by 20 percent, to roughly $36,000. That's when his credit card debt "started skyrocketing," Rick told me. He no longer had any good months that he could use to make larger payments on his debt, and during bad months, he couldn't always afford to make the minimum payment at all. By the time the COVID-19 crisis hit, Rick's credit cards were maxed out and could no longer be used.

At first, Rick lived in his car, while his son went to stay with his mom. Although he applied initially in March, Rick didn't receive Pandemic Unemployment Assistance (PUA) until the second week of May, allowing him to move into a Travelodge, and to make some payments on his credit cards and private student loans, which didn't qualify for the COVID-19 related forgiveness of federal student loan interest. The situation got leaner when PUA expired on July 31st. He stopped making payments on his Capital One card in July, and on his Credit One card in September. Things took a turn for the worse when his unemployment insurance payments were suspended altogether due to suspected fraud; it took over a month for the state of California to verify his ID and restart payments. On December 9th, he had no money left to pay Travelodge and had to move back into his car, this time with his son. His son's mother gave Rick money when she could, which Rick used to try to spend at least one night per week in a motel, so his son could use the Internet to catch up on schoolwork.

Once his unemployment insurance was reinstated in the middle of January, Rick was able to move into an extended stay motel, which pays for using the prepaid Bank of America debit card issued by the unemployment agency. Luckily, Rick told me, the motel only runs a $100 security deposit once per month and refunds it every two weeks, working with him so that the charges are run on Tuesdays, the day after unemployment insurance is deposited.

When we spoke in March of 2021, Rick was applying for jobs and hoped his luck would turn around, but he wasn't optimistic that things would improve right away, even if he was able to find work soon. Because of his low credit score, Rick pointed out that he would likely need to amass a very large security deposit to find a permanent (and less expensive) place to live. If another stimulus check arrived, he hoped to use the money to declare bankruptcy and get rid of some of his debt; without help, he didn't have enough money to pay the bankruptcy filing fees.

Rick's story illustrates how debt rises and falls with the economy. Rick was stretched thin, and he needed the extra cushion provided by the credit card in the years 2015 through 2019, and with the economy booming, credit card companies were happy to lend to him, both when he requested credit, and through credit limit increases when he hadn't asked for more. While the economy was heating up, his balances increased, and so did his minimum payments. By the time the economy crashed, Rick was already maxed out but still kept trying to make payments on his debt when he could. He didn't apply for any new credit, and no credit was proactively extended to him.

For millions of Americans like Rick, the economy is never really doing well: things are either hard, or they're really hard. What does it mean that when jobs are (comparatively) easy to find, people turn to credit cards to stretch their spending a bit further, and that when the economy slows, consumers both seek out less credit, and banks become less willing to lend? It means that we all become vulnerable to a cycle of booms and busts, whether we use credit cards or are able avoid them. In aggregate, the gaps between consumer spending in good times and bad times are made even more extreme by credit cards.

As economists Atif Mian and Amir Sufi explain in their book *House of Debt,* "the bigger the increase in debt, the harder the fall in spending."[16] Economic disasters, they point out, "are almost always preceded by a large increase in household debt."[17] Mian and Sufi published *House of Debt* in 2014, and they pointed out that it was rare for a recession to be caused by anything that changed the "fundamentals" of the economy—how many goods and services people around the world were able to produce. Instead, they argued that when debt burdens become too large, people are forced by rising monthly payments, a loss of housing wealth, foreclosures, or collections lawsuits to curtail their spending, bringing the rest of the country down with them. As I write this chapter, we're living through a global economic downturn that actually does have a discrete, specific cause unrelated to debt: a virus whose contagiousness and deadliness makes going to work or spending money outside the home less safe. The virus may be at the front of people's minds, but for millions of people, the stress of debt payments still lingers in the back.

A family with a typical amount of credit card debt, around $5,000, will have minimum monthly payments of around $150; not surprisingly then, a chunk of federal COVID relief dollars intended for struggling families will be sent immediately to satisfy the requirements of the lenders. Fairbank confirmed in the April 2020 investor call that Capital One saw a spike in credit card payments right after Americans were sent their $1,200 stimulus checks.[18]

AGAINST THE LAW TO LEND

In 1979, Rachel was a newly married nineteen-year-old, with "absolutely no money," living with her husband in rural Wyoming. Her mother-in-law took Rachel and her husband to the bank to cosign on their first credit card. They used the card to rent a U-Haul to move to Colorado, so her husband could attend grad school. It was a no-brainer decision. They couldn't have gotten started in Colorado without a little bit of money. They only borrowed about $300, an amount they paid off in roughly a year. The advanced degree put her family on a different trajectory than most other people from the working-class, small town where she grew up. Now, her household income is around $250,000. Rachel, for her part, eventually became a clinical social worker.

Rachel and her husband lived in Colorado for more than twenty years, having two daughters there. Rachel's husband was an engineer with Hewlett-Packard in Colorado. In 2006, in the midst of layoffs that cut more than ten thousand jobs, he was given a choice: move to the office in Southern California, or be fired. And so, they chose to move to Orange County, where home prices were high and rising by thousands of dollars a month. When they moved to California, Rachel and her husband turned to credit card debt again, this time ending up with $83,000 worth of debt. When I spoke with her in July of 2020, she still had $35,000 worth of debt that she planned to have paid off within a year. "It's horrible," she told me.

Like so many families as the housing bubble was reaching its peak, when Rachel's family moved to California, they felt that if they didn't act quickly to buy an (unaffordable) house, it would become completely out of reach. They put in a $650,000 offer for a home in California before they were able to sell their house in Colorado. But as they were getting ready to close on their new home, the lender asked them to bring an extra $30,000 to closing that they weren't expecting: the house had been appraised for less than the price they offered in order to win in a competitive market. That was when her family's slide into credit card debt started. Rachel assumed they'd sell the house in California within a couple of years, so they took out more credit card debt to add an extra bedroom, assuming they'd recoup their investment. Soon, they were $200,000 underwater on their mortgage. Half of her neighborhood was in foreclosure. In 2010, their oldest daughter, then a twenty-five-year-old married stay-at-home mom, was diagnosed with multiple sclerosis. Within a year of her diagnosis, her husband divorced her, leaving her without an income or health insurance, until eventually the Affordable Care Act qualified her for Medicaid in her state. Rachel and her husband started supporting their daughter and granddaughter, and quickly, their credit card debt ballooned. Like Kathryn G., who we met in chapter 3, wanting what was best for her children made it difficult for Rachel and her husband to spend less than they earned: throughout their financial difficulties, Rachel took a second job so that her younger daughter could stay enrolled in a private high school, and several years later, they bought their younger daughter a car.

In 2013, seven years after moving to California, the year their younger daughter went to college, Rachel and her husband did a short sale on their home: they hadn't wanted to uproot her while she was a teenager. Freed from a $5,000 monthly mortgage payment that they couldn't afford, their credit card debt stopped its upward climb. Although Rachel never felt like the credit card was used for splurges, nevertheless, she was adamant that the credit cards had harmed her more than the credit cards had ever helped. Without them, "I probably would have learned how to set up an emergency fund, which was one of the biggest issues that we had," Rachel told me. "One of the biggest mistakes we ever made was using credit cards," she said. "I spent a lot on things I couldn't afford like, plane tickets, bringing our daughters home to visit. But it's not like we ever went on trips or bought extravagant things." It was only in the last three years that Rachel and her husband were able to make real progress paying down debt. "Before now, we were supporting three apartments, four cars, health insurance, and car insurance."

If the CARD Act had been in place when Rachel was a young adult, she wouldn't have been able to leave Wyoming. As a part of the broader bill, lawmakers initiated a rule called "Ability to Pay," which said banks would have to confirm that borrowers had a high enough income or enough assets to pay their credit card bill before granting a new credit card, or extending a credit limit increase. The rule was a reaction to the lackadaisical underwriting of the early 2000s. In the mortgage business, lenders assumed that every house would rise in value enough that a mortgagor's ability to repay their debt was effectively irrelevant, since the bank could sell the secured asset for a profit. And in the credit card business, the range of tactics banks used to charge high interest rates and fees, some still legal and some not, meant that a borrower with a 50 percent chance of defaulting on their credit card bill might still be profitable.

The Ability to Pay rules are a consumer protection that relied on the borrower's honesty: credit card companies aren't required to check the borrowers' self-reported income unless it is obviously outlandish. If a credit card applicant is under twenty-one, their household income can't be considered—only the individual's own income. The CARD Act effectively made it illegal for a bank to give a loan to anyone who was unemployed, whether or not they had a good shot of finding work in the future, unless, of course, the borrower lied; a loan to relocate, like Rachel had needed, would be off-the-table, even for the modest sum of Rachel's $300 U-Haul.

Rachel's two debt experiences, one a burdensome, self-identified mistake that would still be legal, and the other a transformative opportunity that would now be illegal, seem to illustrate how poorly regulators understand how credit is used. Although they represent a minority of those I've interviewed, I've talked to a number of people who were unequivocally glad they'd used credit cards at least once in their life: like Rachel, Doreen from chapter 3, Jennifer, a Cuban American, first-generation college graduate working as a researcher in Maryland, and Doris, a Black senior citizen whose home was destroyed by Hurricane Harvey.

What these people have in common is that they were all basically broke when they needed to borrow money, and that their situations, in one way or another, were temporary or unusual. Under the new rules, the higher a family's income, the more credit the bank is allowed to extend them. At the same time, a higher income nearly always means a few things that make borrowing unwise. An income of zero is likely to eventually rise: while not every low-income worker will earn more in the future, the typical worker sees her income rise by 60 percent between the ages of twenty-five and fifty.[19] If an income is already high, it is less likely to get higher. Moreover, the higher a person's income, the more likely it is that she could find some strategy, be it comfortable or somewhat uncomfortable, to bring her spending beneath her income, tempting though it may be to try to juggle things indefinitely. In some ways, Rachel's experience in California was also temporary—her daughter's sudden change of circumstances and the challenge of discharging a burdensome mortgage both eventually subsided—but the roughly ten years her elevated expenses lasted, from 2006 to 2016, was certainly a long stretch of "temporary."

When Rachel entered the Great Recession, her credit score was in the 800s. She had never missed a bill payment in her life, she says, and she had such high credit limits on her credit cards that she had no need to apply for any new cards to rack up $80,000 in debt. In 2009, Bank of America closed the credit cards she hadn't used in a while. She says it was frustrating at the time, but she also told me, "It was probably a good thing; otherwise, I'd just have that much more debt." Rachel, like nearly every other debtor I spoke to, borrowed roughly as much as she could on her credit cards, but didn't apply for new credit cards once she reached her borrowing limits: in other words, the amount of debt she took on was heavily shaped by bank policy.

The Ability to Pay rules seem to have effectively banned the one type of credit card borrowing that seems to have the greatest shot of actually being useful to somebody: the loans to people to help them find work, or make ends meet while looking for work. They would have stopped Rachel from getting the loan she needed, while doing nothing from preventing the debt that ultimately became a burden.

As of 2015, about 4.5 percent of all credit card applications were denied solely because of the "ability to pay" regulation.[20] The rules were in part a response to media accounts of the early 2000s that chronicled college students whose lives were derailed by credit cards. The 2006 documentary "Maxed Out" won the special jury prize at South by Southwest, in part for telling the stories of two college students who committed suicide after their struggles with credit card debt. A review by Joe Leydon in *Variety* summarized one the film's key takeaways: "naive college students with limited incomes are encouraged to accumulate massive debt by credit-card issuers."[21] Many college students, of course, work only part time, and some don't work at all, relying on student loans or family support. With a limited income, some would find their credit card debt ballooned before they had a chance to enter the workforce. The public concluded that college student credit card borrowing represented a unique problem, requiring a unique solution.

College students and other low-income, unwitting, presumed to be vulnerable borrowers were an easy target for reform, but the solutions offered mischaracterized the basic nature of the credit card problem. More often than not, credit cards are a problem not because they exploit people who have no income; as we've discussed in this chapter, those with the least money are the most likely to have a productive use for a small loan. Credit cards are a problem because they go after people who *do* have some money, whether that income is $20,000 or $200,000, and tempt them into living, for a while, like their income was tens of thousands of dollars higher, getting in their way of achieving stability, building wealth, or eventually having a comfortable retirement.

After the Ability to Pay rules went into effect, CNBC, NPR, and CNN reported on the story of a stay-at-home mom named Holly McCall who, despite her high credit score, was declined for a Target credit card.[22] Although her household income was high, because she didn't work outside the home, her personal income was zero, and Ability to Pay stopped her from qualifying for credit. McCall, working with a group called Moms Rising, organized a popular online petition, and staged a protest outside the CFPB headquarters. McCall and Moms Rising garnered media coverage, and gained a face-to-face meeting with the CFPB director Richard Cordray, arguing that the law was "demeaning" and discriminatory toward stay-at-home spouses.[23] The CFPB considered her argument, wrote a proposed rule change to allow adults over the age of twenty-one (but not the troublesome college students under age twenty-one) to have their loans considered on the basis of household income, and after public comment, the rule went into effect.

A Roll Call article described her success under the headline "new power for the people."[24] What the CNBC, NPR, and CNN coverage omitted was the fact that Holly McCall had worked at Capital One until 2008, and, at the time of her advocacy, her husband, Chris, was a senior director at Capital One. Chris was the peer of my first boss, and during my first few months of work, we shared the same one-thousand-square-foot enclosed workspace, along with eight or so other colleagues. In exchange for our purportedly less desirable workspace, we got a free lunch each Friday, with the choice of restaurant take-out rotating among us. I mention this not to insinuate that Capital One was secretly behind Holly's activism, although I certainly think the media mischaracterized her success as a populist uprising. *Huffington Post* appears to be the only media outlet to have questioned McCall on her past career, or even to mention her ties to Capital One at all, and speaking to *Huffington Post*, she denied that Capital One played a role in her advocacy, although, of course, her desires and Capital One's were clearly aligned.[25]

In his 2020 book *Watchdog: How Protecting Consumers Can Save Our Families, Our Economy, and Our Democracy*, Cordray told the story of Moms Rising, saying, "If my own mother were alive, I know she would have joined them." The bureau's reaction to the petition was proof, in Cordray's eyes, that "we could be responsive to input and find ways to help consumers who were hurt needlessly by prior regulatory actions."[26] McCall's story, in fact, is the only direct example Richard Cordray provides in *Watchdog* of "consumers" successfully advocating for specific changes in the law. The fact that this described-as-grassroots change was, in fact, engineered by the wife of a credit card executive should give us pause. In the most generous rendering, McCall is a highly educated stand-in for a broader base of consumers, one who needed her prior industry experience to figure out how other stay-at-home moms were impacted by the regulation. Would any other group impacted by the Ability to Pay Rules—college students, those laid off from their jobs, or those looking for their first job—stand a chance of making their preferences heard?

In this chapter, we talked about why consumers borrow the least during recessions and the most when the economy is growing, a phenomenon driven heavily by the fact that consumers grow more cautious in times of turbulence, and more willing to cut the fat from their budgets, painful though it may be; but they are also driven by the fact that banks, during recessions, spend less on marketing credit cards, and decline a higher percentage of applicants. And since 2010, by law, an unemployed consumer would generally be ineligible for a new credit card. In chapter 3, we talked about the fact that consumers are more likely to be in credit card debt if their income is somewhat higher than average, and that consumers are the most likely to be in debt when they're in their late forties, which is for most people, when their income will also peak.

Putting this together, leaves us with two important implications. The first key takeaway is that credit card debt is not only lowering lifetime wealth but also compounding economic volatility. When Americans experience job losses or reductions in income, they're statistically less likely to seek out credit, and less likely to be approved for credit if they apply. In other words, if the economy is like a river that a person tries to cross without drowning, credit cards both make the river deeper overall and exacerbate the difference between the deepest and shallowest points. The second key takeaway is that the rising debt over the last sixty years can't be explained by rising economic hardship, because in times of hardship, Americans reduce how much they borrow. Both takeaways are critical pieces of the principal argument given that Americans do most of their borrowing when the economy is doing relatively well, and they are forced to repay those debts at the same time that they're facing other economic stressors, then lowering the total amount of money borrowed will make it *easier* for Americans to manage bouts of unemployment and other economic stressors. If the debt machine can be slowed—if Americans can hold on to more of their own cash while they're working—they will be better equipped to handle the economy's ups and downs.

5 The Quickest Levers

I am surely not the first person you've heard argue that credit card companies are tricking people into debt through marketing and product design decisions engineered to oppress the American public.

I will tell you that working at Capital One, it didn't feel like our job was to trick people. Work felt like tinkering with anonymous numbers in Excel, being invited to join intramural sports teams, figuring out why your lines of code weren't running correctly, planning diversity initiatives, writing performance reviews, crafting checklists to make sure a new project wasn't going to break any laws, and debating whether it was more important this quarter to reoptimize a credit policy or upgrade some of our technology. My coworkers were relentlessly friendly, to the point, as people new to the company would often point out, of seeming conflict averse. On each floor of our office, there were two coffee makers. I worked briefly with a vice president named Pawel, who, although among the top two or three highest-paid people on the floor, would upon discovering an empty coffee pot, start a brew, and then walk to the other side of the floor to see if that coffee also needed to be brewed, and then start the second coffee maker as a courtesy before returning to the original pot.

Nobody seemed to be a shark. At first glance, there was no scheming. Whenever I met someone particularly crass or arrogant, it occurred to me that they didn't really fit in at Capital One, and usually those people left after a year or two for another company. I fit in, as someone who at the time might have described myself as an outspoken liberal feminist. I spoke the language of a market-driven pursuit of social justice and was promoted quickly. The friendly people around me made me feel like I was a good person by association; it was easy, on one level, to accept the reasoning that if these nice people worked at Capital One, there was probably nothing wrong with what we were doing. People want to borrow money, and we lent them money. It was that simple.

·   ·   ·   ·   ·

Of course, a lot of money went into convincing people that they wanted credit cards.

For a price, the credit bureaus let the credit card companies look up the mailing addresses of all Americans who met whatever criteria they set— for example, everyone with a credit score between 550 and 650, who has a mortgage, who doesn't live in California, with between $2,000 and $20,000 in credit card debt—as long the bank would then send all those people a "firm offer of credit." Alternatively, the bank could build their own statistical models, provide those models to a third-party clearinghouse, who would return the names and mailing addresses of everyone who fell into the designated score range. The question at Capital One was normally not who should be mailed and who shouldn't be mailed, but rather, who should get one piece of mail, two, three, or four per campaign. More lucrative possible customers received more mail, but most consumers were attractive enough to get at least one envelope.

Direct mail is a particularly important marketing channel in the credit card business. In the era before Facebook or Google, direct mail let the credit card companies *personalize* the offers they sent to each prospect. Put another way, it let the credit card companies figure out the very worst product to which a specific person would still be likely to respond. In 2003, the *Wall Street Journal* reported that for the first time in the post office's history, the USPS would offer reduced rates specifically for one customer: Capital One. Prior to the deal being brokered, Capital One, the post office's biggest customer, already sent 1.2 billion mail pieces each year.[1] At the peak of the direct mail business, in 2006, credit card companies in total sent out 7.5 billion pieces of marketing mail. The Internet (and, of course, the Great Recession) put a dent in the direct mail machine, but, before the COVID crisis hit, direct mail was still an important marketing channel for the banks, who had leveled off their credit card direct mail volumes at a sizable 3 billion solicitations per year.[2]

There were a few reasons direct mail remained important, even as the tech giants promised more economical avenues for targeted advertisements. Whereas online advertisements funneled customers to your website, where they would be only a few clicks away from seeing every product offered to every customer, mail made it easier to show something better or worse than what other people saw, making it ideal for testing out new combinations of product terms. And in the mail, you could show people only the product you'd decided was "best" for them, balancing the fact that fewer fees, a lower interest rate, or better rewards would increase a customer's odds of responding, but also making the product less profitable on a per-customer basis. And in your mail solicitations, you could make up brand new products that wouldn't exist on your website at all, keeping these products largely outside of the public view, whether it because the product was unusually good, and you didn't want to your nontarget population to even bother applying, or unusually bad, and you didn't want to scare the public off from your brand.

Most importantly, direct mail remained the easiest way to tell a person they had been *preapproved* for a credit card. It was hard to do that online; you weren't usually certain of who was looking at an online advertisement, and while Google or Facebook might offer data about someone's likely income or hobbies, that wasn't the same thing as knowing how much debt they already had and whether they were paying their bills on time. The implicit guarantee of *preapproval* was especially important for Americans with checkered credit history: these people knew if they applied for the credit cards they saw advertised on television, they'd probably be denied. Every time an American applied for a credit card, that "inquiry" appeared on their credit report, lowering their credit score. Trying to get a credit card and failing would come at a real cost to people; it made every future credit card that much harder to obtain. Preapproval meant something, because in 2018, the overall credit card approval rate was just about 40 percent: under 20 percent for Americans with a credit score below 620, and rising to over 80 percent for Americans with a credit score over 720.[3] And because getting more credit never felt like a guarantee for adults with below-average credit scores, a preapproved offer in the mail sometimes felt like a special opportunity, one that ought to be snatched up before it disappeared.

As James Schenck, the CEO of PenFed Credit Union, the second largest federally chartered credit union in the United States, pointed out to me when we spoke by phone, "American consumers have been educated on the downside of applying too many times for credit, and the repercussions of being turned down for credit. So, when a consumer receives a preapproved offer that has a lot of validity." The importance of preapproval for Americans with average or below average credit scores gives the largest banks a big advantage, Schenck points out: they're able to spend hundreds of millions of dollars on preapproved mail, despite the low response rate, an upfront cost that is hard for smaller banks or credit unions to swallow. "The industry has found a targeted preapproved offer is better than an unsolicited apply-for-credit offer, by many folds," Scheck said, adding, that the conversion rates are "night versus day."

While Capital One competes against companies like Chase, Bank of America, Discover, and Citi, it also had a sizable subprime business, competing against less savory companies, known as subprime specialists, like Credit One, and First Premier. Whether you consider "Credit One" a household name says a lot about what type of household you have. As of 2019, Credit One reported that they had 11 million active accounts, roughly the same number of accounts as the brokerage Charles Schwab.[4] (Rick, who we met in the previous chapter, was one of these 11 million account holders). Although Credit One, of course, has a website, you can't just go there and look at all their products. Instead, would-be customers who haven't gotten a direct mail solicitation from Credit One have to plug their information into their "pre-qualify for a credit card" tool. Clicking on the fine print would reveal that submitting your information into this tool would allow you to be considered for a wide range of credit cards, some with annual fees of up to $99. Helpfully, these disclosures explain, "if you are assigned the minimum credit line of $300 and your Annual Fee is $95, your initial available credit will be only about $205."

Only about 10 percent of all the mail sent by the "mass market" credit card companies like Chase and Discover have an offer of preapproval, but well over half of the subprime specialist solicitations contain one of these preapproval promises.[5] There is a reason not to bandy around a preapproval promise if you don't have to: doing so invites legal trouble if your approval rates aren't sufficiently high. There's not a law that defines exactly what the word "preapproved" means, but there are laws against deceptive marketing. When a credit card company pursues affluent, financially stable people, there is no real reason for them to make the implied promise; financially stable, high-credit score consumers foster no insecurities on the topic, so the promise of preapproval isn't something they care about or notice.

By the 2010s, a new venue to reach Americans with checkered financial pasts would emerge: the sites where you can check your credit score, like Credit Karma and Credit Sesame. On these sites, banks could assess the credit worthiness of applicants with the same type of credit bureau data used in direct mail, so, similarly, the sites were able to reassure stressed out consumers when their approval odds were high. By 2018, more than four in ten new subprime credit cards would come through these "third-party comparison sites," websites that seem to offer unbiased advice, but whose recommendations are driven in part by which banks submit the highest bids. For customers with higher credit scores, the share of new cards that come through these third-party comparison sites is much lower, only about two in ten.[6]

Rarely do these third-party comparison sites prominently highlight APRs in offering their suggestions: for example, APRs do not appear in the first page of Credit Karma's suggestions for cards that also have rewards (only two pieces of key information are listed for each product on the first page of results, so the APR is mentioned for cards without rewards). This fact, that APRs aren't listed on the first page where one compares cards, is true even in the "fair/average" category, primarily made up of subprime cards, targeted at consumers with very high odds of carrying a revolving balance.

The market has evolved in a way that getting credit, if you are one of the many ordinary Americans who struggles to pay bills, feels a bit like fishing. You can't pick and choose between all the fishes in the ocean. You have to reel in whatever fishes come to you. Credit feels scarce: it feels prudent to go ahead and apply for cards as the offers come in, particularly if a credit card offer doesn't have an annual fee, just in case, because there is no way of knowing whether you'll be approved for a credit card when your moment of crisis arrives.

It is this metaphor of *evolution* that is the best way of understanding the credit card market, the first industry in the world to be heavily shaped by constant experimentation. The analysts at a credit card company wouldn't have to plan to oppress the middle class, and, nevertheless, the middle class would be oppressed. By developing engines of experimentation, constantly testing what "worked" and what "didn't work," in a market where typically higher debt burdens for customers led to higher profits, the machine did the dirty work, the analysts were left with clean hands.

.   .   .   .   .

When a person is approved for her very first credit card, her credit limit will generally fall somewhere between $300 and $3,000. When someone applying for her first credit card gets a credit limit above $1,000, it's normally because she already has a checking account with the same bank (especially if she applied in person at a bank branch), or because she already has some credit history. That credit history could be from a student or car loan, or because her parents made her an authorized user on one of their own cards. That latter trick makes the kid's credit report look a lot like the parents: if mom and dad add you on a credit card they've had open since 1980, your credit score similarly reflects forty years of credit history. Part of the reason why authorized user data is reported to the credit bureaus and is considered by lenders stems from the 1974 Equal Credit Opportunity Act, discussed in chapter 2. Congress was worried that if authorized user credit history wasn't considered by lenders, women who were homemakers or otherwise not the primary account holder would be discriminated against.[7] The law has the side effect of working to the benefit of children of privilege, who have a simple route into a super-prime credit score and low borrowing costs: to the extent that it gives these young adults an unfair advantage, it arguably gives young adults with lower-income parents, who are disproportionately Black and Brown, an unfair disadvantage.

Showing up to a bank branch in person to apply for a credit card makes a difference as well, because, it turns out, the hardest part of offering credit cards to people without much credit history is figuring out whether you're handing out money to a real human being, with the actual name and the social security number written on the application. After all, when you're lending at a 25 percent interest rate, if the borrower makes even a passing attempt to repay their debt before eventually defaulting, you stand a good shot of making money. The real risk is that you give out a credit card to a criminal syndicate that's manufacturing fake identities, applying for hundreds of credit cards, never making a single payment. This is a particularly important risk because it can be done at scale: a single criminal syndicate can apply for many accounts.

At Capital One, we called it a "diabolical chargeoff" when a credit card customer defaulted without making a single payment. Sometimes of course, that "diabolical" customer might be a real person, going through a hard time, who applied for a credit card trying desperately to make ends meet, never scraping together the money to pay it back. Other times, it would eventually become clear that the identity that applied was "synthetic:" it was a made-up name, along with a fabricated social security number. Often, there was no way of knowing which of the two things had happened, and there were a range of possibilities in between. The charge-off rate was of intense interest to all the analysts, but the specifics of what happened to our customers when they defaulted was a mystery to most of us, except for the analysts who worked in collections and recoveries, and some of those people who worked in first-party fraud (after all, it was not always clear which customers had fallen on hard times and which were committing fraud).

Diabolical was eventually shortened to "diablo"; this, finally prompted me to say something about the terminology. "Diabolical" was presumptuous, but "diablo" literally means "the Devil" in Spanish! Tepidly, I suggested, we revert to the formal industry term of "first payment default," a suggestion that did not take hold across the company. In the subprime lending industry, it wasn't unheard of to have a first payment default rate as high as 15 percent.[8]

Several financial services companies have, based on current or former employees I've spoken to, internal rules about the maximum lifetime default rate they'll tolerate on their loans, even for loans that are nevertheless profitable. These internal rules are described as a consumer protection, because, as employees would helpfully point out, it would be profitable to lend even to the people with a 45-percent or 50-percent odds of eventually defaulting. Their companies have voluntarily chosen to draw the line somewhere.

If a customer doesn't miss any of his first payments, his credit limit rises quickly. One of Capital One's competitors, Merrick Bank, advertises this prominently, offering what they call a Double Your Line® Platinum Visa®. In the subprime market, the odds that a customer is going to fall behind on his bills is high: over a two-year period, 79 percent of people with a credit score between 500 to 600 will fall at least three months behind on a bill, as will 44 percent of people with a credit score between 601 and 660.[9] When a company lends to people who the economy has not been kind to, to people who live paycheck to paycheck, the question normally isn't *if* they're going to miss payments, it's *when*, and whether or not those missed payments will end up becoming unrecoverable losses, or can be recouped with a lawsuit.

By starting customers out with very low credit limits and raising those credit limits only if the first few payments arrive on time, the credit card companies weed out the people whose situation is already dire; the odds, then, are good, that they'll collect a few years' worth of interest payments (and some past due fees), before the customer's financial situation sours.

REVENUE LEVERS

One of the main jobs for a middle manager like myself at Capital One was to help complete lists of "levers."

On my second or third week of work at Capital One, I went to a SQL class with all the other new analysts, taught by a man who'd worked at Capital One for fifteen years. SQL was the programming language analysts used to fetch data about our customers, allowing us to answer questions like, "Controlling for credit score, do Android users default at a higher rate than iPhone users?" or "By how much do Capital One customer balances increase or decrease after our customer gets a new credit card from another company?"

At one point in the class, the instructor asked all his fellow *engineers* to raise their hands. Of course, he was really asking which of these recent college graduates had majored in engineering. If I remember correctly, it was slightly less than half. I remember thinking to myself, "if these people are engineers, does that make me a mathematician?" If I'd majored in art history, could I call myself an art historian while working at Capital One? I thought they weren't engineers because we weren't engineering anything.

Eventually, I would come to realize our job was to engineer Capital One's balance sheet.

Of course, on one level, all our investors cared about were profits, big profits, and ideally, predictably growing profits. The company's stated mission may have been "change banking for good," but the biggest investors were all just mutual funds, exchange traded funds, or hedge funds seeking a healthy return on the capital they'd invested. The single largest shareholder, Dodge & Cox, was an investment manager who promised their investors a conservative, long-run, value investment strategy, where "value" in this sense doesn't mean values, as in ethics, but value, as in cheap. Lending at a high interest rate to middle America was a money-in, money-out machine: give a person living paycheck to paycheck a dollar, and, on average, they would give you a dollar and six cents back, after having subtracted out the money from the people who never returned your money at all.

But investors couldn't check the gears of our machine, and hence they were constantly afraid things would break, that Capital One would lend to too many people who wouldn't pay it back, and that their whole investment would be lost. As a result, engineering our balance sheet didn't just mean maximizing long-run profit: it also meant tweaking a long list of other portfolio metrics we reported to our shareholders, metrics that made them comfortable and optimistic that everything was humming along as they expected. Cutting into long-run profits was necessary sometimes to help us tweak the other portfolio metrics that investors believed augured the financial future of our company: metrics like the percentage of loans that went to subprime customers, the default rate on our loans, our revenue, our efficiency ratio (the ratio of non-marketing costs to revenues), and how fast we were growing customer balances. Other metrics mattered too: we wanted to climb in the J.D. Power rankings, and, of course, we needed to hit the metrics set by the government, rules requiring that we preserve enough capital, and do enough loans to people living in the low- and moderate-income neighborhoods in the cities where we had bank branches.

Every quarter, it seemed, one of these metrics was veering off track, and so, we would scramble to correct it, in some cases undoing moves that had been made just a year or two ago to move an offsetting number. The clearest of these relationships, where making one number better meant making the other number worse, was between the loss rate and the growth rate: the easiest way to build balances was to be more aggressive in lending to the Americans in the worst financial position.

Middle managers like me were the chefs, writing the menu of possibilities for how to move these numbers around, explaining the likely impact of each menu option, and executives were the restaurant's customers, choosing what they wanted. The first- and second-year analysts were the line cooks and servers, scrambling to execute on orders, and running the monitoring reports to let people know if the refrigerator was broken or if a fire had broken out in the kitchen.

There were a lot of levers at the company's disposal—offering balance transfers to more or fewer customers, offering upgraded rewards to more or fewer customers, closing inactive accounts, raising or lowering fees, spending more or less on marketing. But the quickest, most powerful levers were always credit limit increases.

The idea that a bunch of credit limit increases would yield a bunch of revenue a few months later was treated with great predictability. We were as confident as a pianist placing her finger on the key of a well-tuned piano, not questioning the cause and effect— "If I hit this key, a note will ring." The only question was, after we granted a few hundred million or several billion dollars' worth of credit line increases, whether a few months later 30 percent or 40 percent or 50 percent or 60 percent of the dollar value of those new credit limits would have already been spent by our customers, turning, in other words, from exposure to debt.

If it turned out to be 45 percent and the team had projected 50 percent, well, that was a big problem, even if the credit limit increases continued to be wildly profitable. It would mean our balance sheet had a hole: this was a particularly big issue if executives had already earmarked that planned money for a marketing campaign, a technology overhaul, or a new building. It would trigger a relentless inquiry into the causes—why had things not transpired exactly as our models had predicted? A highly lucrative strategy would still be treated as a failure if it made less money than was expected, or even, if it made money in a different way that had been planned—for example, by generating both more revenue and more loan losses than the team budgeted for.

Credit limit increases made the best levers for a few reasons. The first was that they were fast. If you tried to change portfolio metrics by spending more or less money on marketing new customers, it took a while to implement those changes and to see the results. By comparison, some customers would use their credit limit increase the very same day that the credit was extended. And credit limit increases came with no upfront costs: you didn't have to spend any money on postage or as bounties to online advertisers to book more customers. The only downside was the fact that if customers defaulted, Capital One would lose more money (and, of course, the higher credit limit might be the very thing that triggered their default). Thankfully, as long as you didn't give credit limit increases to people who were currently past due, those chargeoffs wouldn't happen for at least nine months, and, usually, a year or more. Credit limit increases could be targeted to scratch whatever exact itch the company needed to scratch.

As is true at most regulated banks, major extensions of credit had to be approved separately by at least two different people beyond the analysts who'd planned the new scheme for granting credit. The first was an executive who worked within the credit card division; if you were an analyst in the credit card division, this person was probably your boss or your boss's boss. We chipperly referred to our bosses' bosses as our "skips." The second person was an executive within the credit risk management division, a division with the reputation for attracting smarter-than-average misanthropes, because you could be promoted there without having to be anybody's manager. One of the biggest fears of credit risk management was that the credit card division would use up all its "ammunition" with credit limit increases: that is to say, we'd give out so many credit limit increases that in a year or two, when our desire for revenue would presumably be even stronger, there would be no more plausible candidates whose limits could be extended further. And so, the analysts constantly scrambled to prove that we were not clear cutting the forest, that there would be plenty of opportunities to CLIP more people tomorrow even if we CLIPped millions of people today.

After two promotions and about two and a half years at the company, I was asked to lead the "Revolver pCLIP" team—that is to say, the team that would decide which already indebted customers would get a higher credit limit. The *p* in pCLIP stood for proactive, which meant it was our decision to give them a higher credit limit, and that we were not merely *reacting* to their request.

None of what I am saying here is a secret. I am merely echoing what Rich Fairbank publicly explains to investors: "The origination lever and the credit line lever are two separate decisions. And we've always said that for a lot of our business, the real exposure comes on the credit line side, not really the origination side [. . .] As you know from having watched us manage that up through time, we're trying to continue to build the potential energy as carried by the originating new accounts, pulled back for the time being on the credit line, and then trying to get as much information as we can on each customer and watching very carefully their situation. Over time, [we] really open up on the credit lines, but the loan growth will come more on the credit line side, and that is a lever and a dial that we're going to be managing along the way during the downturn."[10]

In other words, the amount of credit received was not really driven by a reflection on what he or she wanted or needed. Credit line increases were "a lever and a dial" for Capital One to get what it wanted, when it was wanted. "Originating new accounts," that is to say, finding new customers, was done only to "build the potential energy" for the credit limit increase machine.

It's hard to see a credit limit increase as a bad thing. The government doesn't think of credit limit increases as a bad thing. There's a whole set of rules about decreasing a customer's credit limit: credit limit decreases are considered an "adverse action," which means the bank is required to send a letter explaining their reasoning, furnishing a credit report where appropriate. By contrast, a bank doesn't need to explain why they raised your credit limit, nor do they need to ask your permission.

In 1970, Congress, believing Americans had a right to understand their financial lives, passed the Fair Credit Reporting Act, which said that when a customer was turned down for a loan, banks needed to explain the reason why, providing a credit report to the consumer if credit bureau information had been a part of the decision. But the rise of credit limit increases would render this law functionally irrelevant when it came to credit cards: instead of declining a customer outright, banks could just give out tiny credit limits if they didn't feel like explaining why they didn't consider a customer creditworthy. All the variables that went into deciding what credit limit to assign would be secret. Some upmarket credit cards, those that say Visa Signature in the bottom left or bottom right-hand corner, have minimum credit limits of $5,000: Visa sets this minimum, and gives banks a higher processing fee per card swipe for these customers. By setting the higher minimum credit limit for Visa Signature cards, Visa ensures that banks don't just give *all* their customers Visa Signature cards, rather than the less illustrious Visa Platinum cards. So, if you apply for any card that says Visa Signature on it, like the Bank of America Premium Rewards card, or the Wells Fargo Visa Signature Card, or the Chase Sapphire Preferred Card, without a decent credit score, you'll probably be declined outright, but otherwise, the more likely scenario is that you'll just receive a tiny credit limit if the bank doesn't think you're up to snuff.

While regulators don't view credit limit increases with much suspicion, consumers certainly do. I can't guarantee what will happen if, while reading this book, you go on Twitter and search 'Capital One credit limit,' 'Bank of America credit limit,' or 'Discover credit limit,' but when I search those terms, along with people asking how to request a credit limit increase, I also see messages like these:

- "Nobody told capital one to increase my credit limit without my permission."
- "Capital one raising my credit limit without telling me"—above an image reading "you raggedy b*tch."
- "The devil so dirty . . . I woke up today with an email from Discover . . . 'your credit limit has increased.' Not today satan."

- "Just paid off my credit card balance & Discover really wants to raise my credit limit by $3,100 tempting me!!!!"
- "Bank of America keep increasing my credit limit like the devil they are."

These statements clearly contradict how my colleagues thought about credit line increases. My colleagues thought nothing bad would happen if somebody didn't want their credit line increase: if a person didn't want a credit limit increase, they just wouldn't use it, they reasoned. But people are unhappy with these limit increases not because they don't expect to use them, but because they know they will. Few people enjoy being taunted with things they want desperately but know aren't good for them. It's the same reason I normally don't buy ice cream at the grocery store: not because I dislike ice cream, but because I love ice cream, and know I'd want to eat the whole pint in a day. And this isn't even just a case of happiness today, discomfort tomorrow. Even at the moment they occur, credit line increases trigger pain for the many consumers who feel dread about the debt they don't believe they have the willpower to avoid.

Credit limit increases are to banks what OxyContin was to Purdue Pharma. Opioids have devastated our country: throughout the 2010s, opioids killed roughly 40,000 Americans per year.[11] Roughly half of those deaths involved a prescription opioid, like OxyContin.[12] And yet, prescription opioids are the only thing that equip some people struggling with chronic pain to go to work, or care for their children. Untreated or undertreated pain can lead to severe anxiety and depression, hypertension, and kidney disease. In *Harper's Magazine,* reporter Brian Goldstone pointed out only about 8 percent of the 10 million Americans who are prescribed opioids for chronic pain are ultimately diagnosed with an addiction.[13] It would be impossible to justify the claim that nobody benefits from credit cards, or that nobody benefits from prescription opioids. When it comes to opioids, and credit limit increases, it's misleading to only ask whether consumers want them, or need them, or are free to decline them. These tools are powerful, desirable, effective, but also extremely dangerous, and each in their own way, difficult to resist. Companies like pharmaceutical companies and credit card companies benefit enormously from peddling these tools, both to people who will benefit, and to those who will suffer. Distinguishing between who will benefit and who will suffer isn't always easy, of course, but the company's incentive is to put their tools in as many people's hands as possible. In both cases, there's a clear asymmetry between the consumer and the corporation: the corporation's incentives are always to sell as much of their dangerous product as possible, while the consumer faces a range of contradictory goals, fears, and impulses.

The most important and most disturbing thing I learned about credit limit increases was that the overwhelming majority of the balances generated for the company would not have otherwise accrued, even though most of our customers could have easily been approved for other credit cards if they sought them out. Comparing the customers who had been randomly assigned credit limit increases against those customers who had been randomly excluded from credit limit increases, this fact was as clear as day: we were driving customers into debt who not only otherwise would have avoided it, but who wouldn't have even thought to apply for a new credit card. There was a "test" group and a "control" group, so we could compare not only the test group's Capital One credit card balance versus the control group's Capital One credit card balance, but also each group's total credit card debt across all issuers, and the number of loan applications they submitted, otherwise known as inquiries on their credit report. The proportion of the higher balances from credit limit increases that had been merely "shifted" from another credit card issuer to us was tiny, and the control group had no more inquiries than the test group. It was hard to marshal any evidence that showed that the control group, saddled with considerably less debt, wasn't better off.

Of course, although most "revolvers" borrowed more and more money with every credit limit increase they were offered, some wouldn't. Some people left their additional credit limit unused. Those people would see their credit scores go up, because utilization, or a person's credit card debt divided by their total credit card limits, is a part of their credit score. This fact is why the media often encourages people to ask for higher credit limits and discourages them from requesting the bank lower their limit. A high credit limit, left unused, is good for your credit score.

Hence, credit line increases would set customers on one of two paths. If a customer didn't use her credit limit increases, she'd quickly find that she became eligible for better credit cards, ones with eighteen- or twenty-four-month-long interest-free periods, and 1 percent or 2 percent cash-back rewards. On the other hand, if she kept using her credit limit increases, her minimum monthly payments would steadily grow until the point when it was hard to pay that minimum monthly payment at the same time that she also had to pay her rent, phone bill, and health insurance. She'd start missing payments, accruing a $25 late fee the first time, and a $35 late fee the second time it happened. With the track record of missed payments, the credit limit increases would stop coming. Some people would stay in this limbo for years, hovering, constantly at razor's edge, falling behind on payments and catching back up, getting hit with late fees, but managing to pay them back.

Credit card companies assessed $13 billion in late fees in 2018, an average of $64 per American with a credit card. Although people with credit scores of less than 720 make up only 40 percent of credit card customers, they paid 80 percent of these late fees. Put another way, Americans with less than pristine credit pay an average of $128 worth of credit card late fees annually.[14] Late fees themselves could drive a customer over the edge into default, especially because they are generally added to a customer's minimum payment, becoming due right away. Sometimes, all the fees and interest would become too much for the person to manage. They'd charge off.

CUSTOMER LEVERS

Middle managers were asked to pull together lists of revenue levers, loss rate levers, subprime credit mix levers, growth levers, but also "customer levers": things Capital One could do that would make customers like us more, or alternately, make us a more ethical company. Nobody at Capital One would have framed it like that, "more ethical." That would have meant that today we were less ethical. But in business, right and wrong is often a gradient.

Customers hated something called *residual interest*; it constantly led to complaints on social media and to regulators, although the practice of charging residual interest is completely legal, and, on paper, makes sense. Let me explain quickly what residual interest is. You are likely familiar with the concept if you've paid off an auto loan or home loan early, but otherwise it may be mystifying. Credit card interest compounds daily. As a result, when the credit card company sends out paper statements, what is listed as the "statement balance" was the balance on the statement date, but since interest compounds daily, every subsequent day, the balance is a little bit higher. Customers who had been in debt for a while would try to pay off their balance by sending in the amount of money they saw listed as their statement balance. The next month, they'd be confused why their balance wasn't zero: they thought they'd completely paid their debt off. And sometimes, thinking their debt had been paid off, they wouldn't even check their next statement, and be hit with a late fee when they missed their next payment. Whether we should waive the residual interest itself, or just the late fees from the people who missed payments due to residual interest, or only the late fees from people who proactively complained, was constantly up for debate. Residual interest wasn't exactly a trick, but it certainly startled and harmed our customers. Everyone could agree that eliminating it would be good. But did that mean keeping it was bad?

Isa, a Black college student I spoke to in Houston, Texas, in 2019, experienced the consequences of both residual interest and credit limit increases firsthand. "There was a point where I'd paid off my credit card, but they still charged me interest on the money I had already paid off," she told me, after I had asked her what she would change about banks or credit card companies if she could only change one thing. Although she used the credit card to pay essential bills, she also told me that she wished she'd never had the credit card to begin with. Without the credit card, she said, "I would have saved money, saved better." Credit card companies "make it too easy to get into debt. Because the more you spend, the more they increase your limit," Isa explained.

By the time I joined Capital One in 2013, executives often bragged about the company's journey of "unassailability"—how the company had abandoned consumer practices that were so slimy as to be impossible to justify. Some of these changes had been forced by the CARD Act, and others, perhaps, were done to curry favor with the newly created Consumer Financial Protection Bureau. Telling the story of "unassailability" at Capital One meant showing a graph of how Capital One used to make money in the old times, around 2004 or 2005, and how it now made money in 2013 or 2014. For the credit card industry as a whole, the percent of profit that came from fees, as opposed to interest, had fallen dramatically, and Capital One was no exception. Most people at Capital One (and the regulators) agreed it was preferable to make money from interest than from fees, since fees were considered less predictable for borrowers, and, in a sense, more punitive. I remember being told that the only fee we "really" had left was the late fee, which was *important,* the executive said, because otherwise customers wouldn't make their payments on time, shooting themselves in the foot, and harming their own credit scores.[15] This was the type of just-so story often told at Capital One: late fees, the executive argued, weren't bad for customers, and, in fact, he claimed they were a win-win.

I wondered, of course, if there was any truth to this idea that late fees were in some sense helpful to customers. My assumption, then and now, was that if there *was* any truth to the claim, a $1 or $5 late fee would be just as effective as a $39 late fee for encouraging timely payments, while less devastating to the people who were just broke. In any case, the idea that late fees were, in fact, a courtesy for our customers, was clearly belied by an ongoing debate over the payment cutoff time.

In 2020, I spoke with a former Capital One executive, who was recruited to join the company from a competing credit card issuer. As she was getting up to speed on her new job at Capital One, she reviewed a PowerPoint presentation that discussed the question of at what exact time on a person's due date his payment should be marked late: customers who missed that time would be hit with a late fee. "It was something like 5pm," she told me, "and there was an entire analysis done that showed if you moved it till 8pm, or 9pm, or 10pm, all the way to midnight, the number of customers that would avoid being late, and therefore that avoid late fees. It was a credit decision, analysis that had been and was being presented so [someone could] make a decision that it was safe and sound. The decision was to not [extend the cutoff time], because of the cost, like we couldn't afford the cost. I was like, 'there are people who literally because they have two jobs that don't get home until 10pm. And that's the day that they get their paycheck. They can't physically make their payment until that time; they are going to be going late and getting a $35 late fee. And you're not going to fix it.' It was just the most inane thing to me."

Clearly, moving the cutoff time to midnight eastern time, or midnight Pacific time, or even to noon the next day, would have been objectively good for Capital One's customers: missed payments aren't reported to the credit bureau until they're a month behind. The people on the West Coast who pay their bill at 6 p.m. (PST) on their due date presumably *believe* they are not making a late payment. There is no moral hazard here, and Capital One accrues no extra costs if you log on to its website at 11 p.m. instead of at 4 p.m. As of August 2019, Capital One's payment cutoff time for some or all customers is 8 p.m. (EST), regardless of where the customer lives, which is, of course, better for customers than 5 p.m. (EST), but also not as good for customers as midnight.

Executives often insinuated that if we could just make more money, we would pull more of these customer levers, things like extending the payment cutoff time, because we could "afford" to do so. At first, I believed this narrative without question: that if I could help the company make more money, we would do more "nice" things for customers. This didn't feel like complete naïveté at the time. After all, the idea that cost savings result in lower prices for customers roughly follows market logic. My long-time boss, an extremely affable and welcoming man named Jeff, told his underlings working in the company's biggest profit center, the credit limit increase team, that our work "powered the mission," as if a dollar earned would be sent directly back to customers. The longer I worked at Capital One, the hazier his calculus seemed. In 2018, the year I left my full-time job, Capital One completed $1.2 billion in share buybacks; as a result, the premise that we simply had no choice but to charge customers who made their payment at 9 p.m. on their due date a late fee struck me as deeply suspicious.

The question of payment allocation was similar. Many customers had balances on more than one interest rate. For example, if they ever took advantage of a balance transfer offer, they'd have some balances on the lower interest rate, or if they took out a cash advance, other balances would be on a higher interest rate. When a customer made a payment, the question was which balance would get paid off first. After the passage of the CARD Act, if a customer made a payment that was larger than the minimum, that extra amount had to be allocated to the highest interest rate first, but the minimum payment could still be applied to the lowest interest rate first, to the benefit of the bank at the expense of the customer.

One former Capital One executive put it this way: "People [at Capital One] said things, like, 'Oh, you know, customers aren't going to really notice payment allocation. It's a pretty opaque concept, and, you know most of them, aren't sophisticated enough to figure it out.'" Describing her initial surprise at the business practice to me, she said, how "insulting is that to the people who give us our money? Can you imagine saying that to a customer: 'You're too dumb to figure out how I allocate your payment, which is why I chose the approach I took?'"

In 2013, Capital One's CEO rolled out a new corporate mission, to "Change Banking for Good": as Rich Fairbank proudly told associates, Capital One had never had a mission before, which is why we were to believe the new mission really meant something. Reportedly, the move to write a company mission was inspired in part by Arkadi Kuhlmann, the head of ING Direct Bank, an online bank Capital One acquired in 2012, that, under Kuhlmann, had a relentless focus on helping America become a "nation of savers." Kuhlmann reportedly told Rich Fairbank that he was shocked Capital One had existed for so long mission-less.

Once established with a glossy rollout speech and a wide array of signage and paraphernalia around Capital One's many office buildings, the mission, "Change Banking for Good," was something employees sometimes mentioned in conversation as a reason to pursue or not pursue any given idea, even if the mantra meant very different things to different people. Managers were, in fact, asked to rate their employees on eight or so competences, one of which was "lives the mission." But if you brought up the mission when discussing something like the fact that minimum payments were allocated to the lowest interest rate debt, colleagues would just argue that if we're going to do stuff for the sake of the mission, it should at least be things that customers would *notice*.

.   .   .   .   .

There's a piece of received wisdom that says the reason the milk is in the back of the grocery store is to trick people who only need milk into buying more stuff as they wind through the aisles. But, as economist Mike Munger points out, when you put milk at the back of the store, it's cheaper to keep it cold, and easier to restock. Munger estimates milk might have to be 20 percent more expensive if stores were going to put it at the front entrance, to cover these additional labor and energy costs. If customers really care about getting just milk as fast as possible, they can head to a convenience store, where the milk is probably more expensive, but faster to reach. If all consumers wanted milk to be at the front of the store, Munger argues that the stores that kept their milk in the back of the store would go out of business: everyone would shop at the grocery stores with the more expensive milk at the front. Munger argues that the customers, in a sense, have actually *chosen* that they *want* the milk to be all the way in the back of the store.[16]

In this narrative, the placement of the milk is partially a parable for the free market: it isn't easy to trick or exploit consumers. And I agree with Mike Munger, a libertarian, when he says it isn't easy.

The problem is when you make the intellectual leap from saying it isn't easy to trick ordinary people, to saying it's impossible to trick ordinary people. I don't accuse Munger of this fallacy specifically, but the assumption that what consumers choose is equivalent to what consumers want, which is equivalent to what consumers need, can be found everywhere in corporate America and on Capitol Hill.

You would think that shopping for a loan could be incredibly easy. After all, money is fungible, so a $1,000 loan from Bank A or Bank B seem like they'd be more or less the same, a commodity. It seems like all that would matter is how much it costs to borrow, and when you'll have to pay the loan back. (It turns out, of course, that people who are struggling actually care deeply about other factors as well, such as their odds of being approved and how quickly the money will get disbursed—two factors that help explain why high-priced payday loans sometimes beat out lower-priced bank and credit union loans.)

But there are dozens of ways banks can subtly alter the price of a credit card. So far, we've discussed the length of the grace period—how many days elapse between when the statement is due, and when you have to repay it—the payment cutoff time, payment allocation, and residual interest. There's also the minimum interest charge assessed.

There's *retroactive interest* (sometimes called *deferred interest*), where a customer is advertised a zero-interest rate period, but if they fail to repay the whole loan amount before the teaser ends, they are hit with the full interest amount instead of just starting to accrue interest on the last day of the teaser. Often, the *precise* date the teaser ends is unclear to the borrower, and the date the teaser ends might be unrelated to a customer's payment due date. Retroactive interest—most commonly found on retail credit cards tied to a specific store rather than the general-purpose credit cards that you can use anywhere—is especially hard to avoid, even if you think you have a clear plan to pay off your bill before the promo period ends: consumers *think* that they're getting a free loan, and that they're on track to pay off the bill in time, and then get hit with a nasty surprise. Consider the complaint of this borrower who used a Comenity Card to purchase a diamond ring:

> "The sales person assured me that 12 installments according to Comenity's payment plan was all I needed to pay off the balance with no interest. He did not give me any paper contract to sign. I got the card for the account about a week later and was directed to the web page with a payment plan set up for me. There were 12 total payments displayed. However, at Comenity they trigger the promotional balance to expire on the actual day the year ends and NOT on the day of the last scheduled payment. After the balance was paid off [. . .] they charged me $880.00 in finance charges. They set you up on a payment plan that will not fulfill the requirements of the plan. So, then you get hit with a huge bill as soon as you pay off the balance. They could have easily helped me avoid this problem by having my first bill be due slightly earlier, or they could have divided my payments by 11. This is unfair and unacceptable. This caused me [to] get charged the interest on the card even though I had an automatic payment coming and was religiously following the plan."[17]

Shoppers with Best Buy cards issued by Citi; Home Depot cards issued by Citi; Lowe's cards issued by Synchrony Bank; or the Amazon Store Card issued Synchrony Bank credit card can expect the same type of treatment.[18]

And there are many more practices, like double-cycle billing and hairline penalty triggers, that were made illegal by the CARD Act. The trend has been for credit cards to get more and more complex in their billing practices over time, except when reined in by regulation. It's not that credit card companies aren't competing against each other at all: research suggests that banks raise hidden fees in part to have the cash to compete more fiercely on the most obvious parts of a credit card, like rewards or the headline interest rate.[19]

You could look at this trend of sneaky fees increasing while banks lower the headline interest rate and say it is proof that consumers *prefer*, for example, a 22 percent interest rate with an earlier payment cutoff time, payments allocated to the lowest interest rate first, and a higher minimum interest charge over a card with a 24 percent interest rate and none of those things, even if the bank has calculated that the first card is generally more profitable (and, in other words, more expensive for the consumer). But in cases like these, it's hard to justify making the leap from what consumers have chosen to what they actually want.

Munger argued that the grocery store designers weren't scheming to get you to pick up twenty things you didn't plan on getting on the way to grab the milk in the back: they were just putting the milk in the most obvious place. By contrast, it is not an exaggeration to say that credit card companies literally run experiments to figure out the least noticeable way of charging you any given amount of money. It is implausible to suggest that this tinkering, this *innovation,* is of any value to the consumer. And while the credit card company can explicitly forecast how any of these toggles will impact any given customer's final bill, the customer herself isn't in a position to see how their total amount due is a byproduct of each of these varying issuer practices. Would a Chase credit card be cheaper than a Discover, a Capital One cheaper than a Citi, an Amex cheaper than a BarclayCard? It's hard to say, and don't expect the media to help you figure it out. After all, even when it comes to the single most influential feature of the credit card, the interest rate, the credit card issuers advertise broadly overlapping interest rate ranges. As of September 2020, Discover It, for example, advertises an interest rate between 11.9 percent and 22.9 percent, while Capital One Quicksilver advertises an interest rate between 15.49 percent and 25.49 percent. The media has no idea what rate each reader would be approved for. Wirecutter or Consumer Reports are great for helping you pick out a vacuum cleaner, a marketplace where most every American can pick between the same vacuums as long as they have Internet access, and be charged, generally speaking, the same price. Wirecutter's credit card recommendations are far less useful because they have no insight at all into the interest rate any given consumer will be charged, let alone how issuer practices impact the likelihood of getting hit with various fees. It should also be noted that Wirecutter earns affiliate fees when consumers sign up for credit cards based on their recommendations.[20] Much of what credit card companies euphemistically label "consumer preference" is really driven by the disconnect between what combinations of fees and finance charges seem cheaper to different people, and which are actually cheaper.

In 2012, the Center for Responsible Lending issued a report documenting twenty-three distinct marketing and pricing practices that make credit cards more complex, and, they would argue, predatory. Nine of these practices were outlawed or fully addressed by the CARD Act, three were partially addressed, and the rest remained legal. Not surprisingly, they found that the banks and credit unions that engaged in one of the predatory pricing practices tended to engage in many. The greater the number of predatory practices the card issuer engaged in, the more complaints they received from the Better Business Bureau, controlling for their size, a clear indication that in fact, customers *do* care about being treated poorly, once the treatment actually begins, even if consumers can't readily identify how bad their treatment will be by reading through the credit card's terms and conditions. According to the report, the more complex and obscure the company's credit card pricing, the higher their credit losses were during the recession. Controlling for each company's prerecession loss rate, the credit card issuers with the worst practices had an increase in loss rate that was about 6.3 percentage points higher than the credit card issuers with the best consumer practices. That's an astronomical difference: a credit card loss rate of about 3 percent is typical, or around 8 percent for subprime lending, so adding on an extra 6.3 percentage points is, as the Center for Responsible Lending observed, "enough to threaten the safety and soundness of the issuer."[21]

The implication is that credit card companies that screw their customers over will eventually pay the price, especially during downturns—a nice thought, if true. Of course, at Capital One, there was more than one school of thought about the best way to prepare for recessions. There was the camp of people who believed the best way to prepare for a recession was to lend conservatively, to be careful of pushing customers into levels of debt they'd then struggle to pay back. But another school of thought was also able to rally logic and evidence for its point of view. That school of thought said being excessively cautious when the economy was roaring would actually shoot Capital One in the foot, and collecting as many fees and finance charges as possible during the good times was the best way to ensure the bank had enough capital to easily weather recessions.

.   .   .   .   .

In the fall of 2020, I spoke on Zoom to a former credit card executive turned venture capitalist. We spoke about how credit cards cause people to borrow much more than they would borrow on an installment loan. He agreed with this point, but he felt strongly that credit cards were both the present and future of lending, because, as he saw it, consumers had a dominant preference for credit cards. As he saw it, the reason consumers so often chose credit cards over the easier-to-understand personal loans was that consumers prized flexibility.

After our conversation, I thought about what Andrea Long Chu wrote in her 2019 book *Females:* "Everyone does their best to want power, because deep down, no one wants it at all."[22] It is sometimes insinuated that consumers like to have power and choice, but the dominance of credit cards over personal loans both supports and contradicts this claim.

The personal loan forces a reckoning; a conscious choice to borrow, at a known price, aware of exactly how much of your paycheck will be dedicated toward the repayment. By contrast, the credit card very often involves forgoing any conscious decisions about exactly how much money you'll borrow, and when, if ever, you'll pay that money back. Of course, on paper, the credit card offers more choice and more autonomy: the consumer has the flexibility to borrow as much as she wants to up to a set limit, and, if after paying down some debt, she wants to borrow some more, she doesn't need to ask anyone's permission. The very small minimum payments provide the borrower more freedom to decide how much money to pay each month: in this way, the credit card gives more power to the borrower, relative to the personal loan. But the credit card also very easily allows the borrower to submit to a go-with-the-flow attitude, avoiding a reckoning, giving up the power and responsibility of making decisions and understanding the consequences. The personal loan is the tool for the *budgeted shortfall:* the person who recognizes a specific mismatch between their income and expenses, with the need for additional money to close the gap (in the modern era, this process need not involve days or weeks of advance foresight). The credit card is the tool for the unbudgeted shortfall, for not having, or wanting, or needing an exact plan.

The conversations I've had with borrowers, overwhelmingly, reflect their ambivalence. Perhaps this is because, unlike the authors of some previous debt polemics, I didn't seek out my interviewees by contacting the subjects of tabloid-esque stories (the nineteen-year-old clerk who feeds his cocker spaniel filet mignon dinners purchased on credit,[23] or the staff major who landed in the Navy brig when she was caught buying an Escalade and getting plastic surgery on her military procurement credit card).[24] I talked to second and third degree connections, happy to interview anyone with any experience of debt, big or small, good or bad, and stood on street corners, in parks, and on a community college campus, talking to anyone who would talk to me. I have provided more details on who I interviewed in the appendix of this book. Most of those I spoke to defended most or all of the purchases they'd made as necessary while also saying that if they could do it all over, they would make different choices, and if they had a time machine, they would find some way to spend less or save more.

WHEN CREDIT IS RETRACTED

If the main story of the 2010s was about credit card companies unilaterally raising people's credit card limits, by the time I'm writing this book, in 2020, the process has started to reverse itself. As the COVID crisis unfolded, one in four Americans with a credit card reported that at least one of their credit card companies had either slashed their limit or completely closed one of their accounts.[25] In the summer of 2020, Capital One closed my girlfriend's dad's account, sending him a check for one dollar and thirty-seven cents, the balance of his unredeemed credit card rewards, along with a letter instructing him to "have a little fun this weekend."

While I worked at Capital One, we launched a campaign to try to encourage our subprime customers, who were already indebted (to us), to open Capital One savings accounts and put money away for a rainy day. On the surface, this is not an objectionable thing to do. Most personal finance books recommend that people establish at least a modest emergency fund, even before paying down high interest credit card debt. The reason this advice is given is because a bank can lower your credit limit at any time. If banks couldn't lower credit limits, it would always make sense to pay off your high interest credit card debt before amassing an emergency fund: if an emergency transpired, you could always just use your now partially paid-off credit card, and mathematically, you'd come out ahead.[26]

But these were *our customers*. Whether or not they got a credit limit decrease (at least from Capital One) was within our control. We encouraged them to save money at a 1 percent interest rate, instead of paying off debt at a 24 percent rate to insure against the possibility that we would lower their credit limit as soon as their debt was paid down. (And of course, whatever money they saved at the 1 percent interest rate would then be lent to other people at the 24 percent interest rate.) We might as well have suggested to them that they should really buy a helmet by reminding them that we could throw a rock at them at any time. The key to this sort of business strategy is to invent and believe a just-so story where the business strategy actually benefits the consumer, because they have more cash savings than they had before.

There's an important sense in which credit limits are a farce. Banks can and do let people go over their credit limits. And a credit limit, once granted, can be revoked without warning at any time (unless, of course, that credit limit has already been used). Your credit limit is just credit that may or may not be available to you at the time you want it: it barely means anything at all. But while credit limits might be effectively a fiction, they are treated as very real by consumers. The industry is more terrible, but less cynical, than it would appear on first glance.

In May of 2020, I spoke to former US Senator Mark Udall by phone. In the early 2000s, first as a member of the US House, and then as a senator, Udall called for reform of the credit card industry. He'd go on to introduce the Credit Cardholders' Bill of Rights on the Senate floor, legislation that would become the CARD Act. We talked about why he prioritized this issue as a lawmaker, and the debates around financial regulation. To Udall, it was all about creating a "fairer playing field," something that was necessary, in Udall's opinion, for capitalism to thrive. But we also talked about Udall's own, generally positive, experience using credit cards as a consumer. Late in 1997, Mark, then a member of the Colorado state house, decided to wage his first campaign for Congress, joining what was a crowded primary with four other candidates. "I needed to raise some money quickly to get my campaign going," he told me, "so my wife and I looked at each other and we took our two credit cards. I think we borrowed $10,000 from each credit card." He added, "It felt very risky, but we needed cash to infuse our campaign right away." As he remembers, the amount he chose to borrow was roughly or exactly equal to his credit limits. Until that point, he'd never borrowed money on his credit cards, and he paid off the cards before the campaign ended. Udall's experience was atypical, in the sense that his choice to borrow helped launch him into the highest echelons of professional and political power, but he was typical, in the sense that his credit limits strictly determined the amount of money he chose to borrow. He didn't apply for other loans (even though he would have likely been approved), nor did he undershoot the limits he'd been granted. Like so many Americans, he didn't first figure out what a reasonable amount to borrow would be, and then seek out the right amount of credit to execute on his own plan; the planning process was outsourced to his banks.

OPTIMIZATION

At a very basic level, the problem of the debt machine is that its quest for optimization necessarily drives its customer toward the dark side of oppressive debt. If a customer defaults on her debt and can't be successfully sued for the unpaid balance, the bank loses; the machine, therefore, does generally try to avoid this scenario. But another scenario is quite lucrative for the banks, which is that the customer hangs on for years by a thread, paying interest and fees, only gradually paying her debt off, or remaining indebted indefinitely. Americans only saving grace, historically, is that these two groups weren't that easy for the banks to distinguish. As a result, for most of the 2000s, America's largest banks (with the exception of upstart Capital One) mostly shied away from direct subprime lending, although they often owned stakes of payday lenders, dipping their toes in the subprime market without assuming as much risk to their own reputation from charging sky-high prices.[27]

There's an amazing video I watched at the Music Center at Strathmore, a two-thousand seat venue Capital One rented out for CEO Rich Fairbank to give his annual speech on strategy to associates. In the video, shown as a part of the day's event, a machine learning algorithm developed by Google tries to play the game Atari Breakout. Even if you've never played on Atari, if you're at least ten years old, you're likely familiar with this style of game: you move a platform to the left and right, to send a ball across the screen as it smashes bricks away. If you fail to catch and return the ball with the platform, you lose a life. You score points based on how quickly the bricks are destroyed. The more times in a row you consecutively hit the ball, the faster it speeds around the screen, naturally increasing the difficulty. As the video explains, "The most important thing to know is that all the agent is given is sensor input (what you see on screen) and it was ordered to maximize the score on the screen." After ten minutes of playing, the algorithm quickly loses all its lives, only managing to return the ball about 50 percent of the time. After two hours of playing, the algorithm plays like a pro, hitting the ball nearly every time. But after four hours, the algorithm has figured out a strategy that would occur to very few humans: it is strategic about its angle in returning the ball, trying its hardest to keep hitting the exact same spot in the brick wall, so as to dig a tunnel through the bricks that the ball can enter. Once the tunnel is complete, the ball enters, and the algorithm-player barely has to move the platform at all anymore until the game is nearly over, because the ball bounces up and down rapidly at the top of the screen destroying the bricks from the opposite side.

I don't remember exactly what Rich Fairbank's commentary was on this video, probably something to the effect of, "Isn't this incredible? Machine learning is the future!" Capital One was not alone in its enthusiasm for machine learning: JPMorgan Chase, Citi, and Bank of America have all bragged about their artificial intelligence capabilities, particularly to their would-be investors.

The Atari Breakout algorithm doesn't know what a ball is and is never told the rules of the game it is playing, but it finds a distinctly nonhuman strategy and batters down on this corner solution until it racks up an impossibly high score. There are some innocuous uses for machine learning by banks, and these are the uses they mostly trumpet publicly—to guess why you might be calling them and route your phone number to the right department, or to get better at detecting money laundering—but, for lenders, the most interesting use of machine learning is to find the sweet spot, the proverbial tunnel in the bricks, where they extract a massive amount of interest from families on the brink without pushing them into literal bankruptcy. At Capital One, there was some recognition that our algorithms often pushed the company toward corner solutions that may not actually be optimal. One former Capital One executive told me that, on paper, it might appear that the best strategy was to have a single customer and charge her 1-trillion-percent interest, referencing, specifically, that it didn't appear that customers were sensitive to higher interest rates at all. But, the executive suggested, good judgment, as he put it, would always draw the company back from the cliff.

His statements were intended as a defense of the company. As a twenty-five- or twenty-six-year-old training new analysts on how to run and interpret our models when I'd worked at Capital One for a few years, I often relied on a particular anecdote, drawn from economist Tyler Cowen's book *Average Is Over*. For decades now, computers have been better than human grandmasters at chess. But, as Cowen explains, some humans with computer assistance can beat computers unaided by humans at chess, fairly consistently. This form of computer-assisted chess, of course, requires you be very good at chess in general, but it also requires other skills: to know when to trust the computer and when to ignore it, to know the algorithms' strengths and weaknesses (ideally, taking the time to run multiple algorithms to see where they agree and disagree). This was the lesson I tried to impart to the twenty-two- and twenty-three-year-old analysts: the best decision-making comes from a skillful combination of human judgment and machine intelligence.

But, expressed differently, what this means is that the only thing standing in the way of the computers running the show were the moral intuitions of some analysts, mostly White, and mostly male, very heavily drawn from families of privilege (most of the time I was at Capital One, the number one school we drew new analysts from was Washington University in St. Louis, literally, the least socioeconomically diverse school in the country).[28] Sure, as the former executive put it, these intuitions would tell us not to charge a 1-trillion-percent interest rate (there was some debate while I worked there about whether or not 24 percent ought to represent a bright line if there would be stigma attached to APRs closer to 30 percent, and you can gauge from the company's website where this debate landed).

But the algorithm-driven march to get each customer into as much debt as possible went mostly unimpeded, as there were relatively few scruples on this topic, and virtually nobody involved in the decisions had any firsthand experience with high-interest debt. The best way to see the extent of machine learning and ethically questionable experimentation regimes at banks is to review their job listings, which are written with much more candor and far less defensiveness than any statements a bank spokesperson might offer, making clear it is common throughout the credit card industry to experiment on human subjects and use the results to tweak product terms such as interest rates and credit limits. In March 2021, American Express sought a machine learning engineer who would "run machine learning tests and experiments." JPMorgan Chase was looking for a new vice president for their machine learning center of excellence, "a world-class machine learning team continually advancing state-of-the-art methods to solve a wide range of real-world financial problems using the company's vast and unique datasets." The posting makes clear that machine learning spans "across all of JPMorgan's lines of business" and has "unparalleled access to the firm." Their ideal candidate would have a PhD in a quantitative field and the "ability to design experiments and training frameworks." JPMorgan Chase also sought a data scientist to develop and implement predictive models in their credit card division "to estimate risk and profitability of the card portfolio and leverage these models to recommend optimal action strategies in credit card price and line management areas."

THE DANGER OF GOOD THINGS

We've talked about hidden fees, and the techniques banks use to extract more of them. But it's not only the fees and the interest that make credit cards dangerous.

Consider the case of Tide Pods, a form of detergent packaging that is uniquely lethal to children and some disabled adults. Tide Pods, however,

don't contain any uniquely toxic ingredients. Accidental detergent poisoning skyrocketed when Tide Pods hit the market, because Tide Pods are
uniquely appealing: they are squishy, and colorful, a delight to hold.[29] The
lessons of Tide Pods are that consumers need to be wary of appealing features: clever packaging can induce accidental poisoning.

The proportion of all direct mail credit card offers that included
rewards tripled between 2002 and 2015, from roughly one in four to three
in four.[30] About 60 percent of all interest-bearing balances are now carried on credit cards with rewards, and it is commonplace for even subprime cards and secured cards to offer cash back or miles.[31] Capital One
offers the Quicksilver One credit card, with a $39 fee, 1.5 percent cash
back rewards, and a 25.99 percent APR. The Amazon Secured Card,
issued by Synchrony Bank, was initially offered in 2019 with a 28.24 percent APR and 5 percent cash back on Amazon, although by 2021, this
interest rate had been lowered to a more reasonable 10 percent.[32] The
Discover It Secured Card comes with 2 percent cashback at gas stations
and restaurants, 1 percent everywhere else, and a 22.99 percent APR. The
Credit One Platinum Rewards Visa has a 23.99 percent APR, and 2 percent cash back on gas and groceries. But rewards are only particularly
valuable to consumers who pay their credit card bills in full every month—
if a consumer isn't paying off their balance monthly, it is hard for them to
have enough available credit to make most of their daily purchases on the
card, and few rewards will ever accrue while interest piles up.

But because the dollar cost of interest is so hard for consumers to estimate, when they don't have a clear idea what their credit limit will be, or
what they'll spend each month, simple binary questions like "Does this
credit card have an annual fee?" and "Does it have rewards?" become the
dominant decision-making factors, even though credit card interest and
late fees are the main money makers for banks.[33]

It should be noted that there are also a range of tactics that credit card
issuers can use to prevent customers from using or redeeming their
rewards. Consider what Jud Linville, the CEO of Citi Cards, told investors
in 2014, "Historically, let me tell you, our rewards programs were based on
breakage. We basically discouraged people from redeeming; capping
the rewards you could earn in a given year and having points expire."
Linville went on to say that Citi had cleaned up their act.[34] He neglected

to mention that a change in accounting rules had forced the hands of Citi and every other credit card issuer: before 2014, the standard accounting rules created by the Financial Accounting Standards Board said that if a customer made purchases, but never redeemed their rewards, those rewards weren't really a cost for the bank. But in 2014, these accounting standards were changed so that credit card companies would need to subtract some of their rewards cost once the credit card rewards were earned, regardless of when they were redeemed, incentivizing them to encourage customers to use their rewards, and quickly.[35] Now, issuers focus more on ways to have consumers earn fewer rewards than they would expect. For example, both Chase and Discover have credit cards with cashback rewards on categories that "rotate" each quarter, but if you do not "opt in" every quarter to the set of categories, then you do not earn the rewards.[36]

A 2015 focus group conducted by the Consumer Financial Protection Bureau (CFPB) shows how effective credit card rewards are at throwing Americans off the scent of the best deal. Participants in the focus groups reviewed five credit card offers, four of which had rewards of varying types, and one of which didn't have rewards, but had a much lower interest rate. Even though many of the people in the focus groups had revolving credit card debt, the credit card with the lowest interest rate was overwhelmingly the least popular. The authors of a report summarizing the focus group findings wrote: "Consumers appeared to be selecting between cards primarily on the basis of rewards, with less regard for non-reward costs and benefits. For example, none of the participants raised the question of how the APR they would be offered would be decided even though participants were presented with ranges of possible APRs they might receive." In what were apparently extensive conversations, not a single participant in the focus group mentioned any estimate of how much money they'd lose in interest charges, compared to how much they'd gain from rewards.[37]

What started as a perk to attract the highest-spending credit card customers became a token to appease the masses. The media has celebrated the fact that now even secured credit cards often come with rewards, insinuating that banks are giving out perks out of the goodness of their hearts, democratizing rewards so that even the poor receive it, instead of recognizing that offering a pittance of rewards distracts the consumer enough that they'll ignore exorbitant interest rates.

THE CONFLICT OF INTEREST

> A firm must pay due regard to the interests of its customers
> and treat them fairly.
> —Principle 6, The United Kingdom's Financial Conduct Authority

In the United States, with very limited exceptions, nobody in banking is obligated to look out for what's best for you. Sure, it's (usually) against the law for banks to brazenly lie or steal, but, for the most part, if a financial product might benefit *somebody* in *some circumstances,* it will be legal on a federal level.

When I worked in the credit card industry, it stuck me that our critics seemed to be speaking out of both sides of their mouth, criticizing the banks for issuing too much credit and driving families into debt, as well as for not being willing enough to give out credit to people who needed a chance. These two opposing accusations struck me as proof that our critics were well-meaning, but they didn't know what they were talking about. After all, it seemed like they couldn't even make up their minds on a single argument. In fact, their points, upon closer observation, made perfect sense: a financial system with little interest in understanding the consequences of its choices on consumers' lives will both underprescribe and overprescribe credit.

And so it is both embarrassingly obvious and remarkably radical that the United Kingdom's Financial Conduct Authority officially formalized Principle 6 (shown earlier) that banks should be required to pay "due regard to the interests of its customers." For decades, the United Kingdom's banking regulators have used a system called *principles-based regulation,* meaning they articulate goals such as *"Behave like you actually care about your customers,"* and then expect banks to act accordingly. By contrast, the United States' system is sometimes called *rules-based regulation:* what is and isn't allowed is spelled out more concretely. The problem, of course, with this approach is that banks, given a clear road map, will figure out all the exceptions and loopholes the regulators didn't plan in advance. In rules-based regulation, you are punished only for breaking the letter of the law and are free to trample all over the law's spirit, like the example we considered in chapter 2 about giving $100 credit limit increases to satisfy the requirements of the Community Reinvestment Act.

Working from Principle 6, the UK's Financial Conduct Authority (FCA; their version of the CFPB), decided to address the obvious mismatch between what is good for consumers and what is good for banks—the problem of what the FCA called "persistent debt." It's clearly good for banks when people spend a decade or longer trying to pay off a credit card bill. But few people, including bank spokespeople, would stand up to argue that it's good for consumers: credit cards, the spokespeople agree, are really meant for short-term borrowing.

When people have been struggling with interest and fees for so long that less than half of their payment dollars go toward the principal of their debt, the odds start to be high that, even if the borrowing was for an emergency, new financial emergencies have been created by the debt itself. As a result, the FCA declared in 2018 that banks would no longer be allowed to trap consumers under the weight of credit card debt, ending, in theory, the era of win-lose credit card economics. The "persistent debt" rules stipulated a set of escalating steps banks were supposed to take. At twelve months of persistent debt (defined as interest and fee payments exceeding principal payments), banks were supposed to not extend any more unsolicited credit limit increases. When a customer had been in persistent debt for eighteen months, the bank was supposed to educate the borrower on the benefits of making larger credit card payments and refer them to third-party debt counseling. At twenty-seven months, banks were instructed to warn customers that their credit cards would be suspended if they didn't increase their payments, providing a specific payment amount that would get the customer out of their persistent debt status, an amount typically significantly larger than a minimum payment. People who had dug themselves into deep holes (with their bank-provided shovels) would have their shovels rescinded. And, at thirty-six months of persistent debt, banks would have to put customers on a plan that would repay their debt over a reasonable period, converting their credit card into a lower-interest installment loan, and, if those payments would be unaffordable, forgiving some or all of the debt. This last clause is of course the most radical: banks wouldn't be allowed to profit from extending unaffordable loans, because they'd have to forgive the interest and fees if they pushed customers too far.

On paper, this would seem to solve the problem of credit card debt, effectively banning banks from getting consumers into serious trouble

with debt. If banks had to waive interest and principal every time someone was truly struggling, presumably they would back away from predatory lending to begin with.

Paul Davies, a *Wall Street Journal* reporter, wrote that losing the revenues from persistently indebted customers would "likely give the card
industry a bloody nose."[38] But in January 2020, *The Mirror,* a British daily
newspaper told the story of Mike, a preschool teacher whose wife was
recovering from a recent stroke.[39] Over the past twenty-seven months,
Mike had paid more in credit card interest and fees than he'd paid down
toward his principal: BarclayCard sent him a warning letter saying his
account would be suspended if he didn't increase his payments by £612
per month (roughly $850), an amount that was half his monthly pay-
check. The letter didn't contain any instructions about what Mike should
do if that amount was unaffordable, other than suggesting that he continue to make at least the minimum monthly payment. Mike told *The
Mirror,* "When they suspend my cards next month, I really don't know
what I will do." The FCA's vision to end the cycle of crushing debt didn't
appear to be going as planned. Debt write-offs were supposed to be widely
available to people who would have otherwise needed to choose between
a nearly endless cycle of minimum payments or prioritizing their credit
card debt over their basic needs. But banks weren't exactly making it obvious that help was available. StepChange, a UK—based debt advice charity
that provides assistance to over six hundred thousand people annually,
had received only about six thousand inquiries about the persistent debt
letters as of August 2019.[40]

Sue Anderson, a StepChange spokesperson wrote, "Perhaps it means
that people have not noticed or not understood the information (or the
signposting to advice) that lenders have been sending them—or that they
feel it doesn't have anything to offer them. We certainly think that some of
the information lenders have been sending has been very poorly worded."[41]
As the thirty-six-month deadline approached, neither the FCA nor the
banks shared any information about whether borrowers were increasing
their payments. The public was left in the dark about whether any of the
earlier interventions had been successful. And advocates feared that UK
residents might be prioritizing the larger credit card payments over basic
necessities, not realizing that under the rules, assistance was supposed to

be available. In February 2020, the FCA sent a warning letter to the banks not to engage in widespread credit card suspensions. We are "concerned that some firms may be planning a 'blanket' suspension," they wrote, clarifying that the measure should only be taken if a customer either fails to respond to bank communications, or if the customer "confirms that one or more of the proposed options are affordable but that they will not make increased payments." In other words, BarclayCard was supposed to offer Mike forbearance if he couldn't increase his payments, and not suspend his card unless he refused to cooperate (not if he couldn't afford to make larger payments). But the strategy that BarclayCard, like most UK banks, appeared to be following was to hope their customers didn't contact them. The communication *The Mirror* printed certainly failed to make it obvious that Mike was likely eligible for a reduction in his interest rate. A spokesperson for BarclayCard declined by email to provide me with any examples of emails or letters that Mike or other customers would receive, but said, "If the paydown plan offer is not affordable, customers should get in touch with us, and we will work with them on a case-by-case basis to establish an affordable payment amount that enables the balance to be paid off within four years—this may involve further interest rate reductions or other concessions." In March 2020, COVID hit: the FCA told banks to call off the credit card suspensions of customers who hadn't contacted them, until October 2020 at the earliest.[42]

The term "suspension," of course, sounds deeply punitive. The most typical pattern of behavior for credit card revolvers is to make purchases and payments on a credit card at roughly the same rate, keeping the credit card balance roughly constant, that is to say, having a credit card limit of roughly $3,000, and a balance of roughly $2,500. Every month, a typical customer might make roughly $45 worth of new purchases each month, be charged $55 in interest, and make a payment of $100, keeping their balance roughly constant over time.[43] For a person in that situation, a credit card suspension could throw your life into chaos, regardless of how much warning you've received: after all, you might be relying on the credit card for the $45 of monthly liquidity it provided. But over time, the situation becomes more and more dire, and it is hard to say, in this context, whether the credit card would still be necessary if the borrower hadn't already spent hundreds of dollars on credit card interest each year.

The FCA's position, that citizens, already saddled with burdensome debt they had little capacity to repay, shouldn't take on more debt, was both intuitive and deeply controversial. With the suspensions postponed by COVID, the future of the law remains up in the air. Perhaps, as some have said, a principles-based regulatory system only works if the bankers themselves are principled. The persistent debt rules set out a road map to make lending fairer and less punitive. The FCA appears to have believed that by failing to specify the precise turn-by-turn directions, banks would use the broader road map to innovate. The FCA specified the outcome they had in mind—fewer Britons trapped under long-term credit card debt—and gave banks some freedom to figure out how to get there. But, of course, the banks had every reason to avoid offering interest rate reductions or principal write-downs. Thus far, British banks seem to be tiptoeing around what they ought to be doing, and it isn't clear whether the FCA will consider their behavior egregious enough to warrant any form of punishment.

LOANS WITHOUT LEVERS

There is an obvious and simple alternative to credit cards, which is that when Americans wanted to borrow money, they could apply for a loan that was for roughly or exactly the amount of money they needed. Maybe that loan would have a fixed monthly payment schedule, like a personal loan. Or maybe the large monthly payments required to pay down the debt in one or two years would merely be a suggestion, and payments as small as credit card minimum payments (roughly 3 percent of the loan balance) would still be allowed. The very low minimum payments of credit cards are often criticized, but they have one obvious benefit to consumers: they give consumers the choice of making either a large or small payment, depending on what fits into their budget that month, something that on paper is clearly a good thing.

In the pre-computer era, preapproving people for high credit limits that they'd draw down when needed made sense: the architecture is far less clearly suited for a world in which a person could be approved in a few seconds for a loan sent directly to their smart phone. Credit can be granted instantaneously, with funds transferred in minutes to a checking account or mobile wallet (and while, of course, not everyone has a cell phone or a checking account, generally speaking, the people who today have credit cards are not so dispossessed). To be clear, I'm not necessarily suggesting a consumer pursue this strategy in lieu of having credit cards, but rather pointing out that a system where this was commonplace is technologically feasible.

Credit limit increases have never been a big part of the debate over indebtedness in the United States, but, I'd argue, the practice of unsolicited changes to customers' credit lines is central to understanding why Americans are so deeply in debt, and, in turn, critical to the principal argument. Two facts, pulled together, completely changed how I viewed the relationship between credit card companies and their borrowers: first, the fact that most indebted Americans predictably increased their debt every time they received a limit increase, and the second, that the people who *didn't* get unsolicited limit increases were unlikely to apply for any new credit cards, or ask for a higher credit lines. Credit limit increases weren't anticipating customers' need for credit: they created the need. A few countries have banned unsolicited credit limits in one form or another. Since 2012,[44] Australia has required its banks to get customers' consent before raising their credit limits, and since 2018, Australian banks have been forbidden from marketing credit limit increases in any form.[45] Canada, since 2011, has banned banks from raising a consumer's credit limit without receiving consent first, and in the United Kingdom, since 2018, banks can't raise the credit limits of consumers who've been in persistent debt for twelve months or longer, a rule estimated to have stopped more than one million credit limit increases annually.[46]

It's a remarkably simple concept: get a customers' permission before raising their credit limit. A consumer can always call their bank to ask for their limit to be lowered (to my knowledge, no credit card companies in the United States allow consumers to do this online). A few consumers do go through the trouble of calling their banks to lower their credit limits, but of course, it's a lot of work to go through just to avoid temptation, and most news articles and personal finance websites strongly discourage the practice. Americans with high credit scores probably don't think much about the significance of limit increases: after all, they generally get high credit limits out of the gate. In the high-FICO segment, banks don't rely on limit increases as a risk management strategy, and they are afraid of offending the customers with the most credit options with a spending limit that's too anemic, so, for high credit score customers, starting credit limits are high and credit limit increases are relatively less common. But because banks rely so heavily on credit limit increases for low-FICO customers, and because these limit increases are so irresistible, reigning in these limit increases is one of the most obvious way to reduce unwanted credit card debt. And, of course, just requiring banks to get a customer's permission before raising their limit can't be said to be cutting off access to credit in any meaningful way: while a consumer might miss an email or a letter, if they really wanted a higher credit limit, they could request it. It wouldn't exactly make sense for banks to argue that any given consumer is so unsophisticated that she doesn't realize that she could request a higher credit limit over the phone or online but is simultaneously so sophisticated that she understands exactly how credit cards work and is at no risk of becoming overly indebted.

More generally, if part of the problem with credit cards is that they are loans that don't feel like loans until the borrower is already drowning in interest payments, the solution to the credit card debt problem must be to find ways of preventing people from slipping into debt without having ever made a conscious choice. After all, debt can financially burden a family and reduce their wealth, even when the interest rate is zero.

The most obvious risk of regulating credit limit increases is that banks will respond by just offering higher credit limits at the outset. This, presumably, is no better for the customer, and by encouraging banks to lend more with less information, could have the knock-on effect of increasing defaults. But banks that are today in the habit of handing out $300 credit limits and successive limit increases that push each customer to his or her particular breaking point wouldn't suddenly hand out $5,000 initial credit limits if banned from raising credit limits except upon customer request: doing so would often mean throwing their cash out the window. And, of course, regulators could also require credit card applications to inquire about a consumer's desired credit limit. The result of regulating credit limit increases would be a much smaller credit market, one in which credit would be roughly as accessible for those who want it, without being so liberally heaped on the people for whom credit is an unwanted temptation.

There's another possible answer here, one that would be hard to regulate into law: this next proposal relies on banks acting in the best interest of their customers, which means we can't trust or expect that it would come to life. I want to articulate it nevertheless, because it's worth fleshing out what lending would look like if lenders were in fact committed to only doing the loans that evidence suggested were likely to have a positive effect on the customer's life.

Because banks rely so heavily on credit limit increases to manage their risk, by the time most credit is granted to customers, banks know quite a bit about the people they're lending to. The people who I've spoken to who are glad that they used credit cards, like Doreen in Fresno, typically had a few things in common. They understood that credit cards were very expensive, which led to a few behaviors. They made the largest payments they could on their credit cards: circumstances sometimes dictated they make only the minimum payment, but, when possible, they paid more. Similarly, they didn't borrow money on their credit cards except in an emergency, for things they really needed. They didn't fall into the trap of using credit just because it was available to them: often, their credit cards weren't anywhere close to being maxed out.

Importantly, each of these behaviors I just described is the type of data that is available to banks making credit limit increase decisions: If a customer is paying finance charges, did those charges result from buying groceries and motel stays, or from video games and concert tickets? (I don't judge people who look for happiness where they can find it; I'd only observe that borrowing money outside of emergency spending in unusual circumstances tends to make one's financial situation more and more stressful over time, forcing one to further deprive oneself in future periods.) Not every purchase can be neatly categorized by an analyst who wasn't there in the moment as discretionary or nondiscretionary, but many purchases can be. Has the customer consistently maxed out her credit card, or have there been sustained periods where she avoided using all the credit available to her, illustrating an awareness that credit can and should be left untouched when possible? And does the customer make much-larger-than-the-minimum payment at least occasionally—for example, when she gets her tax refund, illustrating an awareness that carrying high-interest debt is quite costly? The credit card companies brag about hiring rocket scientists, but if a person cares to know, it doesn't take a rocket scientist to see if somebody is on track to be crushed by credit card debt. Banks already use these variables, in one form or another, to set credit limits, but banks are using these variables to help them answer their own question, the question of what credit limit for each customer will yield the bank the highest profit, instead of answering the question of what credit limit is *right* for each customer.[47]

·   ·   ·   ·   ·

Some people would suggest that it may be inappropriate, even, paternalistic, for banks not to give out as much credit as someone might otherwise be eligible for just because they expected that customer to become overly indebted. After all, our culture is much more highly attuned to people being unfairly deprived of credit than it is to people being pushed into debt. Consider the uproar in November 2019 when technologist David Heinemeier Hansson posted on Twitter that Apple and Goldman Sachs, the two partners behind the Apple credit card, assigned him a credit limit that was twenty times higher than the credit limit they gave his wife. "The @AppleCard," he tweeted, "is such a fucking sexist program. My wife and I filed joint tax returns, live in a community-property state, and have been married for a long time. Yet Apple's black box algorithm thinks I deserve 20x the credit limit she does," receiving over 28,000 likes.

It is worth unpacking both why Apple and Goldman Sachs may have assigned the credit limits in this way, as well as the cultural framework that generates Heinemeier Hansson's reaction.

To begin with, there is no law or rule saying that credit limits should align to what people "deserve"; banks today are under no obligation to assign credit limits according to one's income or according to any concept of responsibility, real or imagined. If a bank believes that two people have the same exact income, and they believe the first person, in accordance with sound financial advice, saves 15 percent or 20 percent of each paycheck, and the second person doesn't save anything at all, a profit-maximizing algorithm would be inclined to give the second person a higher credit limit than the first, because that higher credit limit would actually be used. The algorithm doesn't care what you "deserve" or don't "deserve": that is not the question the algorithm is trying to answer. And suppose there are two people, we will call them Jane and Paul. Jane has $1,000 worth of monthly expenses that she intends to pay for using their credit card: she'll make the same purchases if her credit limit is $1,500 or $3,000 or $30,000. Paul, without realizing it, is more influenced by whatever credit limit his bank gives him, whether that's because Paul read online not to spend more than 20 percent or 30 percent of their credit limit and he intends to stick to that rule of thumb, or because Paul thinks the bank has figured out what he can "afford" to spend each month, and Paul assumes his bank can estimate that number better than Paul can. At the $1,500 credit limit, maybe Paul only spends $450 on his credit card each month, but with the $30,000 credit limit, Paul doesn't bother to keep track of the purchases he's making, knowing he's not going to max the card out, and suddenly Paul has racked up a bill that he can barely afford to make minimum payments toward. If the algorithm can predict Jane and Paul's behavior, the algorithm will give Jane a credit limit of only $1,500, and Paul a credit limit of $30,000 (assuming Paul's risk of default is not too high). In other words, the high credit limit may not be a medal for good behavior: Heinemeier may have gotten the higher credit limit not because Goldman Sachs's model predicted he was more responsible than his wife, but, in fact, because they assumed he was *less* responsible, for reasons entirely unrelated to gender.

When you have access to the right data, it's not too hard to figure out whether a credit risk score—a score that predicts a person's likelihood of defaulting on a loan, like FICO—is racist or sexist. To see, for example, if the score is sexist, you wouldn't just check whether men and women have different credit scores (although that may be informative). You would then see if, for the same credit score, men and women have different odds of defaulting on a loan: if, for example, women with a FICO credit score of 600 defaulted on 15 percent of their loans, while men with a FICO credit score of 600 defaulted on 20 percent of their loans, it would be clear that FICO wasn't fair toward women, giving them a lower score than what they "deserved." But with credit limits, as opposed to credit risk scores like FICO, it's not so simple. Banks aren't legally required to assign credit limits just based on a person's likelihood to default; they can and do assign them based on to what extent a higher credit limit will drive the customer to carry a higher balance on their credit card. To assess whether a credit limit assignment algorithm was racist or sexist, you would need to also have data on each individual's marginal propensity to increase the credit card balance as the credit limit was raised.

Credit card liquidity isn't a straightforward good thing: it is very useful, but often very dangerous. If one group gets a lot, and another group gets very little, you can't conclude, without a careful analysis, that the group who got a lot was better off for it. And in a country where Americans with credit card debt spend an average of $1,100 each on credit card interest annually, it is not so clear who the winner is and who is the loser when the banks give one person a higher limit and another person a lower limit: we understand what it means to be unfairly deprived of credit, but not what it means to have the toxic gift of credit handed to you.

Madison, one of Isa's classmates, a nineteen-year-old Black woman studying to be a nurse, opened a Discover credit card when she needed a new laptop for school. "It's very tempting," Madison said, "to spend on the card, knowing you have a credit card. It's very tempting. I have to try not to spend so I can go and get that balance down." Her language is significant. The very existence of the credit card turns the act of not spending into something that requires constant effort. In fact, the level of temptation she felt was, overall, what surprised her most about having a credit card. Even finding the $35 to make minimum payments is hard, Madison told me.

Nearly every company tries to alter our behavior, to shift our courses of action, in whatever way suits the company, which usually means trying to get us to buy more of its product, or, sometimes, to use their product more often so they can serve us more advertisements paid for by a third-party. Manipulation isn't necessarily sinister, even when it happens below the level of our conscious understanding, like product placement in a television show or movie. And while some might disagree with me on this point, it's not the use of involuntary experimentation that renders the manipulation unethical: if a company wants to run two advertisements, see which one yields more purchases, and then only runs the second advertisement, this doesn't strike me as any real tragedy or breach of ethical norms, even if the people who saw the advertisements had no chance to consent to the experiment. But it is hard to make excuses for the experiments when on the other side of the manipulative practices there is real suffering, impoverishment, and despair.

In 2010, economists Steven Pressman and Robert H. Scott III set out to measure how many people are made poor by debt alone—that is to say, how many had enough income to fall above the poverty line, but, after subtracting the interest they paid to their debtors, fell below the poverty line. Pressman and Scott excluded mortgages (and home equity loans), and only considered the interest payments, not any payment of principal. They also didn't consider credit card fees, like late fees. In 2007, the last year with available data at the time of their study, they found that there were over 4 million people who couldn't afford life's basic necessities because of their crippling debt interest payments. The 2007 poverty rate rose from 12.3 percent to 13.4 percent once these debt interest payments were considered. In chapter 2, we talked about the First Debt Boom, from 1977 until 1989, when credit card debt exploded for the middle class, and the Second Debt Boom, which kicked off when Capital One and its now defunct subprime cousin Providian brought less fortunate Americans into the fold in 1989. The Second Debt Boom is quite evident in Pressman and Scott's analysis: between 1988 and 2007, while the proportion of Americans who met the government's definition of poverty fell slightly, the proportion of Americans who were debt-poor more than doubled.[48] Of course, it's not as if a family that was earning just $16,000 or $17,000 annually, but then spent $2,000 or $3,000 on debt interest payments (as was typical for the debt-poor families that Pressman and Scott studied) would have an easy, stress-free life if it weren't for their debt: things would have been hard either way. And yet it is obvious that the debt machine is willing to take the last of whatever a family has left, ensuring that it gets paid before people are fed, babies diapered, or gas tanks filled.

THE CHANCE TO ESCAPE

It is worth detouring for a moment to talk about the choice Americans make in paying or not paying their bills. When somebody signs up for a credit card, they're signing a contract obliging them to repay the debt they use the card to accrue. But people and corporations think of contracts very differently. Many people view it as dishonorable, shameful, even unethical to breach a contract, or not to repay a debt. That's true if their counterparty is someone they know, but also true if their counterparty is a faceless corporation. But corporations don't view their contracts in this way: cooly, they assess the costs of exercising the contract's exit clause, or the stated penalty for noncompliance. If it's cheaper to stay in the contract, they stay; if it's cheaper to leave the contract, they leave.

In the early 2000s, banks spent roughly $100 million lobbying for legislation that would make it harder for middle-class Americans to declare bankruptcy.[49] They won their battle, when President George W. Bush signed the 2005 Bankruptcy Abuse Prevention and Consumer Protection Act (BAPCA). The titans of finance and industry often make use of bankruptcy protection—think Delta, General Motors, Hertz, J. Crew, and JCPenney—and many Americans do as well, to the tune of roughly 750,000 personal bankruptcies in 2018.[50] But for every working-class or middle-class person who declares bankruptcy, there are many more who would benefit from wiping their slate clean, but don't. There are two main costs for declaring bankruptcy: the cost of filing, including attorney's fees, and a ten-year-long mark on your credit report. But for people struggling to keep up with bills, bankruptcy often ends up improving their credit score: after all, if you're often or always late on your debt payments, your credit score will drop anyway. Since bankruptcy often reduces your debt payments to an affordable level, and, for working-class people who file for chapter 7 bankruptcy, generally eliminates debt payments altogether, bankruptcy can improve a credit score, relative to the alternative of frequent missed payments. In fact, after reviewing a 5 percent random sample of all American consumers' anonymized credit reports, economists Stefania Albanesi and Jaromir Nosal found that one year after filing Chapter 7 bankruptcy, the credit scores of those who filed were about fifty points higher than the credit scores of similarly situated indebted adults who chose not to or were unable to file for Chapter 7 bankruptcy. "Bankruptcy offers relief from financial distress," Stefania and Jaromir wrote, "not only because it provides debt discharge and stays collections, foreclosures, wage garnishment and other court actions against the borrower, but also because it allows filers more access to new lines of credit."[51]

Of course, insolvent families often don't declare bankruptcy because they can't scrounge together the filing fee—like Rick, who we meet in chapter 4 of this book. There are two types of bankruptcy for consumers: in a Chapter 7 bankruptcy, you must forfeit your assets of value, but once you've done so, your debt is wiped clean. In a Chapter 13 bankruptcy, you get to keep your assets, but you're put on a five-year-long payment plan. In a Chapter 7 bankruptcy, the better deal for most working-class families, who generally don't have any assets that they'd be required to forfeit, you need to assemble the money to declare bankruptcy up front. For a Chapter 13 bankruptcy, attorney's fees can be included in your post-bankruptcy payment plan, but Chapter 7 bankruptcy forbids it. People, very literally, have to "save up" to declare Chapter 7 bankruptcy, often forgoing basic necessities to do so.

One of the most significant consequences of BAPCA was that it made declaring bankruptcy more expensive. Before BAPCA, a typical Chapter 7 bankruptcy cost $663 to file. BAPCA created new paperwork requirements, and made bankruptcy attorneys personally liable for any errors in the forms that were submitted. As a result, the Chapter 7 median filing cost rose to $986, a change that put bankruptcy out of reach for families who desperately needed debt relief.[52] But, these dry costs are just a piece of the puzzle explaining why few people declare bankruptcy. Bankruptcy usually makes sense if you have a low credit score, at least $10,000 in unsecured non-student-loan debt, and an income around or below the median for your state, but in a 2020 survey, Americans said they wouldn't consider bankruptcy on average unless they had more than $40,000 in credit card debt. In the same survey, 47 percent of American adults said they would never consider bankruptcy, regardless of how much debt they had.[53]

Before the passage of BAPCA, estimates by economist Michelle White suggest that about one in six Americans would have been better-off financially if they'd declared bankruptcy. That number, she noted, would be closer to 50 percent, if families first took a few steps that were at the time available to help people in bankruptcy protect their assets (for example, using any of their spare cash to pay down their mortgage, since most home equity is protected in bankruptcy). But bankruptcy rates pre-BAPCA were never much higher than 5 percent: only about one in ten people who should have walked away from their debts did. Nearly half of Americans could have "gamed" a system that had some loopholes that worked to debtors' advantages. What is shocking isn't that a few people took advantage of the system, but that most Americans didn't. There was a shred of truth in the argument banks made, that the system was rife for abuse before the BAPCA's passage. But most Americans behave by a very different moral code than the bankers who govern their financial lives: they feel obliged to repay their debts, while their bankers feel no sense of reciprocal obligation. Kathryn G., the former nurse who we met in chapter 3, with over $60,000 in credit card debt, expressed her sentiments about bankruptcy in a familiar way. Whether or not bankruptcy would benefit her, she said, "It's just not something I want to do. You know, I spent the money, I'm liable for the payments."

In a sense, the better of a person you are, the more vulnerable you are to getting beaten down by the system. Whatever character trait it is—perhaps some sense of honor—that leads some people to prioritize repaying their creditors above taking care of their own needs, you can bet that the bank's algorithms will eventually find that variable, much in the same way that the Breakout algorithm learns to dig a tunnel on the side of the Atari screen. It is precisely those people that the algorithms will find a way to pummel.

SOLVING THE PRINCIPAL PROBLEM

I've attempted to make the case in the last few chapters that Americans in debt very often haven't consciously chosen how much they want to borrow; instead, they fall into debt through use of a product that, after decades of scientific experimentation, has been engineered to encourage them to borrow more and pay less. The tripling of per capita consumer debt between the beginning of the First Debt Boom in 1977 and today, by my argument, hasn't been driven primarily by Americans wanting or needing to borrow more money. Instead, it has been driven by the fact that deregulation made lending more profitable, and the banking industry's desire to supply credit rose.

In 2018, NerdWallet reported the results of a nationally representative survey of two thousand adults, indicating that 86 percent of adults who have been in credit card debt regret it.[54] In Part II of the book, I'll talk about the cost of credit, but, I think it is important to remember that it is not only the *cost* that matters but also the amount. To break the debt machine, we have to dismantle the tactics banks use to push people on the margins into debt. We would know we have succeeded if the people who are actually looking for loans can still find them, but far fewer Americans would say they regret borrowing money. This, to recap, is the principal problem: Americans are induced to borrow unnecessarily, creating a financial burden that isn't just because of high interest rates, but also because the principal of the debt itself is hard to repay. So how do we solve the principal problem?

Consumers, not the banks, need to drive the decision about the amount of money they'll borrow; it may make sense for banks to set the ceiling of the maximum amount they're willing to lend each person, but in the current environment, they succeed at goading millions of Americans into borrowing more than they originally intended. When a person applies for a credit card, they should state the credit limit they'd like, and banks shouldn't exceed this amount without new instructions from the consumer. And banks shouldn't be allowed to increase customers credit limits, except at customer requests. These proposals may seem shallow to people who have never struggled with credit card debt, but both my experience in banking and my time spent talking to debtors around the country have left me convinced that credit limit assignment has a deterministic impact on how much customers *choose* to borrow, not only on the maximum amount they can hypothetically borrow. In an era in which banks can and do increase credit limits instantaneously upon customer request, giving consumers more say in their debt limits would never have to cause a consumer hardship for lack of credit: it would only make it easier for consumers to avoid debt. And because, for Americans who revolve on their credit cards, roughly half of the exposure from credit limit increases turns into new debt, the overall amount of debt that would be avoided by this seemingly small change is significant.[55]

More generally, if Americans would like to be left only with the debt they've consciously chosen, not the debt they semi-consciously assented to after repeated provocations, credit card rewards need to go. They serve no positive function: they only transfer wealth from the less-well-off people, those who have credit card debt, or no credit cards at all, to the already financially blessed, who can easily pay their bills in full each month. Credit card rewards are financed by the processing fees that merchants pay to accept credit cards, and these processing fees raise consumer prices for everyone in America, at the gas station, supermarket, the pharmacy, the discount store, and everywhere else, importantly, raising consumer prices both for those who have credit cards and those who do not have credit cards, who are usually lower income.[56]

More importantly, rewards make people feel like suckers for avoiding a game that is not designed for them to win. In a credit card market without rewards, interest rates would once again become the most important feature people would look for when comparison shopping. People who didn't expect to borrow money may not even choose to have a credit card at all, reducing the substantial temptation that credit cards create.

The European Union and Australia both set caps on the maximum amount of processing fees that credit card companies can charge to the merchants that accept credit cards—the United States has a similar rule, but it applies only to debit cards, and not to credit cards, explaining why debit card rewards are somewhat rare. As of 2015, credit card interchange rates in Europe are capped at 0.3 percent while the same fees in the United States average 2.25 percent.[57] Because of Europe's interchange cap, credit card rewards are relatively rare across Europe, and where they do exist, they're paid for mostly by the annual membership fees some credit cards include, instead of, as in the American system, by raising the prices every consumer pays when they shop for groceries or buy a new TV. Lowering interchange rates would be a blessing in particular to the nation's small businesses, who unlike America's mega-chains, are unable to negotiate with Visa and Mastercard for preferential treatment.

When franchise owners of 7-Elevens around the country organized a petition drive in 2009 to ask Congress to cap interchange fees, collecting more than 1.5 million signatures, Mastercard responded that 7-Eleven owners were just asking their customers "to claim that they want to pay more for their payment cards so 7-Eleven can increase its profits."[58] Mastercard, Visa, and the Consumer Bankers Association would have Congress believe that the credit card industry competes more fiercely on price than 7–11 does, or Walmart does, or that grocery stores do, and that lowering credit card processing fees would just be a windfall to these companies, without ultimately lowering consumer prices.[59] But the profit margins, of course, on gas stations and grocery stores, are much lower than the profit margins of Americas banks—both gas stations and grocery stores earn a roughly 2 percent profit margin. The profit margin on credit card lending is roughly twice as high.[60] The idea that credit card companies are more likely to "pass through savings" to their customers than, for example, gas stations, just doesn't stand to reason. Every time the price of crude oil falls, the price Americans pay for gas at the pump falls too, but when banks' cost of borrowing falls, credit card interest rates continue to rise. Only in competitive marketplaces are cost savings passed along to consumers: while supermarkets and gas stations compete fiercely, credit card companies have market power. I'll prove this claim in more depth in chapter 6.

The brawl over credit card interchange continued into 2021: in the midst of the pandemic, Visa and Mastercard weighed raising interchange rates further, by roughly $1.2 billion, while lawmakers, including Democratic Senator Dick Durbin, urged them to call off the fee hikes.[61] Visa and Mastercard agreed to a one-year delay, but appeared to be gearing up for a fight. The CEOs of Visa, Mastercard, Discover, and American Express teamed up in March 2021 to form the Payments Leadership Council, a move that reporters from industry mags like Payments Dive and PaymentsJournal attribute to planned clashes with Congress over the high interchange fees, and the duopolistic, anticompetitive power of the payment processors.[62] The Payments Leadership Council hired Raj Date to be its first director; Date held the number two position at the CFPB until January 2013.[63] Before that, Date spent five years as a vice president at Capital One, and five years as an engagement manager at McKinsey. A few weeks after the Payment Leadership Council formed, the group earned a meeting with the US Department of the Treasury.[64]

In the absence of widespread credit card rewards, fewer people would apply for credit cards, and those with credit cards would be less inclined to overspend. And, like ending unsolicited credit limit increases, ending credit card rewards would make it no harder for people who need a loan to get a loan.

When I think about the people who I've met who *are* glad they borrowed money—Doreen from Fresno, Doris from Houston, Jennifer from

Silver Spring, and others around the country—I feel deeply cautious about what I suggest, afraid of yanking away the only lifeline some Americans are offered. But I feel a knot in my stomach untangle when I realize that it is possible to have fewer people slide into debt, while keeping credit available to those who need it. Making customers state their intended credit limit only helps people avoid the temptation of *unwanted* credit. Ending unsolicited credit limit increases wouldn't stop banks from giving more credit to those who request it. Lowering credit card interchange rates would drive rewards out of the marketplace, but not alter the basic economics that make consumers profitable or unprofitable to lend to.

Next, banks should no longer be able to use their customers as unwitting test subjects, conducting experiments on their customers without consent, and without sharing their findings. Randomly approving or denying someone for a loan, randomly altering their loan amount, randomly offering lower interest rates or more generous rewards is a categorically different type of intervention than just randomly showing some customers a red button and others a blue button. It isn't the act of experimentation itself that I object to here. Understanding the consequences of access to credit on people's lives is vitally important, and the randomized controlled trial is the most effective tool for gathering knowledge we have. But while the findings of drug trials are published in journals, the public is never made aware of the grim truths known only by the credit card analysts who manage and analyze the experiments.

As Harvard Business School emeritus professor Shoshanna Zuboff points out in her book *The Age of Surveillance Capitalism: The Fight for a Human Future at the New Frontier of Power*, all federally funded scientific research has to follow ethical guidelines known as the Common Rule: "informed consent, avoidance of harm, debriefing, and transparency."[65] And, as she explains, the need for ethical standards of research is even stronger for corporations than it is for academic and government researchers: the profit motive of corporations gives them little reason to act in the public's best interest, particularly if they're convinced their experimentation won't become visible to the public. If banks wish to conduct experiments on the American public—for example, to determine how access to credit impacts Americans' lives—there should be strict independent review of these experiments prior to their implementation (for example, by the CFPB). The full, unredacted results of the experiments should be public, and consumers should have the right to opt out of participation.

This very mismatch itself, between what is profitable for banks and what is good for consumers, is the root of our problem. Very often the issues associated with a crummy product can be solved by someone coming along and inventing something better. But rarely is it the case that when people start borrowing money on a credit card they realize how frustrating and painful the experience will ultimately be; at the outset, the product strikes them as extraordinarily convenient.

Any new competitor to credit cards will have to do the heavy lifting to convince people *before* they become dissatisfied with their credit cards. For the competitor to solve the principal problem, the competitor would have to do more than offer a lower interest rate or pricing structure: they'd have to prevent the consumer from taking on so much debt to begin with. It is hard to monetize convincing people not to borrow. If this competitors' product itself was a loan, the company's reward would be a much smaller lending industry. Economist Mary Zaki makes this point: if someone tries to disrupt the credit card market by competing fiercely on price, they will have to contextualize how much money a person could stand to save with, say, lowering an interest rate from 18 percent to 15 percent, which just as often convinces the borrower not to borrow money at all. Existing market participants would prefer not to trigger a race to the bottom on price, and, perhaps more importantly, they don't want to persuade people away from borrowing money in general by prominently highlighting the costs of borrowing.[66] Companies and start-ups who want to explain why their product is better than the alternatives typically do so through paid marketing; any start-up in the business of convincing people not to use credit cards is likely to be outbid and outspent on advertising by orders of magnitude by the banks who control a very lucrative market. We've seen already quite some "disruption" when it comes to refinancing people's credit card debt, mostly through personal loan companies like LendingClub, Payoff, and SoFi, but also through products like Tally, an "automated debt manager" that helps people save money on interest by automatically allocating their payments and also refinancing parts of their credit card debt when Tally sees fit. This disruption has succeeded because it takes effect at the moment in which people recognize their debt has become a problem—not at the outset when the money is first borrowed. But very often borrowing begets more borrowing, because spending money on credit card interest only causes one's financial shortfall to grow more severe over time. There is one exception to my point about most competition taking place *after* Americans are already indebted, and that exception concerns point-of-sale lenders like Affirm and Afterpay, which I'll talk about more in the final chapter.

When I first heard about the UK's persistent debt rules in 2018 (while I still worked at Capital One), I was, for a moment, tremendously optimistic for the realignment of incentives it seemed to create. I have heard for years that banking is "ripe for disruption," made by quasi-idealistic entrepreneurial types who seem to believe bankers have done nothing for decades but collect fat paychecks. The fact is that banks do have the deep pockets to hire many "innovative" people.

At Capital One, the most talented designers, engineers, data scientists, and product gurus seemed to fall into two categories. For people who loved the algorithm itself, the technology itself, or the process itself, Capital One was a delightful place to work, a place where you could enjoy Silicon-Valley style amenities and cash in generous paychecks as you explored new strategies to keep the company's statistical modeling or technology at parity or ahead of its peers. One Capital One director, Mili, formerly the cofounder of a meal delivery start-up, told an audience at South by Southwest, "I actually feel like I'm still living the startup life." *American Banker* magazine, reporting on her talk, said Mili was delighted on the date of her job interview to find not cubicles or spreadsheets but, instead, walls plastered with sticky notes, a sign, allegedly, of "creative minds at work."[67]

The second category of people were those with some enthusiasm for the apps, tools, and, on rare occasion, even for credit policy changes that might help American families struggle a bit less, have more in savings, or less in debt. Pilot projects along these lines were often put into beta and then dashed a few years later. In 2015, Capital One acquired the popular budgeting app Level Money, best known for a feature that told people how much of the money in their checking account was considered "spendable." Capital One shut Level Money down in 2017. Capital One's Seattle office piloted a "financial advisor in your pocket," targeted at helping Americans with credit card debt in 2018. Although their financial guidance tool could generate nineteen personalized recommendations, the tool, along with the whole Seattle office, closed down in 2019. (At the time, the company was struggling with the outsized costs of integrating the Walmart credit card portfolio they'd just acquired.) Everyone at Capital One seemed to agree, in loose terms, with the idea that you'll also hear from self-proclaimed fintech "thought leaders" on Twitter: the future of banking would belong to whoever was the best at genuinely solving Americans' financial problems. But as years passed, the present, with all the profits the company was earning at a high interest rate, seemed to stretch out longer and longer. Anything that actually helped customers financially, generally speaking, drove down profits. In a crunch, it would be hard to argue why software engineers on these pilot projects shouldn't be rededicated to a more urgent need; it was hard to justify something money-losing in a quarter with anemic profits. The people in the second category—the people interested in changing how banking worked—would leave when their favorite pilot project was dashed.

When the persistent debt rules were first implemented in the United Kingdom (the only market outside of North America where Capital One operates), it seemed to transform the incentives so that lenders would only make money if customers did well. I imagined this would mean all the experts and tools at the bank's disposal—the designers, data scientists, product managers, self-styled behavioral economics experts—would be harnessed to stop people from getting into persistent debt. The United Kingdom example shows that we can't expect such a tidy resolution. But with enough regulatory willpower, the underlying approach could make sense: punish banks that cause their customers to struggle, instead of setting rules, as the United States has done, dictating who banks should and shouldn't lend to.

The general trend of consumer lending has been to get increasingly complicated over the last seventy years, completely abandoning the sorts of loans, once common, where the customer and the lender could calculate all the costs using pencil and paper (a necessity in the era when much of the loan administration wouldn't happen on a computer).

Suppose we reverse all that complexity: make each loan as simple as possible without changing the average prices charged. If the price that is charged to each individual consumer were to remain roughly constant, but product terms were simpler, economists would predict that credit availability would also remain roughly constant. My argument is that, faced with very simple loans with clear prices, many more Americans would opt out of borrowing altogether.

Chile gives us some evidence to understand how much consumers can benefit from this process of radical simplification. Chile is the wealthiest country in South America. Like most relatively wealthy countries, Chile saw consumer credit skyrocket during the first few years of the 2000s, and then, during the Great Recession, faced painful economic conditions and a series of financial scandals. In the most notable instance of financial wrongdoing, the major department store La Polar, was found to have illegally changed the loan terms and interest rates of roughly 1 million Chileans without their knowledge.[68] When conservative president Sebastián Piñera took office in 2010, both the left and the right in Chile agreed on the need for major financial reforms, and a new consumer financial protection agency, Servicio Nacional del Consumidor (SERNAC for short), was established to oversee banks and lenders.[69] While roughly 50 percent of Chileans have a retail credit card and 20 percent have a bank credit card, Chileans, much more so than US residents, take out personal loans when they need to borrow money. Roughly 15 percent of Chileans have a personal loan outstanding (these are unsecured loans, not mortgages, and the average loan amount is $3,400).[70] These loans were often saddled with hidden fees and costs, especially add-on insurance products that weren't useful to most consumers, raising the price of credit by roughly 20 percent, and often coming as a surprise to borrowers. In 2011, a new law (Chile's Law 20.448) cracked down on these hidden fees in a few ways. Anytime a Chilean shopped for a personal loan for under 1,000 UF (roughly $36,000), banks had to offer them a loan with a special "Universal Credit" contract. Universal Credit loans sharply limited how many terms banks were allowed to tinker with: basically, they could only adjust the loan size, the annual interest rate, the repayment term, and an optional one-time fee. All the Universal Credit loans were presented in the exact same format, always stating the monthly payment, the total cost of the loan, and the combined interest rate inclusive of fees. Banks weren't forbidden from adding on insurance products; those had to be sold separately and, optionally, with an obviously separate price. Banks could also make more complicated loans, but if they were going to lend to you at all, they had to show you what Universal Credit loan you qualified for. In other words, the law did two major things: it *standardized* loans, so they were stripped down into simpler products that were nearly identical from bank to bank, and it also *improved disclosures.* The standardized loan contract meant you wouldn't have to read the fine print of your bank's terms and conditions anymore, because the contract you'd get would be *literally identical* from bank to bank other than the highlighted terms. Law 20.448 was wildly popular, and a year later, Chile passed Law 20.555, which required larger loans (those worth more than 1,000 UF) to have the same improved disclosure requirements, although they wouldn't have to follow the same standardized contract.

A team of researchers studied the impact of Law 20.448 and 20.555 to see how each of the two changes impacted consumers: standardizing and simplifying loans so they were more similar across banks and increasing disclosure requirements. The results were striking. It was obvious that the hidden fees and insurance products were catching many Chileans by surprise, so much so that they often couldn't afford the payments they were signing up for. By comparing loans just above and just below Law 20.448's cutoff point, the team found that the increased disclosures reduced loan delinquency rates by 40 percent, from roughly one in three Chileans falling behind on their loans, to roughly one in five. When the team did a deeper look, separating out Chileans with higher and lower levels of education, they found that the improved disclosure requirements made a huge difference for those with higher levels of education but did little for those with lower levels of education, while creating the much simpler, standardized product made a huge difference for those with lower levels of education, while it did little for those with higher levels of education. [71]

It's worth asking the question, who in America (other than the bankers) would lose if every single loan was stripped down to its most basic form, just an interest rate and a term length? When loans went from having a maximum of three or four terms of understand, to an average of twenty-one separate price points, banks gained a much wider set of levers to tinker with, but American consumers didn't gain any more flexibility, or any more freedom.[72]

PART II   The Interest Argument

6 Divergent

The amazing thing about credit cards is the fact that the cost of using them keeps going up and up.

Over the last twenty-five years, the price of TVs and computers have both fallen by roughly 95 percent. Cars haven't necessarily gotten cheaper, but in many ways, they're much better: more fuel efficient, safer, often equipped with backup cameras, and Bluetooth speakers. Even simple things like socks and t-shirts have been getting cheaper: since 1994, their prices have fallen by roughly 8 percent.[1]

But the price to borrow money on a credit card has risen consistently over the past twenty-five years. By 2019, the average interest rate Americans paid on their credit cards (considering only Americans' assessed interest, not the credit card interest rates for people who pay their cards in full) had reached a record high of 17.4 percent. The steady climb of credit card interest rates is particularly jarring when you compare these interest rates to prime rate, the rate that banks charge their best customers for low-risk loans, or the federal funds rate, the amount of money banks have to pay to borrow money themselves. Throughout the 1990s, the prime rate never dipped below 6 percent, and it was mostly north of 7 percent.

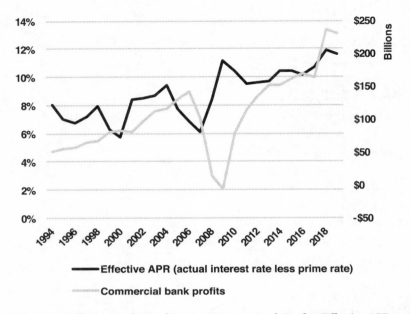

Figure 8. Effective Credit Card Interest Rate vs. Bank Profits. Effective APR is a Federal Reserve data series G. 19 [Commercial bank interest rate on accounts assessed interest] for Nov. of each year, minus *Wall Street Journal* prime rate for Nov. of each year. Commercial bank profits is total net operating income of FDIC-insured commercial banks and savings institutions.

Twenty-five years ago, consumers with credit card debt were paying, on average, 8 percentage points more than the prime rate to borrow money. By 2019, that lending margin would reach 12 percentage points, a 50 percent increase.

Competition and innovation are supposed to make things cheaper and cheaper over time, or at least better and better. But with credit cards, the opposite is happening; they are getting more and more expensive, with no obvious improvements in quality. It's not that banks haven't been innovating; they've been hard at work figuring out how to extract more interest from each American family, with great success. Their efforts have paid off. Over the same twenty-five-year period, US banks' profits have grown twice as fast as the wages of the typical American worker.[2]

Of course, you could argue that the interest rate doesn't reflect the whole cost of borrowing money on a credit card, and, therefore, the fact that credit card interest rates have been rising doesn't necessarily mean credit cards are getting more expensive.

After all, as we've discussed, credit cards are riddled with hidden fees, and their pricing is obscured by rewards like cash-back and miles. And credit card reward programs are only getting more common. But the extent to which rising interest rates might be *related* to the increasing frequency of credit card rewards, in some ways only proves my earlier point: banks have succeeded at obscuring the cost of borrowing money.

The CFPB studies the total cost of credit cards, taking into account not only interest rates, but all the fees that consumers are charged (their calculation excludes any money refunded by credit card rewards or other perks). In the immediate aftermath of the passage of the CARD Act, the CFPB found that banks lowered the total cost of credit cards significantly. Between 2008 and 2012, the total cost of using a credit card, inclusive of all fees assessed, fell on average by about 2 percentage points, from roughly 17 percent to roughly 15 percent. The CFPB speculated, cautiously, that this might be attributable to the fact that the CARD Act set maximum late fees, made it harder for banks to charge over-limit fees, and stopped banks from charging multiple fees for the same transaction. The 2 percentage-point decrease in the total cost of the credit reflected the fact that fees had fallen sharply, and banks had only partially made up the difference by raising interest rates.

But the story doesn't end there: in 2016, and 2017, and 2018 (the last year covered by the CFPB credit card reports at the time this book was written), the total cost of using a credit card rose again each year, for every group of consumers, from those with the most checkered credit histories, to those with the most pristine credit scores.[3]

Meanwhile, it is cheaper than it ever has been to run a credit card company. We've already talked about the fact that the federal funds rate, the cost at which banks borrow money, is significantly lower now than it was in the 1990s. Just as importantly, the credit card companies are big data companies, and the cost of storing data has decreased by more than ten thousandfold since 1994.

And looking at credit card delinquency rates, it is obvious that American banks have been able to keep their loan losses down; risky lending can't explain why Americans are being charged higher interest rates than ever before. In 2019, the delinquency rates on credit cards stayed below 2.7 percent. By comparison, between 1996 and 2004, the delinquency rates on credit cards were always above 4 percent.[4]

You can't chalk the rising cost of credit up to the banks expanding access to credit. In chapter 1, we talked about the First Debt Boom, which lasted from 1977 to 1989, when the middle class gained access to credit cards, and the Second Debt Boom, which lasted from 1989 to 1998, when credit cards would become accessible to basically everyone who hadn't very recently defaulted on a loan. Since the Second Debt Boom ended, the number and the types of Americans who can get credit cards has stayed relatively constant, with the exception of a brief dip in the immediate aftermath of the recession. In a sense, it would be impossible to increase access to credit cards, given that the credit card companies will often lend to people who've just declared bankruptcy, or had their car foreclosed, or whose only income is their social security check. As Shailesh Mehta, former head of Providian told PBS's *Frontline*, when he first joined Providian in 1989, then called First Deposit, the company was growing quickly by giving credit cards to people who had never had access to credit before. But by the mid 1990s, as he explained, "As [the credit card] market became saturated, our ability to find underserved markets became harder and harder, because everybody was entering in every market." He added that there was "No underserved market in reality. Even in a FICO score 500, I had people giving solicitations."[5]

In the last decade, a number of start-ups have tried to disrupt the credit card industry—none have broken through. Raj Date and Marla Blow, two former Capital One executives turned CFPB regulators, started a sub-prime credit card company, FS Card, in 2014 with the goal of helping lower-credit-score Americans "save billions of dollars in fees and interest compared to available alternatives."[6] The project was sold to Continental Finance for an undisclosed amount just five years later. As of 2020, Continental no longer books new accounts into the product that FS created. (Raj Date, you may remember from the previous chapter, now chairs the Payments Leadership Council.) Fair Square Financial, launched in

2016, has had some success beating the big banks' interest rates by a few percentage points but is hardly a household name. A similar story could be told of credit card startups like Mission Lane, Petal, Jasper, and Deserve. These startups have succeeded in attracting at least a handful of customers, and have some reasonable basis for claiming that they are better than major bank credit cards for their target segments. (Whether you see a meaningful amount of daylight between these fintechs, and the big banks from which these startups draw their executives, is a matter of opinion.) None of these companies seems poised, after multiple years in the market, to become one of the top five largest credit card issuers in America.

In the previous section of the book, I argued that banks have succeeded at getting Americans to borrow far more than the consumers themselves really intended to borrow, pointing out that borrowing can create future financial stress, even when the price of borrowing is manageable (or even free). In this section of the book, we'll turn to the interest argument: Americans are charged far too much to borrow money. The fact that credit card interest rates have been rising steadily over time, with no relationship to banks' costs (other than the inflated salaries of their corporate employees), is but one piece of evidence that prices could be lower.

Lowering credit card prices, of course, is key to helping Americans get out of debt: with lower interest rates, each payment a consumer made would go further in paying down her principal balance. In this chapter, I'll show that most Americans aren't paying the *competitive* price for their debt—that is to say, the cheapest price any bank or credit union would bid to be their lender.

Banks have led the media to believe that Congress couldn't cap interest rates without causing millions of Americans to lose access to credit. For the most part, this is untrue, and in the next chapter, I'll explain how the government could make loans more affordable for Americans, without pushing anyone into the arms of loan sharks.

·   ·   ·   ·   ·

Just how profitable are credit cards?

It's not an easy question for a journalist or another outsider to answer, in part because the credit card industry has two different profit models smushed together. In the first profit model, the "transactor" model, banks charge a processing fee to the merchant every time a customer swipes their credit card or makes a purchase. That fee is generally between 1.8 percent and 3 percent, sometimes a bit more for American Express cards or Discover cards, and it averages a bit over 2 percent. The bank has to pay some of that processing fee to whoever handled the payment—Visa, Mastercard, Discover, or American Express—and then they give money back to consumers in the form of credit card rewards. There's a reason so many credit cards offer rewards that are roughly equal to 2 percent of the value of all your purchases: that leaves them with a fairly small but healthy profit margin on every purchase you make. It's a common misconception that banks don't like the customers who pay their credit card bills in full every month. If those people are rich and have a lot of money to spend, the processing fees add up big time. Banks compete with each other fiercely to win the business of the nation's affluent spenders—and of course, in our era of inequality, a small number of people do an awful lot of the spending. It is true, however, that someone who spends just a few hundred dollars a month on their credit card and pays that amount in full every month may or may not be profitable, depending on how expensive it is to service that account: how often they use the call center, whether or not they get paper statements, and how often they lose their credit card and need it to be replaced. Those operational costs hover around $40 per customer per year.[7] The profit margin on the transactor business is small: well under 1 percent, but banks love to be in the business, because it doesn't scare them. The hard part is luring in the wealthy customer: banks will spend hundreds or thousands of dollars in marketing and early spend bonuses to convince them to open a card, but after that, the bank just effortlessly collects money every time a new purchase is made. They don't worry very much about those customers defaulting, and, while the business model may not be good for society (after all, those rewards have to paid for in the form of higher prices at the stores where everyone shops), unlike subprime lending, it doesn't attract a lot of negative scrutiny from the media or from the government

The second profit model is the "revolver" profit model, where you collect interest and late fees from customers who borrow money on their credit cards. The biggest expense in this business are loan losses, when a customer borrows money and then can't afford to pay it back (and the bank isn't able to sue them to garnish a paycheck, or sells the debt to a third-party collector for pennies on the dollar, or spends a lot on money on legal fees in the process of garnishing the paycheck). The revolver model is far more lucrative: even at the peak of the Great Recession, from 2008 to 2010, as defaults skyrocketed, the credit card industry earned a profit margin north of 10 percent for lending to customers with credit scores between 520 and 560.[8] In a good year, the profit margin on subprime lending, taking into account all the expenses of running a credit card company, can easily exceed 15 percent. Another way to put this is that you could cut interest rates and fees almost in half for the riskiest consumers, and still break even on your lending. A finance reporter might look at the profit and loss statement of a big bank and see an overall credit card profit margin of around 2 percent and think they're covering a highly competitive industry, without much juice to squeeze out, when they're really seeing the combined average of two separate businesses—banks earning slim but steady profits catering to the whims of the wealthiest people in the country, and a very high-margin business carting money away from needy families.

In the midst of the COVID crisis, it became clear to me that most Americans, including journalists, had little concept of just how much money banks make. Angry consumers who canceled their vacations because of the coronavirus turned to Twitter demanding full refunds from airlines and hotels: it can often feel like all major corporations are rolling in dough. But the *entire* United States airlines' industry made less money in 2019 than *any* of the country's largest banks—that is to say, all the airlines in the United States earned a combined total profit of $15 billion that year,[9] while JPMorgan Chase alone booked $36 billion; Bank of America booked $27 billion; scandal-battered Wells Fargo booked $20 billion; and Citi booked $19 billion in profit. Some banks, of course, like Goldman Sachs, make money by taking a cut of major transactions between large corporations and investors, charging fees for coordinating mergers, acquisitions, the issuance of bonds, and the initial public offering of companies; whether this work is good, bad, or neutral for society is outside the scope of this book. But many other banks make all or most of their profits from arranging the financial lives of ordinary families and small businesses, thriving even though many people feel that their finances have never felt less secure.

.   .   .   .   .

You're right to treat my claims with skepticism. After all, if banks could slash all of their customers' credit card interest rates by 10 percentage points and still make money, why doesn't a start-up come around doing exactly that?

This is, roughly speaking, the business model of several of the startups I mentioned earlier in the chapter. They face two obvious challenges. The first is that their costs of doing business are much higher than that of the big banks: everything is more expensive when you have thousands of customers, instead of tens of millions. Most importantly, the big banks can fund their loans very cheaply; when they offer checking accounts or savings accounts, they have a source of cash they can lend out, while generally paying their customers with checking accounts 1 percent interest or less. By comparison, the startups have to spend a lot of money to have any money to lend: they have to pay 3 percent or more to have any money to lend out.[10] So while the big banks often earn a profit margin of between 10 percent to 15 percent on their revolver businesses', the startups can only afford to slash interest rates compared to the big banks by a few percentage points.

More importantly though, the way Americans shop for credit cards makes it nearly impossible for them to figure out when they're getting a good deal and when they're being taken to the cleaners, making it hard for new entrants to break through. A family can easily save thousands of dollars by reducing their credit card interest rate by just a few percentage points, so the choice of a credit card ought to be of great significance to most borrowers.

But a number of barriers stand in customers way, preventing the power of competition from making things better for indebted Americans.

The first, as we've discussed, is the fact that consumers very often shop for credit cards before they realize they'll actually use them to borrow money. Roughly half of Americans with credit cards are using them to borrow money at any given moment in time, but a 2019 NerdWallet survey found that only 29 percent of adults said that the APR was the most important factor when they were deciding which credit cards to apply for.[11]

And, frustratingly, by the time consumers have a wake-up call about their credit card debt, struggling to make their monthly payments, their options for credit have often narrowed considerably: the consumer is often less creditworthy than they were before, and it's harder to find a good deal.[12] This was Kathryn R.'s experience. Once she'd racked up $28,000 in credit card debt, she looked around for a way to consolidate her debt and lower her interest rate. The best deal she could find, a secured loan against her car, only covered a portion of her credit card debt, and didn't offer a much better rate. "It was like pouring a cup of water into a volcano," she said, "hoping it'll put it out."

Perhaps more importantly, consumers face a cost every time they submit a credit card application: the act of applying for a credit card itself lowers your credit score, making it harder to be approved for future loans, and less likely that you'll get a good interest rate. When people shop for car loans or home loans, they're allowed to submit multiple applications within the same month; the credit bureaus are then supposed to "bundle" all these applications together and treat them as a single credit report inquiry. But no such generosity is administered to people who apply for credit cards. Often, there is no way of knowing what interest rate you'll get on a loan before submitting an application. (The one "hack" I often tell people in credit card debt is that some of the major issuers have preapproval tools on their websites that will tell you if you're likely to be approved for a particular card, with only a "soft" pull on your credit report, thus, not hurting your credit score. These preapproval tools usually also tell you what interest rate you'll be assigned. From talking to people in credit card debt, it is clear that the availability of this hack is not common knowledge.)

Imagine if you wanted to buy a pair of shoes, and the shopkeeper told you the shoes would either cost $50, or $100, or $150, and you couldn't find out the price until you purchased them. If you were unhappy with the shoes or the price charged, you could return them, but would have to pay a sizable return shipping fee and try your luck at another shoe store that follows the exact same system. That's what it's like to look for a credit card in the United States.

The problem isn't just that Americans have a hard time translating between interest rates and the total amount of money it will cost to borrow, although that's also true. The problem is also that the credit card shopping process often hides the interest rate until the application is submitted. The consumer is left almost entirely in the dark about how much the credit card will cost her—meanwhile, the credit card company has a prediction, down to the penny, on the exact amount they expect to earn from each customer in interest and fees.

There's a school of thought that says that people should have the right to see all the data that is collected about them, including any predictions that companies make based on their data. You could imagine how this would transform the credit card industry if any time a person applied for a credit card, a giant, bold, pop-up appeared explaining all the forecasts the bank had made. The fact that they expected you, Jim, for example, based on your unique history, to wind up paying them $2,095 in interest, another $273 in late fees, that they expected to pay you back $75 in rewards, and that they figured out had a 38 percent chance of eventually defaulting on the card.

Ultimately though, there's an even more important reason why competition hasn't been driving down the cost of borrowing. In the first half of the book, we talked about the fact that the amount of debt Americans carry isn't really driven by how much they want or need to borrow: it's driven by how much lenders have decided to lend. If Americans decided in advance exactly how much they wanted to borrow, and only borrowed up to that amount, more competition would mean consumers could be choosier about what lender they picked. But few Americans think about credit cards in this way, and, as a result, when more companies are peddling loans, Americans just end up in more debt.

Consider the rise of fintech installment lenders, companies like LendingClub, Avant, and SoFi without any bank branches, who, in 2017, issued more than $50 billion in loans.[13] Very frequently, the fintech installment lenders give out better interest rates than major credit card companies.[14] For example, as of October 2020, the lowest interest rate offered online by Chase to their most creditworthy borrowers, was 13.24 percent. By comparison, in the same month, the most common interest rate that the fintech lender Prosper offered customers with average credit scores was 10.74 percent.[15]

These fintech loans are often marketed as a way for consumers to consolidate and pay off their credit cards, and over the short term, that's often what happens. A team of researchers from Georgia Institute of Technology found that immediately after getting a fintech installment loan, Americans pay off, on average, 42 percent of all their credit card debt. When they do so, they suddenly have a significant amount of unused credit limit on their credit cards. But the lure of the wipe out game remains as strong as ever. The researchers found that it only took Americans an average of nine months to wind up with exactly the same amount of credit card debt as they had when they took out the installment loan. At the two-year mark, their total debt burden, combining credit cards, the fintech installment loans, and any other debt other than their mortgage, is $4,000 higher than it was when the person first tried to consolidate their debt. Not only that, but over those two years, the typical fintech installment loan borrower has watched her credit score decline, and she is increasingly likely to fall behind on one of their credit card payments.[16]

Start-ups like Lending Club and SoFi have succeeded at making some founders and investors rich, and building sizable businesses, but their success didn't come at the expense of the credit card industry: the debt was all additive. The lesson is that you can't lower Americans' borrowing costs by introducing a new, cheaper loan, because they'll take that loan and keep their old, expensive loan too.

7 A Fair Deal

So what would a fair price for credit be?

As a starting point, let's say we were to return to the credit card profit margins that banks earned twenty-five years ago. If credit card interest rates dropped from an average of 16.9 percent to an average of 13.3 percent, the resulting 3.6 percentage point change would save Americans $28 billion per year, the equivalent of the banks writing a check of $224 to every family in the country.[1] And returning to the lending margins of 1994 would leave a still very generous amount of profits for the lenders: even at those lower prices, banks were excited to expand their credit card businesses and peddle their debt.[2] The resulting interest rates would start to more closely resemble what credit unions generally charge for their credit cards, rates between 7 percent and 18 percent, instead of the prevailing bank credit card interest rates of 14 percent to 27 percent. Even a larger reduction in interest rates might be possible.

This type of change, a 3.6 percentage point reduction in credit card interest rates, isn't so different from what Senator Bernie Sanders and Representative Alexandria Ocasio-Cortez suggested when they introduced the Loan Shark Prevention Act in 2019, a bill which would cap loan interest rates at 15 percent. My own simplistic and easy-to-understand estimate, which is that banks overcharge consumers by at least 3.4 percentage points, aligns with economists Kyle Herkenhoff and Gajendran Raveendranathan who concluded that credit card companies charge interest rates that are between 3.6 percent and 8.8 percent above the "competitive" interest rate—that is to say, the lowest price that a profit-seeking bank would be willing to accept to win a customer's business.[3]

But, of course, saying you could lower *average* interest rates by nearly 4 percent and still be left with extremely profitable credit card operations isn't equivalent to saying that you could implement an across-the-board cap of 14 percent or 15 percent. After all, banks don't give every customer the same interest rate.

The invention of *risk-based pricing*, which means giving different consumers different interest rates depending on how likely they are to repay a loan, is either the root of all evil in finance or the cornerstone of a more socially inclusive financial system, depending on who you ask. Risk-based pricing is in a sense terribly regressive: wealthy people get low interest rates and poor people get high interest rates, making the rich richer and the poor poorer.

The other side of the story of risk-based pricing is what Capital One told me and about forty or so other Duke students in a ballroom at the Washington Duke Hotel one winter day in 2012. Based on the recruiting presentations they use to attract college juniors and seniors, Capital One considers itself to have introduced risk-based pricing into the credit card industry. According to their own accounting, in the mid 1980s, before Fairbank and Morris entered the market, every bank offered a flat 18 percent interest rate on their credit cards. At that interest rate, roughly half of all Americans didn't qualify for credit cards: it wasn't profitable for any banks to lend to them. The audience, primarily Duke's many Econ majors, sees a graph appear on the PowerPoint slide. Capital One enters the market, and suddenly the lowest-risk Americans can get much better deals, with interest rates of under 15 percent, and the higher-risk Americans can get a credit card for the first time. In this story, everyone wins. I'd see that PowerPoint slide many times over in the years that followed, although the template was updated at least once to look more modern. I saw the slide when, as a Capital One analyst, I visited colleges for recruiting trips, and later, as a manager, when I presented the slide. Thanks to the helpful notes we were provided, all the presenters hit on the same themes: Capital One used technology and big data to disrupt the industry and make people's lives better. I ate this story up.

And when I started working at Capital One, I was in awe of how smoothly the machine ran, how neatly it seemed to match the lessons in my economics textbooks—most importantly $MC = MR$, or marginal revenue equals marginal costs. In other words, banks will lend to the riskiest customer that still turns them a small profit: the interest and fees collected are the "marginal revenue," and the money you expect you might lose if they fail to repay, times the probability that they won't repay, is the "marginal cost." *Marginal* is one of the most important words in economics, and it was one of the most important words for an analyst at Capital One. Our *marginal* borrower was the very riskiest customer we would still approve for a credit card, and, similarly, we thought about the *marginal* impact of giving a customer an extra $100 or $500 or $1,000 in credit limit. Every small perturbation in revenues or expenses changed the calculations: the rising cost of postage, a quarter-of-a-percentage-point change in the prime rate, or tiny tweaks in the processing fees charged by Visa and Mastercard to merchants might all be reasons to rerun the company's optimizations, changing who was approved for a credit card and who was declined, what credit limits they received, and how many pieces of preapproved direct mail any particular American would receive in a month.

When you know that fact, it becomes obvious that the free marketers are correct about one thing: some people who currently could get a credit card wouldn't be able to get a credit card anymore if Congress implemented an across-the-board cap of 15 percent. There is a "marginal" customer who gets a credit card at a 27 percent interest rate, who wouldn't get it at a 26 percent interest rate, and another customer who gets a credit card at 26 percent interest rate, who wouldn't get one at a 25 percent interest rate. By comparison, a hypothetical law in which banks had to subtract 3 percentage points from every customer's interest rate would have a much smaller effect on credit access (and a much bigger effect on how much money Americans would save) than a single across the board cap on interest rates. Such a rule, however, would be difficult or impossible to write and enforce. If there is one thing I admire about Bernie Sanders specifically, it's that he seems to understand the benefits of having laws be very simple—why it's a good thing to have a law fit on a single page. What is lost in efficiency is gained through the creation of smooth and glossy policies, policies that don't give special interest groups a foothold to bend things toward their will.

Governments around the world have a long history of attempting, with mixed success, to stop lenders from exploiting their borrowers. As we talked about in chapter 1, until the 1970s, state-level interest rate caps of 18 percent were common, and some states had toyed with interest rate caps under 10 percent. Perhaps not surprisingly, these laws came with a number of unintended consequences, especially for borrowers who wanted small loans, or for borrowers with a spotty credit history. Retailers who sold furniture or radios to the poor on credit would markup the cost of the product itself since they couldn't mark up the loan's interest rate. Some lenders would refuse to issue small loans, forcing a borrower who, for example, wanted a $100 loan to borrow $1,000 instead. (This might not be a problem if the customer could just repay the $900 immediately, but these lenders charged interest on the original loan amount, rather than the declining balance of the loan, meaning the borrower couldn't avoid interest through pre-payment.)[4] States responded to the second problem, of banks refusing to offer small loans in the presence of interest rate caps, by creating different interest rate caps for different loan amounts. And often, different types of loans had different levels of caps— for example, revolving loans, like credit cards, often had higher interest rate caps than installment loans, because in the era before computers, revolving loans were more expensive to administer. But not many governments opted to vary the interest rate cap based on the perceived risk level for the borrower. After all, many lawmakers reasoned that it is precisely the people the banks label as risky that can least afford to pay high interest rates.

.   .   .   .   .

I was asked by a documentary producer in the fall of 2020 if credit card companies were as evil as they seemed. And I struggled to answer the question, because the reality is that the credit card executives, at least at Capital One, don't seem evil and don't believe themselves to be evil.

The moral reasoning of most people who work at credit card companies has only a few steps, which are easy to follow and elegant in their simplicity, reflective, generally speaking, of these people's true beliefs. The reasoning goes as follows: Consumers choose to borrow money on credit cards. The fact that consumers have freely chosen to borrow money on credit cards must mean that credit cards make their borrowers' lives better. These credit card companies are doing something good for the world. Of course, the logic continues, people who find themselves in need of credit card debt are probably in a tough situation, however, the credit card itself must be making the situation better. The credit card executives view the banks as aiding people facing tough situations, at what they see as a very reasonable price, when the rest of the world refuses to offer any assistance at all. Key to their intellectual framing is that the executives assume that the alternatives to the high-price credit they offer are either even higher-priced credit from payday lenders or loan sharks, or no credit at all. There is, of course, another possibility, one that is completely ignored: the banks themselves could offer lower-priced credit, while still turning a significant profit.

Credit card executives aren't philosophers, but if they were, they might say that it is obvious what they are doing is ethical, because the loan transaction is *consensual* and *mutually advantageous* between the borrower and the lender. But according to late philosopher Alan Wertheimer, virtually *all* exploitation is both consensual and mutually advantageous. As he explains in the aptly titled book *Exploitation,* the act of exploitation doesn't require one person to be made better off and the other person to be made worse off: all it requires is that the benefits of an agreement not be shared fairly.

During the years I worked at Capital One, from 2013 to 2018, I watched us raise the interest rates we offered to new borrowers, not because we needed to in any objective sense, but simply because we realized we could, and we'd make more money in doing so. Any given executive might feel like raising interest rates were necessary: after all, Wall Street investors aren't satisfied with merely large profits; they demand large and growing profits, and no Fortune 500 executive can feel secure in his or her job in the face of a declining stock price. But in a broader, more abstract sense, the only real reason to raise interest rates was so that people with huge amounts of money could have even more money.

I was never directly involved in setting the interest rates for Capital One's biggest subprime credit card, Platinum, but in my last role with the company, I was the manager in charge of Capital One's secured credit card. The Platinum team had just raised their interest rates; wouldn't it make sense, my boss asked, for the Secured Card team to do the same? In his mind, it was effectively illogical for the secured credit card to have a lower interest rate than Platinum, because the typical customer of the Secured Credit Card had a lower credit score. We didn't have any relevant data in front of us, so our conversation was all theoretical.

I made two arguments. The first was that the secured card customers had put down a substantial security deposit, often a deposit fully equal to their amount of available credit: in that sense, there was nothing "illogical" about granting them a lower interest rate, because, although their credit scores were generally lower, they had already paid a separate price, the price of putting down the deposit. There was not an industry standard on this point: some companies charge secured card customers their highest interest rates, others charge secured card customers comparatively low interest rates, particularly given their generally subprime credit scores. The second argument was that a higher interest rate wouldn't make it any easier for Capital One to approve more secured card customers: generally speaking, people are only declined for the secured card if the government requires it, or if it's presumed to be particularly likely that the person would commit fraud. After all, on a secured credit card, you really have to make a significant effort to abscond with any of the credit card company's money: if you put down a security deposit of $200 for a credit limit of $200, and then max out your credit limit, the company has effectively broken even. It is only if the customer figures out how to rack up more than $200 in credit card debt—for example, by stealing a third person's checking account credentials to make fraudulent payments—that the creditor stands to lose. My boss and I were probably both guilty of wishful thinking. I didn't want to raise customers interest rates, because I didn't want workers to have even less money to pay their bills, so I made a business case against raising the interest rate. My boss wanted to raise interest rates, so suggested that it wasn't purely an issue of profits, but also, in a certain sense, of fairness, to the customers on the Platinum card being charged more than the Secured Card customers.

We reached an impasse. While my boss could have forced the issue, or overruled me, he didn't. Almost as soon as I left the company, the team's new manager raised the Secured Card's interest rates to match Platinum's. The sorts of moral arguments held between employees of corporations seem to make some difference around the edges of an otherwise unrelenting machine of capitalism.

The definition that Wertheimer employs applies neatly to all sorts of situations, from sweatshops that pay pennies an hour, to pharmaceutical companies that charge outrageous prices just because they can, to the hardware store operator who triples the price of snow shovels during a storm. Sure, the sweatshop worker is better earning poverty wages than being unemployed; the diabetes patient is better off paying $6,000 per year for insulin than she would be dying without medicine; and the snowed-in customer buys the shovel because she figures, even at the outrageous price, that it's still a good use of her money. In these cases, there is some "zone of agreement," Wertheimer says, between the lowest price at which the seller (or lender) would still turn a profit, and the highest price the buyer is willing to pay. The zone of agreement in the case of something lifesaving may be the last dollar that a consumer has. At any price in the "zone of agreement," the buyer and seller, or the lender and borrower, could hypothetically strike a deal. Exploitation is when the more powerful party gets his way about where within the "zone of agreement" the price will be set; the less powerful party is still better off relative to a baseline where no deal occurs but is worse off relative to the baseline of a fair deal. And, when you're talking about the credit card industry, the choice to move APRs from a lower rate to a higher rate will mean that families who, very obviously, already struggle to pay their bills will be forced into making even more difficult decisions. Will the working dad drive more hours for Uber, at the cost of not being home to tuck his children in for bedtime? Will the twenty-six-year-old elementary school teacher spend another few years living with her parents so she can finally afford to rent an apartment in the city where she teaches? Will the senior slowly cut down on the portion sizes of her meals?

.   .   .   .   .

The hope with usury caps is usually that banks will lend to the same people but will charge lower prices for the loans. But another question emerges: are there people who are so likely to be unable to repay their loans that it would be harmful or unfair to lend to them? The US government believes this idea to be true. It's why, for example, they required in the CARD Act that credit card companies ask borrowers to state their income before giving them a credit card, and why they put special restrictions on lending to college students. There are two basic reasons why some people hold the belief that people who are at an especially high risk of default should not receive loans at all: The first is that they observe that defaulting on a loan can cause hardship—for example, if a borrower is sued by their lender and their paycheck is garnished. The second reason is that they observe that lenders will only choose to lend to insolvent borrowers if they can charge such outrageous fees that it doesn't matter whether or not the loan is eventually repaid.

In some ways, I think this framing by Congress and regulators reflects a pro-industry bias: by focusing on the hardship faced by borrowers who default, it is easy to ignore the hardship faced by the borrowers who manage to keep their heads barely above water, and who succeed, despite difficulty and sacrifice, to make their payments. After all, when a customer defaults on their loan payment, it is often lose-lose, especially if the default occurs when the account has only been in existence for a year or less. The company can potentially recoup some or all of their principal with a lawsuit, but doing so isn't cheap, which is why many lenders sell their unpaid debts to collection agencies for pennies on the dollar. Meanwhile, when a customer struggles, successfully, to repay a loan, it is a win-lose. It is this win-lose scenario that the credit card companies are most attached to.

So while I don't think looking at the percentage of customers who eventually default is the right way to judge a lender, it is nevertheless a useful metric to think about. I'd encourage you, the reader, to think about what number would feel wrong to you. Would you think it's wrong for a bank to lend to a customer with a 90 percent chance of defaulting on their loan? How about a 75 percent chance? A 50 percent chance? A 30 percent chance?

Capping interest rates ends up being a way to cap how many Americans will default on loans, because it is the people who the banks have predicted have the highest odds of default who lose credit access in the presence of an interest rate cap. The specific interest rate cap you set, whether it is 15 percent, 18 percent, 36 percent, or 100 percent, translates into something important: who should the market deny credit to?

I'll do some arithmetic here, to help illustrate my point. Suppose you simplify things and assume there are two types of people who will use a credit card: non-defaulters and defaulters. The non-defaulters, we'll assume, immediately max out their credit limit and then pay it off gradually over the course of four years, at which point they stop using the card. The defaulters immediately max out their credit limit, make minimum payments for two years, before running into financial trouble—for example, the loss of a job. They max out their credit card again, and then default without making another credit card payment. Although these are simplified assumptions, they are a good way of approximating the economics of subprime lending, where virtually 100 percent of the consumers will use their credit card to borrow money, as opposed to paying their bill in full every month.[5] And, importantly, most people who default on their credit cards won't do so right away: it will be after years of struggling to make payments. I'll assume that there is also an operating cost to run the credit card, but I'll ignore all the money the bank earns from late fees, from the processing fees charged to the merchants where the customer spends, and I'll assume that if the customer defaults, the bank doesn't make any effort to collect on the debt, so they don't spend money on collections, but they also aren't able to successfully garnish the person's paycheck.

The credit card with a 15 percent interest rate will make money as long as less than one in four customers defaults. The credit card with an 18 percent interest rate will make money as long as less than one in three customers default. The credit card with a 24 percent interest rate can make money even if nearly half of the customers default. The credit card with a 36 percent interest rate can make money even with more than two in three customers defaulting. And, hypothetically, a credit card with a 60 percent interest rate would make money even if all the customers defaulted, because you'd make so much money off of each person before they fell from hard times to harder times.

Leaving aside the question for a second of whether we should demand banks do risky loans when they would be expected to lose money, these

Table 2   Break-Even Default Rates for Credit Cards

Interest Payments Received per Customer

	Assumptions	CARD INTEREST RATE (APR)				
		15%	*18%*	*24%*	*36%*	*60%*
Non-Defaulters	Non-defaulters max out the credit line immediately, pay down gradually over 4 years, and then stop using the card	$1,007	$1,230	$1,694	$2,699	$4,965
Defaulters	Defaulters max out the credit line immediately, make minimum payments for 2 years, max out again, and then default	$804	$964	$1,286	$1,929	$3,215

Total Profit or (Loss) per Customer

	Assumptions	CARD INTEREST RATE (APR)				
		15%	*18%*	*24%*	*36%*	*60%*
Non-Defaulters	Non-defaulters max out the credit line immediately, pay down gradually over 4 years, and then stop using the card	$912	$1,135	$1,599	$2,604	$4,870
Defaulters	Defaulters max out the credit line immediately, make minimum payments for 2 years, max out again, and then default	$(2,291)	$(2,131)	$(1,809)	$(1,166)	$120

Table 2 (continued)

Break-Even Default Rate for Credit Card

	CARD INTEREST RATE (APR)				
	15%	*18%*	*24%*	*36%*	*60%*
Maximum Profitable Default Rate for Given APR	28%	35%	47%	69%	>100%

NOTE: Based on a $3,000 credit limit and funding/operating costs of $5 + 3% of credit limit. These assumptions make several simplifications: They ignore interchange revenue and late fees. They ignore the cost of collections and recoveries, but they also assume the bank does not recover any money lost from defaulters via legal action or collections activity. The cost of funds varies significantly between credit card issuers depending on their funding structure and could be as low as 1% or as high as 4% of balances, with an average of under 2%. A study of credit card issuer practices by Sumit Agarawal and coauthors found an average non-marketing, non-collections operating expense of $36.58 per account per year between 2008 and 2011, or 2.7% of credit card balances; this figure includes both fixed expenses, which would not be expected to substantially alter the break-even default rate, along with variable expenses.

figures lead us to some conclusions, especially if you believe that when a person can't repay a loan they are worse off for having borrowed money. Cutting off APRs at 15 percent would stop banks from lending to people who are very likely to repay their loan, although perhaps saving some other consumers a significant amount of money. Meanwhile cutting off APRs at 24 percent would only stop credit card companies from lending to people who have a nearly fifty-fifty chance of defaulting anyways. There are no obvious answers to the ethical questions at stake here: if two in three Americans will succeed in repaying a loan, while one in three will struggle and fail, is it a good thing or a bad thing to deprive the two in three the opportunity to borrow? In questions of degree, any cutoff point set is ultimately arbitrary. Questions of degree are nevertheless worth grappling with. My own intuition says that it wouldn't be good to stop people with only a 25 percent chance of default from acquiring credit, for example, by setting a 15 percent interest rate cap, while an 18 percent interest rate cap provides a bit more leeway for Americans to get a second chance with credit.

There's an important way in which credit cards are more usurious than they seem, while payday loans are a bit more reasonable than they might

Table 3   Break-Even Default Rates for Payday Loans

Interest Payments Received per Customer

		LOAN INTEREST RATE (APR)				
	Assumptions	15%	18%	24%	36%	60%
Non-Defaulters	Repay the loan in one month	$4	$5	$6	$9	$15
Defaulters	Don't make any payments	$-	$-	$-	$-	$-

Total Profit or (Loss) per Customer

		LOAN INTEREST RATE (APR)				
	Assumptions	15%	18%	24%	36%	60%
Non-Defaulters	Repay the loan in one month	$(10.25)	$(9.50)	$(8.00)	$(5.00)	$1.00
Defaulters	Don't make any payments	($300)	($300)	($300)	($300)	($300)

Break-Even Default Rate

	LOAN INTEREST RATE (APR)				
	15%	18%	24%	36%	60%
Maximum Profitable Default Rate	n/a	n/a	n/a	n/a	0.332%

NOTE: Based on a $300 loan size and funding/operating costs of $5 + 3 percent of loan size. These cost estimates are illustrative and are an underestimate for payday lenders operating via storefront. Cost estimates may be reasonably accurate for online-only payday lenders, excluding marketing costs and the cost of collections/recoveries.

appear. Let's assume that the cost structure of a payday loan somewhat resembles the cost structure of a credit card: there are some fixed components of the cost—the amount it costs to file all the paperwork, get the account set up within computerized system, and send by mail any statements or disclosures the borrower needs to receive. If this is all fully automated and online, the best-case scenario is probably that these fixed costs would total around five dollars per loan. (On top of that cost, there will be other lender expenses that are proportional to the loan size, the most important of which is the amount of money it costs the lender to fund the loan, usually at least 1 percent or 2 percent of the loan amount. Payday loans are often for fairly small amounts of money—for example, $300 to $400.[6] And, on paper, they are usually supposed to be repaid within one month, although very often the borrowers can't afford to do so and continuously roll over the loan. If a $300 loan comes with $14 in operating costs for the lender and is to be repaid in one month, it's not profitable at a 36 percent interest rate, even if every single customer repays the loan. At a 60 percent interest rate, only one in three hundred customers can default and have the lender still break even. The most common misconception about payday loans is that their prices are outrageously high because their borrowers are so risky. In fact, the default rate on payday loans isn't that different than the default rate for subprime credit cards; the biggest difference in their profit models are the operating expenses.[7] Historically, some governments have tried to balance the relatively high costs of small dollar lending and their desire to mandate fair lending practices by letting lenders tack on a relatively small flat fee—for example, the equivalent of $10—outside of the bounds of whatever interest rate cap the government set.

.   .   .   .   .

Of course, in this argument, I assume that banks will lend if they can turn a profit and will refuse to lend at a loss. But there are other possibilities. The government could mandate that banks do a certain amount of unprofitable lending. The government could grant these risky loans themselves. Or, finally, the government could provide support and encouragement to credit unions or other nonprofit lenders to issue loans.

The idea of a government lending mandate for banks isn't an unfamiliar concept. In fact, that is roughly the idea behind the Community Reinvestment Act, which we discussed in chapter 1. Interestingly, the proponents of the Community Reinvestment Act often insist that loans induced by the law *are* in fact profitable, eschewed by banks only for discriminatory or unknown reasons. There is a great taboo in this country against risky lending. Nobody wants to be held responsible for a bank collapse, which means that advocates for increasing lending to the poor often argue that the lending is not as risky as it may seem, instead of acknowledging that the lending is risky, but that banks maybe ought to do it anyways.

But it's not exactly clear why banks should be doing these riskier loans, instead of the government doing the lending itself: after all, if you think that banks don't give back enough to society, it's much simpler to raise their taxes instead of asking them to make unprofitable loans. If you believe, as I do, that banks can't be trusted to do the right thing by their own accord, it isn't obvious that the Community Reinvestment Act successfully induces them into good behavior.

People who believe the government shouldn't get into the lending business because they think the banks are simply better equipped to do the lending are probably not thinking about all the lending the government already does.

Consider, for a moment, the $1.6 trillion federal student loan program. Certainly, it has its critics. Most commonly, people suggest that the government should be offering a free or less expensive education rather than offering loans, or they argue that the government is too indiscriminate in how much it allows students to borrow. Critics also point out that the advice given to borrowers by the student loan servicers (contractors, not government employees) is not very helpful and is sometimes inaccurate, or they suggest that the government is too rapacious in their attempts to collect on delinquent student debt from people who can't afford to make payments. In other words, the most common criticisms of the government as a lender are not that the government fails to live up to some high standards set by banks. Rather, the biggest criticism of the government as a lender is that it behaves similarly to the universally despised big banks.

By some other measures, the student loan program is a massive success. The highest interest rate the federal student loan program has charged new borrowers since 2013 is 7.9 percent, a rate much lower than what is offered by any credit card company. And the current rates for new student loans issued by the federal government for undergraduate borrowers are lower still: only 2.75 percent as of June 2021. By most accounts, the federal government has been able to offer these comparatively low rates without dipping into taxpayer dollars, turning a small profit.

The federal student loans made directly to undergraduate students (as opposed to parents and graduate students) have no minimum credit score and no minimum income. And every borrower with federal loans is eligible for a variety of payment plans that make their payments proportional to their income, providing an important form of insurance that isn't generally available for credit card borrowers or other bank borrowers, although these programs appear to be vastly underutilized, reflecting a failure on the part of student loan servicers to fulfill their job responsibilities.[8] Last but not least, the government has been able to offer these trillions of dollars of loans at interest rates well under 10 percent without engaging in risk-based pricing: poorer students and wealthier students get the same interest rate. Of course, the federal government has some built-in advantages that private lenders lack: the government doesn't need to pay taxes, and the government can borrow money very cheaply. But using these putatively unfair advantages to the benefit of indebted Americans, at the expense of bank shareholders, seems eminently reasonable.

Another example is the federal government's Small Business Administration disaster relief loans, issued after floods, wildfires, hurricanes, and other catastrophes. Confusingly, based on the agency's name, nine times out of ten the recipients of these loans are ordinary individuals, with no connection to a small business.[9] (These figures represent pre-COVID disaster relief loans, not the COVID-related programs such as the Paycheck Protection Program.) Although some people get grants from FEMA, more often than not the major form of assistance that the federal government offers after a natural disaster is the low-interest-rate SBA loan. As of 2020, homeowners could borrow up to $200,000 to rebuild or replace their homes after a disaster, while renters could borrow up to $40,000 to replace or repair their cars, furniture, or other property.[10] In the aftermath of Hurricane Harvey, for every $1 that FEMA offered as a grant, the SBA issued $2.13 as loans, usually with interest rates under 2 percent. Very often loans are the only helping hand a person receives.[11] No collateral is required for the SBA disaster relief loan if the loan amount is under $25,000.[12] And, like the student loan program, the federal government breaks even on the SBA disaster relief program, avoiding the use of taxpayer dollars, despite the fact that they don't engage in the risk-based pricing presumed to be necessary by bankers. In fact, the government does the opposite of risk-based pricing: as of June 2020, they charged an interest rate of 1.563 percent if the agency concluded you had "no credit available elsewhere"—for example, if your credit score was comparatively low—while they charged a higher interest rate of 3.125 percent if you fell into the "credit available elsewhere" category.[13]

But this policy to offer one or two flat low interest rates comes with its own set of problems. Because the program is designed to break even, the federal government only approves about 40 percent of the disaster relief loan applications that it finishes processing. In 2019, the Center for Public Integrity reported that "ninety percent of SBA disaster loan denials since 2001 have been for 'unsatisfactory credit history,' 'lack of repayment ability' or both."[14] In other words, the government's desire to offer a single low rate, without offering a subsidy, means that nearly half of Americans are turned away. Any lender, whether public, corporate, or nonprofit must decide: will their loans be offered at a single low interest rate, will everyone be eligible for the loans, or will the loans break even?

The government's success at offering low-interest rate loans to vast swaths of the American public certainly suggests that they could, if they tried, beat the credit card companies at their own game, offering interest rates at roughly half the prevailing level to people who need short-term loans. I'm hardly the only person to suggest that the government should take a bigger role in offering Americans an affordable banking option: in the 2020 presidential primary, Elizabeth Warren, Bernie Sanders, and Kirsten Gillibrand all campaigned on postal banking, although in Gillibrand's proposal, the post office banks would offer checking accounts, but not small-dollar loans. From 1911 to 1966, Americans could open a bank account at any post office in the country; some believe it's time for the United States to revisit such a system.[15] Lending money doesn't have to be complicated: what lending ought to be is affordable and transparent. The state of North Dakota has operated a public bank for over one hundred years, offering low-cost student loans, agricultural loans, and business loans, along with checking and savings accounts (but no credit cards). While their policy is explicitly to limit the extent to which they compete directly against the private sector, the state has nevertheless proven that governments have the capacity to offer affordable financial products, without putting taxpayer dollars at risk.[16]

Over the course of this book, I have largely ignored the fact that, in the presence of a stronger social safety net, there would be little need for credit cards, payday loans, or any similar alternatives. In the presence of a more expansive unemployment insurance program, paid family leave, adequate public transportation, affordable housing, and public health-care coverage, Americans wouldn't be so reliant on high-priced loans to save them from the brink of catastrophe. A universal basic income would roughly double the size of the federal budget, representing a fairly radical break from the structure of our current economy (although, some would argue, a necessary break). A more modest proposal would be to offer the equivalent of a universal emergency fund for every American. In 2018 Senator Cory Booker proposed a program that would give every eighteen-year-old money, inversely proportional to their parents' income, guaranteeing, in effect, that poorer kids would start out their lives with the types of safety net that richer kids already enjoy. The initiative, whose grants would be up to $47,000 each for the lowest-wealth eighteen-year-olds, would cost $60 billion per year, a tiny fraction of the scale of a full UBI program.[17] Starting every young adult with a financial safety net would make it much less likely that Americans would become trapped in a cycle of debt. But I have purposefully constrained the scope of this book to talk only about the debt machine itself, to imagine the best financial system possible, holding constant the rest of the economy. Readers interested in the expansion of the welfare state have plenty of other sources to turn to.

Finally, we have the possibility that credit unions could be the purveyors of our fairer deal. The nation's credit unions count a total of 122 million members, representing a sizable chunk of the adult population, even if a handful of people have multiple credit union memberships.[18] A report by the Pew Health Group suggested that credit union credit card interest rates are typically about 20 percent lower than bank credit card interest rates.[19] Nearly all the credit cards available with interest rates under 10 percent come from credit unions.[20] Federally chartered credit unions, by law, aren't allowed to charge credit card interest rates in excess of 18 percent, virtually guaranteeing that a credit union credit card will come with cost savings for the many Americans whose bank-issued credit cards charge interest rates of 20 percent or more. Fees are generally lower as well. Credit cards issued by banks have an average of 4.57 different fees, compared to an average of only 2.73 different fees charged by credit unions.[21]

But even though credit unions generally offer lower prices than the big banks, only 4 percent of new credit cards are issued by credit unions.[22] For boosters of credit unions, advocates of usury caps, and believers in the idea that consumers will find the best deal available in the marketplace, this fact raises a thorny question: if credit unions offer a much better deal than banks, why does anyone get a credit card from a bank instead?

It's worth comparing the credit card industry to two other products where credit unions dominate: personal loans and auto loans. More than a quarter of all new personal loans and auto loans are issued by credit unions, and, in fact, in both markets the credit unions have a bigger market share than the banks. (Credit unions are no. 2 in the auto loan market to "captive" auto lenders—e.g., the lenders affiliated with the auto manufacturers, like Toyota Financial Services and American Honda Finance— while credit unions are no. 2 in the personal loan market to fintechs.)[23]

Auto loans and personal loans both make their costs pretty clear: not only are Americans told an interest rate; most Americans with a high school diploma can contextualize the loan's total cost based on the monthly payment and the number of payments made. When a person *realizes* very clearly that they're going to spend thousands of dollars in interest charges, it induces a much stronger motivation to shop around and find the best interest rate. When that shopping process is done, very often, credit unions come out on top. Without credit card rewards thrown into the mix, the better deal offered by credit unions shines clearly.

As Pentagon Federal Credit Union CEO James Schenck pointed out to me, it would be impossible for credit unions to match the scale of marketing that banks use to maintain their dominant position: after all, as he notes, JPMorgan Chase alone has roughly $3 trillion in assets, nearly double the level of assets of all of the nation's credit unions combined. The largest banks, he said, "have the scale to market-bomb the country using, not only analytics, but also direct mail offers into the right mailboxes not just once, not just twice, but persistently." The smaller scale of credit unions forces PenFed and their peers to be "extremely selective in who we market to, in order to get the return on our marketing dollar, compared to a large bank that's hitting [consumers] every week on the airwaves, television, and direct mail, and social."

Moreover, most federally chartered credit unions have a limited field of membership: according to the Federal Credit Union Act of 1934, all the members of a credit union need to share a predefined "common bond," like sharing the same employer, the same religion, or living in the same neighborhood. Nearly all Americans are eligible to belong to one or more credit unions, but the field-of-membership rules can create one more barrier for Americans looking for a good deal. PenFed is relatively unique among credit unions, in that it has an open field of membership: in 2019, it merged with Progressive Credit Union, which had an open charter because it was founded in 1918, prior to the passage of the Federal Credit Union Act. As a result, PenFed is one of the only credit unions in the country legally allowed to market their credit cards across the country.

The only way for a credit union to have an open field of membership is for it to be grandfathered into the system, like PenFed. The National Credit Union Administration has threatened legal action against credit unions that falsely imply they are "open to everyone." It's possible that credit unions could gain a larger market share, especially if consumers become aware of the lower prices they offer, but under current law Americans would have to rely on the nation's existing credit unions to save the day. Under the field of membership rules, any new credit unions have to be limited in the membership. It's not impossible to start a new credit union, but it's effectively impossible to start one with a broad, nationwide reach, even if you have deep-pocketed donors willing to support the cause.[24] Perhaps not surprisingly, the American Banker Association, the most important industry lobbying group, has fought to stop the National Credit Union Administration from opening up field of membership rules, and has even fought to strip credit unions of their tax-exempt status. The very idea of financial institutions that work in the best interest of the American public, rather than in the best interest of wealthy shareholders, threatens major banks.

The 18 percent interest rate cap doesn't stop PenFed, Schenck said, from lending to Americans with average or below-average credit scores. "We have very high acceptance rates, and we can market broadly." The 18 percent cap might present an issue, he noted, if the prime rate were to rise, which would in turn make it more expensive for PenFed to borrow money. But he was very clear that in the current rate environment, "17.99 [the interest rate limit] does not limit PenFed or any of the other credit unions from reaching out broadly across credit [score] bands, making credit card products available to our consumers."

In a sense, auto loans and personal loans reflect the debt that Americans have consciously chosen for themselves, the loans that, correctly or incorrectly, Americans explicitly decided would improve their financial condition. By comparison, credit cards very often reflect the debt that is induced purely by marketing, debt that Americans weren't completely sure if they needed or not, but that they slid into, nevertheless. The very aggressive marketing of the banks keeps them on top of an industry where consumers must be convinced of their desires, even if the banks are relatively feeble competitors when Americans have made up their minds about what they need.

So how do we solve the interest problem, and help American workers hold on to more of their own wealth? Part of the answer would come from making it easier for Americans to comparison shop for credit cards. Some of the solutions discussed in the first half of the book would help—capping credit card interchange rates to reduce the prevalence of misleading credit card rewards, and creating "universal credit contracts" like those found in Chile. The credit card market has clearly failed at what markets are supposed to do best: encourage competition. To help Americans find lower prices more effectively, the federal government should introduce a comparison-shopping marketplace, like Healthcare.gov, where consumers could submit a single application and see the interest rate that every credit card issuer would offer. Existing comparison-shopping websites, like Credit Karma and CreditCards.com do little to help Americans find the best deal, instead steering them toward banks with the biggest advertising budgets. And, finally, the government needs to remove barriers faced by credit unions—most importantly, by eliminating the common bond requirement. Most Americans are fed up with Wall Street. That should be "common bond" enough. If nonprofit lenders can achieve scale and lend to Americans all over the country without having to be coy about who is eligible, the public will benefit. Credit unions and other forms of non-profit lenders would also, importantly, have much better odds against big banks if consumers could effectively shop, for example, through a portal where they could compare interest rates, because the problem of credit unions being outspent in marketing would become less important.

And finally, Congress should implement a nationwide interest rate cap tied to the prime rate, at roughly 18 percent (e.g., the prime rate plus 15 percentage points). At this interest rate cap, only Americans with relatively high odds of default would lose access to credit in the private market. To the extent that Congress deems that access to credit is still valuable for these Americans, the government should lend to them directly.

PART III   The Future

8 The Last Frontier

One of the strategies I used to learn about Americans' experiences with debt was to stand in public places and ask people, "If you could change one thing about banks or credit card companies, what would it be?" Most conversations were brief. Some conversations were very long. Many people either didn't have the time to talk or weren't interested in speaking with me. But even the short conversations could be informative.

Near a Greyhound station in Houston, Texas, when I asked one man what he would change about banks, his answer was brief: "Me and my friends don't really f*ck with banks anymore."

Roughly 15 million Americans, 6 percent of adults, don't have a checking account. A somewhat larger group, 45 million adults, roughly 18 percent, don't have a credit score, which means they don't have any open or recently closed loans. The group of Americans who don't have a credit card is only slightly larger than the number without a credit score, at 47 million.[1]

The financial industry, of course, views this as a problem. When Americans with a credit card already have an average of $4,600 in credit card debt, even aggressive lenders might question if they're pushing consumers a bit too far. Banks are clearly content with growth that comes from driving indebted Americans more deeply into debt, but their appetite for reaching new Americans, naturally, is even stronger. The last frontier, the manifest destiny for the banks, is that every American have a credit score. The natural corollary to this mission is that every American ought to be in debt.

Around the country, in Michigan, Minnesota, Iowa, Texas, and Louisiana, I talked to Americans without any type of bank account. Some of these people were paid in cash, which could mean either unstable employment, doing odd jobs, or a slightly steadier situation, like bartending. Others made use of check cashers to convert their paychecks into hard currency. Some felt excluded by the financial system, like Vernon, who couldn't get a bank account because he didn't have any ID, or Nick in St. Paul, whose bank had closed his account after an overdraft. But very often, these consumers had intentionally never opened a bank account or had voluntarily closed their accounts, fed up with the fees they'd been charged.

You can certainly have a bank account without getting into debt, but it's somewhat unusual to get into debt without having a checking account. Although consumers of payday loans are sometimes lumped into the category of "unbanked," in a literal sense this is almost never the case. The vast majority of payday lenders require a checking account to open a loan. Traditionally, to get a payday loan, you had to provide a postdated check, although increasingly, customers are asked to provide their checking account routing number and account number instead.[2] It's more unusual for credit card companies to refuse applicants on the basis of not having a checking account, although it does happen.

CREDIT INVISIBLES

The Consumer Financial Protection Bureau calls the roughly 26 million Americans who don't have a credit report "credit invisibles." By their definition, a consumer is only "credit invisible" if the three major credit bureaus are completely blind to their existence, lacking a record of any sort. An additional 19 million Americans, they report, aren't credit invisible, but they still don't have credit score: their name and social security numbers appear in the records of the credit reporting agencies, but they don't have enough recent credit history to be given a FICO score.

The Bureau makes it quite clear that credit invisibility is, in their minds, "a problem."[3] This way of thinking about Americans without any debt didn't originate with President Donald Trump's pro-business appointees. Richard Cordray, the Consumer Financial Protection Bureau director appointed by President Barack Obama, has described the state of lacking a history of indebtedness as "a huge hindrance to personal opportunity."[4]

The popular press echoes the framing that the rate of credit invisibility ought to be driven to zero, insinuating that many Americans who've never used credit are desperately seeking an entry-point into the system. In Politico, Colin Wilhelm wrote, "There's a catch-22 at the core of the U.S. financial system: To get credit, you need to already have established a credit history. Millions of Americans never find a way around the contradiction, and as a result, are locked out of things like credit cards or student loans that the rest of the population can take for granted."[5]

These narratives sometimes elide a basic fact, which is that any American can turn themselves from "credit invisible" to "credit visible" simply by submitting an application for any credit card, along with most other types of loans, whether the loan application is approved or declined. When a consumer applies for a loan from any bank or lender that consults the major credit bureaus—Equifax, Experian, and Transunion—the credit bureau will make a note of the loan application. That record of an application, successful or unsuccessful, is called an "inquiry." An American who applies for her first credit card and is declined will then have a credit report with her personal information (for example, her name, address, and social security number), and a record of her single unsuccessful "inquiry" for credit. By the Bureau's own definition, such a consumer isn't "credit invisible." So, to some extent, being completely "credit invisible" reflects a conscious choice to avoid credit, and to not submit any loan applications.

Of course, there are undoubtedly some Americans who really would like credit but have no idea how the system works or where to begin, particularly if their relatives have never had credit or owned a home. As one young woman in Houston told me, "I feel like some people who don't have credit, it's because they never use their credit like me. I don't have credit, because I don't use my credit. But I'll be so scared to lose my credit, cause I don't wanna mess up my credit." For many people, she pointed out, the system is inscrutable and inaccessible. Several interviewees I spoke with, not just young people in their twenties, but also middle-aged men and women, said they believed it was too hard to get credit in the United States, but they also said they had never applied for credit, or hadn't applied for credit within the last decade, and they weren't sure what types of criteria banks used to assess creditworthiness.

Not having any credit is very strongly associated with economic dispossession, low income, and living in a high poverty area. This is, to some extent, an inevitable byproduct of a system in which the banks' profit motive occasionally discourages them from lending to people without the means to repay a loan. Moreover, the fact that the government forbids banks from offering credit cards to people without an income strictly links wealth and credit access. This well-established and highly visible association between having credit and being well off leads Americans toward a range of conclusions. While some Americans look at the association and conclude that credit is only available to those of means, others look at the association as evidence that credit helps people build wealth.

This association between credit and wealth means that some people seek credit *specifically* because of the association: they have internalized the idea that using credit is associated with being middle class or rich, and that not having any credit is related to being poor. So many people I spoke with, Kathryn R. and Alisha and Naomi and Isa and Madison and Tasha and Joe, expressed this basic idea that getting a credit card is simply what *one does* as a part of entering the middle class or staying middle class. On an emotional level, staying outside the system can feel riskier than entering it.

Others conclude that the system isn't designed for them to win, or, like the woman in Houston, identify themselves as lacking the confidence that they wouldn't "mess up."

In *Seeing Like a State: How Certain Schemes to Improve the Human Condition Have Failed*, anthropologist James C. Scott documents the discomfort that governments have historically felt when some of their subjects are, as he would say, "illegible," unmapped, or undocumented, when citizens cannot be fit into the state's literal or metaphorical databases. Scott describes free-flowing but messy forests transformed into timber plantations by German bureaucrats, destroying the underlying ecology for the sake of making mappable plants, and Spanish colonists entering the Philippines, forcing new surnames onto the islands' original residents for the sake of standardization. Scott quotes philosopher Isaiah Berlin, who said, "If the facts—that is, the behavior of living human beings—are recalcitrant to such an experiment, the experimenter becomes annoyed and tries to alter the facts to fit the theory, which, in practice, means a kind of vivisection of societies until they become what the theory originally declared the experiment should have caused them to be." [6] For the contemporary bureaucrat, it may very well be that the individual who doesn't render herself as a *consumer* poses an epistemic threat.

Naming as a policy goal that more Americans ought to be credit visible ignores the active attempts many people are making to avoid credit—rodents in a game of cat and mouse where the banks are aggressively feline. A study of the financial behaviors of low-income women by Texas Law professor Angela Littwin found that 52 percent engaged in one or more "anti-temptation" strategies to avoid credit card debt—most commonly, tearing up the credit card offers that they received by mail. [7]

And why should it be surprising that some people would prefer to avoid debt? Why is it considered a defect of our economy that some Americans prefer to save up for their purchases in advance, avoiding paying interest in the process? After all, those who cannot, for example, afford to save up to purchase a car are often those who find their auto loan payments to be unaffordable. It is not as if credit, generally speaking, can solve the problem of having a low income merely by rearranging the timing of when bills come due.

It's not surprising that banks would like to grow and they consider Americans without credit scores to be their only natural growth opportunity. What is perhaps more shocking is the extent to which the public buys into the premise that this expansion is socially beneficial, even necessary, under the banner of what banks often call "financial inclusion." The premise of financial inclusion does not accept the possibility that many Americans reject banks, that they have opted out of a system that they know was not designed for them to succeed.

Advocates of universal credit "visibility" might acknowledge that it is merely a means to achieving more salubrious goals, like increasing the number of Americans who own their homes, or reducing the costs of credit for the now-invisible consumers who might in the future choose to borrow.

In the United States, it is rare to get a mortgage without having first established a credit history through other types of credit accounts. This doesn't necessarily have to involve paying any interest: an American can achieve a high credit score through paying their credit card bill in full every month.

But there's also no real reason why credit cards or other types of loans should be needed as a precursor to a home mortgage. In many countries, including Australia, Belgium, Denmark, Finland, France, and Portugal, the credit bureaus primarily track negative information about borrowers, like missed payments, or loans in default, and don't report positive information, like loans repaid on time.[8] This may sound punitive, but it also means the absence of a credit record doesn't count against a person when it's time to apply for a mortgage. There are downsides to this "black marks only" style of system: hypothetically, those people who *do* have a long credit history might receive better interest rates in the countries where this history can be evaluated by lenders. But if we think, as a country, that it is important for Americans to be able to own homes, we should seriously consider why we've designed a system where, unlike in other countries, people are expected to go through the rigmarole of other loans first.

And how hard, exactly, is it to access credit if you don't have a credit score? I'll speak only about credit cards here, although, of course, home mortgages and auto loans are perhaps even more important. Contrary to Wilhelm's account that "To get credit, you need to already have established a credit history," most Americans seeking credit find it easy to circumvent the alleged Catch-22.

A small proportion of Americans, roughly 15 percent of adults with a credit score, establish their credit history by "piggybacking" on the credit reports of a parent or loved one; they build a credit record after being added as an authorized user onto somebody else's credit card. Student loans are also a relatively common way for people to establish a credit record, but by far the most common method of obtaining a credit score is by getting a credit card. 95 percent of the time, the credit cards that these "new to credit" consumers receive from banks or lenders are unsecured cards.[9] Nearly all the indebted Americans I talked to have had no trouble getting their first credit card, although starting credit limits were often relatively low. Personal finance experts sometimes suggest that Americans getting their first credit card should look for a secured card: in practice, evidence suggests that this is rarely necessary. The exception would be someone who has negative marks on their credit report before they've ever been given a loan—for example, a cell phone bill that entered collections.

The problem is hardly that credit is a walled garden. Although the prices charged by lenders are often high, as we discussed in chapters 6 and 7, those high prices aren't simple byproducts of lending costs and, hence, can't be solved purely by better underwriting. The media, regulators, and bank executives often lump people who are new to credit in with those with low credit scores, but the reality is that these groups of consumers are in very different boats.

Part of the media's misunderstanding seems to arise from the very big disconnect between "not having a credit score" and "being new to credit." We've already discussed the truly "invisible" consumers who have no record with the credit bureaus at all, a fact which, as mentioned, also means they haven't applied for a credit card or a traditional loan at any point within the last two years.

Let's now turn our attention to the somewhat smaller group who appear in the credit bureau's records but who don't have a FICO credit score. The term of art sometimes used by bankers for these Americans are "invalids," because the credit bureaus don't produce a "valid" credit score for these consumers. According to a report by Quantilytic, which studied the credit reports of Americans without FICO credit scores, 65 percent of these invalid-score Americans *do* have a record of debt, either in the form of a past bankruptcy, tax lien, or debt in collections. PPI (Progressive Policy Institute), the center-left think tank, calls this group the "involuntarily inactive." A lender who reviews the credit report of one of these "involuntarily inactive" consumers is likely to treat them similarly as a consumer who has a relatively low credit score. An American's credit score will become invalid once all of her loans have been closed or charged off at least six months ago.

The next largest group, making up 25 percent of invalid-score Americans, are the people who paid off or closed all their credit accounts at least six months ago, and who don't have any records of defaults or delinquent debts on their records. The credit bureaus consider these very dated loans to be largely irrelevant, and so they won't produce a credit score for these consumers. Notably, the median age of this second group of consumers is seventy-one years, not necessarily an opportune time to be taking on new debts. The smallest group, only 10 percent of the invalid-score Americans, are those who are new to credit.[10]

For credit cards and auto loans, those who have difficulty gaining access are generally those who have struggled to repay loans or other bills in the past. Gaining access to small business credit is notoriously more difficult, but, of course, roughly half of all small businesses fail within the first five years. My point isn't that these people deserve a lifetime of punishment, or should never get a fresh start, but rather that credit scores are often a sadly accurate picture of real, and still-unresolved, financial distress, a state of affairs that may or may not be improved through additional borrowing.

CREDIT REBUILDERS

When Americans with low credit scores apply for secured cards, or credit building loans, it doesn't always end well for the borrower. When I first took charge of Capital One's secured card product, I was proud, believing that my work would help people who had fallen on hard times rebuild their credit scores and, in turn, their financial futures. Secured cards work the same way as other credit cards, except the borrower is required to put down a security deposit to open the card, usually, a security deposit equal to their entire credit limit. Only about 20 percent of secured card customers are ever able to get their security deposit refunded by their bank, unless they close their account.[11] For the consumer, this obviously isn't an ideal setup: once the consumer closes a credit card account, her credit score is likely to drop, at least if that secured card was her oldest open line of credit. Although secured cards are marketed as a way for consumers to build credit, as opposed to a way for consumers to borrow money, in any given month only about one in three secured card customers uses the secured card and then pays their secured card bill in full. The most common behavior is to carry a revolving balance on the secured card, paying an interest rate that is, in most cases, above 20 percent.[12]

My sense of pride quickly turned into a grim desperation realizing how many consumers put down a $200 deposit, to get a $200 credit limit, and then borrowed money against their own deposit at a 26.99 percent interest rate, often hit with late fees of up to $39. Across the industry, one in ten secured card customers misses their payment in any given month.[13] As a result, late fees are a major source of revenue for secured credit cards. Research by Larry Santucci of the Federal Reserve Bank of Philadelphia suggests that the median customer with a secured card sees only an eleven-point increase in their credit scores over a two-year time period, a number that reflects the fact that many secured card consumers can't keep up with the bill, and see their credit scores drop by sixty points or more.[14] The eleven-point increase in credit scores is especially disappointing when you consider the fact that Americans with a troubled credit history will often see a score improvement as older missed payments recede into history and eventually fall off their credit report. Companies and organizations that tout their credit building products or loans rarely present a counterfactual: what would have happened to a consumers' score if they *did nothing at all* but wait?

Undoubtedly, some people find secured cards to be useful. One of my former colleagues got a Capital One Secured Card shortly after he moved to Virginia from India. For a recent immigrant with a considerable income and little short-term need for liquidity, the secured card served its purpose rather nicely: he could easily rent cars, book hotel rooms, and build a credit history. By putting down a security deposit of several thousand dollars, he ensured he could travel without hitting his credit limit. If he had applied for an unsecured credit card, his limit would have been much lower. Critically though, the secured card was only more useful than an unsecured credit card because he really didn't need credit at all, at least not right away. Banks allow a few success stories to justify a greater number of more lucrative failures.

Many nonprofits, credit unions, and fintechs offer credit building loans, geared at helping Americans improve their credit score. Consumers of these products don't necessarily fare much better. In 2014, the CFPB conducted a study of credit building loans (CBLs), in partnership with a midwestern credit union that already offered this product. Most credit building loans have a similar structure: a bank, credit, or fintech gives an American with a low credit score a loan, but the loan is deposited into a locked savings account that the borrower isn't immediately allowed to access. The borrower is required to make a certain amount of payments, and it is only after those payments have already been made that the borrower gets access to the loan in escrow. Unlike a secured card, the borrower doesn't have to front any money upon account opening, but like with a secured card, the lender is not at a risk of loss unless the customer finds a way to commit fraud. By partnering with a credit union who already offered CBLs, the CFPB could assess the impact of the product on the types of consumers who naturally gravitate to it, or would otherwise have been recommended it by their credit union.

The study found that 40 percent of the CBL customers missed at least one CBL payment. Overall, the CBL appeared to have little or no effect on consumers' credit scores, even though it was beneficial for the borrowers who made all their payments on time: the net effect was zero, because so many people had a *decline* in their credit score. For the CBL customers who already had one or more existing loans—70 percent of the total—the researchers concluded that the CBL made them somewhat more likely to fall behind on those other payments, presumably because the CBL created a new monthly expense to juggle. For all this, the consumers were charged interest and fees of roughly $50 per customer.[15] Keep in mind that this is the price offered by a nonprofit credit union. The for-profit company *Self*, recommended by writers for *Forbes*, *Travel and Leisure*, and NerdWallet, charges $80 in interest and fees for their cheapest similar offering.[16] These types of products are no magic bullet.

It's not surprising that the American public is grasping for ways to build a system of credit that is more equitable and less costly. Changing how credit scores are constructed or creating products like secured cards and CBLs both appear promising on the surface, in part because the banks are eager proponents; they love the idea of having more data on each American in the country, and more products they can use to extract money from each consumer. Reforming how credit scores are constructed, though, won't change the basic fact that many Americans struggle to pay their bills, and ultimately default on their loans. And as we discussed in chapter 6, as banks have developed more innovative and sophisticated credit scoring methods, they haven't shared any of the dividends with consumers in the form of lower prices, in part because it's so difficult for Americans to measure the cost of credit or effectively comparison shop.

One proposal is to allow or require a greater range of companies to report payments to the credit bureaus—for example, landlords, utility companies, and cell phone providers. Under the current system, rental, utility, and cell phone accounts only appear if the consumer falls very far behind on the bill, and the company or landlord then sends their account to collections. Adding these sorts of noncredit accounts to credit reports would likely help the subset of people who always pay their rent and cell phone bill on time, but don't have any other types of debt.

Around the country though, utility companies report that the percentage of their low-income customers that pay bills late ranges from 17 percent in California to a whopping 75 percent in Washington, DC.[17] Many municipalities have laws stopping utility companies from shutting off customers' heat in the middle of winter: low-income customers often use that time to catch up on other bills, knowing both that they won't lose gas, and that, in most circumstances, those late payments won't be reported to the credit bureaus. There is no guarantee that adding extra forms of information to Americans' credit scores will make life easier for everyday people: however, it will make everyday people much easier for banks to surveil and monitor.

There is one important way, though, in which adding rental, utility, and cell phone data might help Americans avoid debt. A 2018 survey found that nearly one in four Americans who had carried a revolving balance on their credit card did so mistakenly believing that the revolving balance would improve their credit score.[18] Making it explicitly clear that there is a path to home ownership that doesn't involve credit cards or other non-mortgage debt payments could prevent some people from getting tangled up in dangerous products.

The Department of Housing and Urban Development estimates that there are roughly 10 million landlords in the United States,[19] roughly one thousand times the number of banks and credit unions combined. It is hard to imagine that all 10 million will ever accurately report rental payments. But researchers at HUD studied what would happen if rental payments were added to tenants' credit reports, by looking at the roughly ten thousand individuals living in public housing authority–owned buildings in Seattle, Louisville, and the Chicago-metro area. The consequences were mixed. Two separate credit scores were evaluated, FICO and Vantage.

HUD called these two scores "Score A" and "Score B," although to protect the proprietary credit score formulas, they didn't say which score was which. When rental data was added to credit reports of previously credit invisible or "invalid" credit score tenants, under Score A, 35 percent landed with a prime credit score, 35 percent with a near-prime credit score, and 29 percent with a subprime score. Under Score B, tenants fared worse: 17 percent landed with a prime credit score, 15 percent with a near-prime score, and 44 percent with a subprime score.[20]

And as Chi Chi Wu, a staff attorney at the National Consumer Law Center explained to Congress, "For some purposes, the lack of a credit history could be better than a negative history. Employment and insurance are two uses of credit report information where no history may be better than solely negative information, and where invisibility may be a benefit. For example, a number of state insurance laws are designed to ensure that a consumer with no credit score is not treated worse than someone with an average credit score."[21] Moreover, the low-income consumers who generally avoid credit are also the most likely to occasionally fall behind on other bills.

American journalists, bankers, and regulators have all seemingly bought into the potent mythology that many, many people are unsuccessfully chomping at the bit to gain access to credit, a problem that can allegedly only be solved through the development of more extensive apparatus to surveil and record each American's behavior. This narrative clearly serves the best interest of their banks, who would like us all to believe that their biggest shortcoming is that they do too little of a good thing, rather than too much of a bad thing. If the biggest problem with banks is that they don't lend enough, the path to solving America's economic woes may very well run through larger, more profitable, and less encumbered financial institutions. On the other hand, if the biggest problem with banks is that they lend too much, and at too high of a price, then America's ideal financial system would be much smaller and much less profitable.

9 Transformational Lending

What is debt for? It's a simple question, but it doesn't have an easy answer. Credit cards are elusive because they're used in many different ways. Doreen used her credit card to move to a town with cheaper rents, ultimately escaping a cycle of homelessness. Joe bought food and nice clothes and plane tickets to see his long-distance girlfriend. Michael bought records. Kathryn G. bought groceries and used the money to attend the weddings of close friends. Peggy bought a mattress and a cell phone. Madison bought a laptop that she needed for college. Some were purchases for survival, a few were purchases for opportunity, but most debtors and their purchases defy a simple categorization.

What happens if we recognize that debt sometimes acts as a safety net, but more often acts as an unanchored buoy, floating at sea? The borrower swims toward the buoy, but he may never reach it, no matter how hard he kicks, and his perception of the distance is always changing. A better life is often out of reach. On average, the most typical consequence of debt is that it equips Americans with some level of income to live as if their income were a few thousand dollars higher, in exchange for a much longer period of time of living as if their income were a few thousand dollars lower. We can acknowledge that some borrowers reach the buoy, that the buoy may even stop them from drowning, without losing sight of the full range of outcomes of debt, some positive, and many negative. Although I have focused this book on ways to better regulate credit in isolation from other changes to the economy, I should emphasize my own personal belief: that Americans can afford to, and morally ought to, build a system where nobody feels like they must turn to high priced credit to survive, through better policies around health care, childcare, housing, labor, basic income, unemployment insurance, and disability insurance. The recommendations on credit that I have offered, though, are those meant to still do more good than harm even if our social safety net remains weak.

As Rich Fairbank told investors on an earnings call in April 2021, "It is really striking that of all the asset classes, [the] one [that] really stands sort of unique in the industry is the one asset class that shrank since the start of the pandemic, and that's credit cards. And of course, that's because it is a discretionary spending and borrowing product." Suppose we take Fairbank at his word: that credit cards are primarily a *discretionary* borrowing product (knowing that there are hundreds of millions of debtors and, hence, millions or tens of millions of exceptions).[1] After all, Fairbank has access to the data that shows exactly at which specific merchants credit card revolvers accrued their debt. Much of the data I have shared in this book supports his claim: Americans borrow more when they are feeling *less* stressed financially and avoid borrowing as much as possible when under stronger financial pressure. His claim, if true, is proof that we do not need to passively accept the inequality that the debt machine creates— it is at our discretion.

While credit card debt dipped during the COVID-19 recession, as of April 2021, Brian Doubles, the CEO of Synchrony Bank, which issues many retail credit cards in partnership with brands like Gap, Lowe's, Verizon, and Citgo, was certain that debt would once again begin its upward climb. "You're going to start to see that pretty soon as the confidence gets better, you tend to see consumers take on more debt and revolve a little bit more, which will help on balances and margins as well," he said.[2]

The debates about the purpose of credit have a long history. Some Victorians tried to reign in the "salary buying" or loan sharking industry because they worried that workers were just borrowing money to get drunk, while other Victorians tried to reign in the loan sharking industry because they thought that access to *cheaper* loans was vital to the well-being of the working poor (the Victorians who supported the loan sharking industry didn't leave an extensive written record behind). Loans for consumption became fashionable and respectable when the American middle class started using them to outfit their homes with critical status icons and functional items—pianos, encyclopedias, sewing machines, furniture, and appliances—but there were always spoilsports around to declare these purchases to be wasteful.

When we situate our current moment in the broader arc of American history, we see a set of debates that have repeated, for centuries, along somewhat familiar political, economic, and religious lines, about the purpose and morality of lending. But in a few critical ways, our current moment is different. The last several decades, by which I mean the years since the First Debt Boom began, are different than the preceding years because the American working class can no longer count on predictably rising wages. As a result, high costs of borrowing, whether for survival or for enjoyment, aren't absorbed by rising incomes in the way that they once were. The gap in power, money, and data between lenders and borrowers has never been greater: while per-capita, inflation-adjusted debt levels may have been a bit higher before the Great Recession than they are today, credit card industry profits have reached their peak. And ten years after the passage of the CARD Act, the most important legislation ever written about credit cards, which eliminated so many of the obvious tricks and gotchas, it should now be completely clear that the problem with the debt machine was never a few bugs in the system. It was the system itself.

Before I say goodbye, I want to take a second look at the definition of the debt machine: the system of parts that transmits wealth from ordinary American families to bank shareholders, bank managers, and to a lesser extent, bank savers. The managers of banks and credit card companies choose the interest rates, fees, marketing strategies, litigation tactics, and credit lines of credit cards, or they choose the algorithms that will choose these features, and, in doing so, they imbue their own values and goals into their company's plan of action, reflecting their attitudes about who matters and what matters. Perhaps most importantly, they set the constraints along which the algorithms will optimize, and which set of possibilities are considered ethically or practically out of bounds, and they choose the objective function of the algorithms: what, exactly, will be max-imized. The bank shareholders reap the profits, and importantly, large shareholders and investment managers create the climate where manag-ers know that their jobs are only safe as long as Americans' debt burdens and credit card interest rates continue to rise. The payment companies, like Visa and Mastercard, not only maintain the infrastructure of the debt machine, but they also lobby against changes to the debt machine as seemingly disinterested intermediaries.

The debt machine is powered by legislators and regulators, some lib-eral, some conservative, who have absorbed arguments put forward by the banks, even if they consider themselves critics of Wall Street. These argu-ments include the following, and many others: "Banks are too unwilling to lend"; "No American should be credit invisible"; "It is too hard to get access to credit"; "We should help Americans improve their FICO scores." There are shreds of truth in every one of these arguments, but they each miss a fundamental point. Many of these talking points have been repeated since the 1970s, an era when loan interest rates were relatively low, infla-tion was high, and lending margins were slim. In that environment, many people were shut out of the system of credit, sometimes for reasons of profit, and sometimes for reasons of bias. Banks no longer solicit deposits from consumers they'd never lend to. Instead, they lend to consumers but won't offer the same consumers free checking accounts without high min-imum balance requirements or punitive overdraft policies. Americans have ready access to credit, even immediately after a bankruptcy, even when they already have a large amount of high-interest debt, and even when they're falling behind on their existing payments. It is too hard to get access to *good* credit. Americans need better pathways to affordable housing, including better pathways to homeownership for those who'd like to put down roots. Meanwhile, there is little evidence that Americans need a greater variety of options for short-term credit at high interest rates. Banks are highly willing to lend when there is no constraint on the prices they can charge: the risk today isn't that they lend too little; it is that they lend too much. Expanding the system of financial surveillance to encompass more Americans is unlikely to improve the cost of credit for ordinary people, because, as discussed, credit card companies have signifi-cant market power. When the price of crude oil falls, Americans pay less at the gas station, but when the cost of lending falls, the interest rates Americans pay continue to rise. Because Americans can't effectively comparison shop for credit, banks don't "share" the gains associated with better technology or better credit scoring data with consumers by lowering their rates. Legislators, regulators, and advocacy groups must abandon their focus on raising consumers' credit scores, reducing the number of Americans without a credit score, and changing how credit scores are calculated: the fact that banks don't fight them on this issue should be all the proof that is required that they're fighting the wrong battle. The path to prosperity for the working class and middle class will not be a win-win for everyday people, or for the biggest existing banks and market participants: it will be a win-lose. Anything the banks are willing to compromise on will represent at best a minor improvement for the American public. Luckily, in a democracy, banks are not *supposed* to call all the shots. Instead, legislators and regulators must regroup and redouble their efforts to lower the price of credit, and curtail the strategies that banks use to induce unwanted debts.

And what about fintechs, aspiring entrepreneurs, community banks, and credit unions? For the last two decades, when new competitors have entered the market, their main contribution has been to simply *add* to the total amount of debt Americans carry, rather than helping Americans find better deals or to achieve financial stability. This isn't necessarily the fintechs' fault: it is a byproduct of a system where consumers have a hard time making specific choices about the amount of money they'd like to borrow, and very often they end up borrowing exactly as much money as is made available to them, regardless of the long-term consequences. While we've seen some limited successful examples of fintechs lowering the cost of credit for consumers, it hasn't been enough to change the basic shape of the market, enough to slow the rise of credit card debt, or enough to force credit card companies to lower their rates.

In January 2021, speaking to investors, Roger Hochschild, the CEO of Discover said, "in my decades in this business, there's always something that's going to kill off credit cards. But so far, the growth trajectory of the industry remains solid."[3]

Congress could unleash the power of credit unions to fully support the American public by eliminating the rules that require them to have limited membership criteria. Bank lobbyists assert that large credit unions, even at their current scale, don't deserve to be considered non-profits or to be tax exempt, and they shouldn't be allowed to grow to serve a nationwide, unrestricted audience. They say that very large credit unions have an unfair advantage when it comes to competing against banks, because they're tax-exempt. But who cares if profit-seeking banks can't compete successfully against credit unions, as long as credit unions continue to offer lower prices to American consumers? As I researched this book, and researched the credit union movement in the United States for articles for *Forbes.com* and *The Outline,* I came across many types of credit unions, and many types of credit union leaders. Some credit union leaders are visionary community activists; others are former bankers who continue to align themselves, politically and philosophically, with their former employers, rather than fully advocating for the credit union member–owners who pay their paychecks. Many fall somewhere in between. I don't currently believe that this problem necessarily can or should be fixed by legislation, nor do I think this problem is sufficient justification for Congress to continue to thwart credit unions. But I hope that credit union boards and credit union members will think more carefully about how to create pathways for tellers and other branch employees, or other community members, to become credit union managers and executives, rather than recruiting so heavily from banks.

Congress could also empower credit unions, community banks, and consumers by establishing a simple comparison-shopping portal for credit cards, so every American could see the absolute lowest prices that any financial institution is willing to charge them to carry their debt; this move could save American families a significant amount of money, and would benefit the financial institutions who focus on offering reasonable prices, rather than spending huge amounts of money on direct mail solicitations.

Fintechs and aspiring entrepreneurs must take a clear-eyed approach to their business and their social impact. Many successful fintechs are highly implicated in the debt machine. Consider, for example, Credit Karma, the website that offers credit score monitoring and other financial services to roughly 100 million customers.[4] One of Credit Karma's largest investors was Nigel Morris, the Capital One cofounder whose venture capital firm, QED Investors, led Credit Karma's Series A round of funding. As Stacy

Wakefield, Credit Karma's director of affiliate marketing explained on a podcast in 2012, "Credit cards are a huge industry and people are constantly searching for new credit cards and looking for ways to compare credit cards. And at Credit Karma, the main offer that we give to our users is credit cards." Stacy added, "Because we do so well monetizing Credit Karma with credit cards, we have great relationships with all the major card issuers. We work with Chase, Capital One, Citi, Discover, and Amex, those big five and some other smaller issuers, that we have decided that it makes sense for us to take the way that we display credit cards and offer that to other credit card comparison sites or credit card domains."[5] It is rare to find a US-based fintech that is not substantially funded by either QED Investors, Citi, Goldman Sachs, Capital One Ventures, JPMorgan Chase, Fenway Summer, the venture capital firm founded by Raj Date, or the Financial Health Network, a nonprofit that receives donations almost exclusively from America's largest banks and insurance companies. What looks like fierce competition between fintechs and banks is closer to peaceful coexistence, with fintechs generally carving out niches that support, rather than challenge, the dominance of their funders—for example, by becoming vendors to banks or advertisers for banks.

Too many fintechs justify outrageous pricing by making false claims about the availability of credit in the United States. Take, for example, Sasha Orloff, the founder of LendUp, a company that markets itself as "a better alternative to payday loans," funded by QED Investors, along with Google Ventures and other venture capital firms. LendUp offers short-term loans with interest rates up to 458 percent.[6] Arguing for the importance of LendUp, Orloff wrote on the Google Ventures Medium blog, "A full 56 percent of Americans—more than half!—can't get access to traditional banks because their credit score is too low. Instead, their options are limited to payday loans, title loans, and other dangerous products." He linked to an article from the Corporation for Enterprise Development, stating that 56 percent of Americans have a credit score under 700. The problem with his interpretation is that consumers with credit scores under 700 get approved for credit cards and bank loans every day: 80 percent of consumers with a credit score between 620 and 659 have at least one credit card, as do 60 percent of consumers with a credit score between 580 and 619. Orloff effectively overstated the percentage of

Americans without access to formal bank credit by roughly twofold, perhaps more.[7] You could argue that I am mincing hairs—after all, if one-quarter of Americans lack access to bank credit, isn't that also a problem? Perhaps, but Orloff's error reflects a common and critical bias among fintech founders, investors, and managers: the assumption that there is a massive undersupply of credit in the United States, and, therefore, offering more high-priced credit is socially beneficial.

Fintechs and their investors must ask themselves the following questions.

One: "Are my company's loans helping my customer *avoid* other types of debt, or are my company's loans generally *increasing* a consumer's total debt burden?" Raising a consumer's total debt burden isn't *intrinsically* a sign that a business is harmful. After all, if you were lending to consumers who truly had no other opportunities to access credit, their debt burden would logically increase after your loan. This situation is the exception, not the norm, because very few Americans lack access to credit in America today. A corollary to this question is, "Did my loan cause my customer to borrow when she otherwise would have avoided debt?" For credit limit increases, and other types of loans that aren't initiated by a customer, this question is especially important.

Two: "What evidence do I have that I am offering my product at a lower cost than a consumer's other available options?" The baseline point of comparison here shouldn't necessarily be payday loans, because even subprime consumers often *do* have credit card access. Lenders cannot safely assume that just because a borrower chose their loan, that their loan was their best or cheapest option. The more a lender spends on marketing, the more questionable the assumption becomes. Of course, marketing isn't intrinsically unethical: if a consumer never finds out about a valuable product, it's effectively as if the product didn't exist. But where cheaper options *do* exist and they're simply not visible to consumer, entrepreneurs should be highly skeptical about the extent to which they are acting in their consumers' best interests.

Three: "What would happen if all the predictions my company made about a consumer were shared with the consumer?" It is common practice, not only in the financial sector, but across many other parts of the economy (especially in subscription-based businesses, like streaming services, gym memberships, software and apps) to calculate an expected lifetime profit for each individual customer or type of customer. This practice is morally neutral on the surface, and these predictions aren't always very interesting. Take the example of a streaming music service like Spotify: their predicted lifetime value for a specific consumer with a paid subscription might just be equal to the consumer's monthly rate, multiplied by how many months the consumer is likely to use the service before canceling, minus expenses like the royalty payments made to musicians. The predictions made by banks and lenders are far more informative: they tell the story about how any given American's financial life is most likely to unfold, and what percentage of a consumer's lifetime wealth will ultimately be diverted to line the pockets of bank executives. This total cost, the dollars and cents a consumer loses to interest and fees, is rarely foreseeable by any given American, who has no way of predicting all the levers the bank will pull, or how the presence of the credit card (or other type of fintech product) will shape how they spend money. But this data is known by the lender. When one party in a deal knows *so much more* than the other party in a deal, the transaction, at best, skirts the line between honest and deceptive, ethical and unethical: in practice, withholding all these predictions you have made about a customer, predictions that clearly could influence whether she wants to buy the product, is not so different from selling a car you know has a faulty part, and doing so not just one time, but millions of times.

Because we are all prone to wishful thinking and to justifying our own behavior, I would encourage each fintech to try to assemble the strongest possible argument *against* the ethics of their business model based on their available data, not necessarily because the pessimistic argument is the correct one, but to avoid cherry-picking evidence to suit the story they wish to be true—that they are not only making money, but also making a difference.

"Buy now, pay later" (BNPL) lenders like Afterpay, Affirm, and Klarna increasingly make headlines, especially after Affirm's eyepopping IPO in 2021, which catapulted the company to a valuation of $24 billion, a giant multiple of Affirm's 2020 revenue of $510 million. Afterpay, Affirm, Klarna, and their competitors give shoppers, usually online shoppers, the ability to make purchases by getting approved for an installment loan, integrated into the checkout processes. These lenders usually offer the type of transparent pricing that I celebrate in this book, the type of easy-to-understand loans that were popular before the credit card was introduced. Interest rates are often similar or lower to credit card interest rates. Some of these loans don't charge interest at all and are paid for exclusively by the merchant. Overall, I think BNPL products are a bit better than credit cards. But they share the same basic risk as other types of installment loans. So far, it appears as if consumers aren't choosing BNPL loans *instead of* getting into credit card debt, but rather *in addition to* getting into credit card debt—or simply using these loans, which are sometimes offered at a 0 percent interest rate, to spread out the cost of large purchases like Peloton bikes over multiple months instead of paying up front. Even if the consumer saves money on that purchase by using a BNPL loan instead of her credit card, that substitution frees up credit card liquidity that history shows us will likely be used elsewhere. The extraordinary investor optimism around BNPL seems to be rooted in the assumption that most or all borrowing is to make large purchases, like buying furniture or plane tickets. But most credit card borrowing is for ordinary daily purchases, and, as a result, BNPL does not have an easy answer for displacing the credit card debt Americans accrue on ordinary daily purchases. There's still room to create a product that truly combines the transparency of installment loans with the versatility of credit cards; many talented people are working on this problem specifically. The hardest challenges here won't be technical or creative, but political and economic: even once the lending alternatives are vastly superior, it will be hard to displace the credit card goliaths.

There are a few bright spots: I am especially inspired by nonprofit fintechs like finEQUITY and Onward Financial. Brooklyn-based finEQUITY offers credit-building loans and credit education to Americans who have experienced long-term incarceration, while Onward, in Washington, DC, helps small- and medium-sized businesses set up emergency savings accounts for their workers, to reduce the likelihood a worker will need to rely on high-priced credit. (Both aspire to build outward from their successes in these areas.) I would encourage any entrepreneurs who are truly committed to creating positive change to follow in the footsteps of finEQUITY founder Briane Cornish and Onward founder Ronnie Washington. As nonprofits, finEQUITY and Onward have less access to the capital that might allow a for-profit company to scale quickly, but Briane and Ronnie's teams are building products that truly put the American public first. Being a nonprofit doesn't mean a start-up must rely exclusively on donor funding—for example, Onward collects subscription fees from the employers who want to offer the emergency savings accounts to their employees. A typical start-up has only three possible end states: failure, acquisition by another company, or an IPO or initial public offering, the process by which a start-up becomes a publicly traded corporation. None of these exit paths can protect an ethical, socially conscious business strategy: once a corporation goes public, it can't choose which investors purchase its stock and become its owners. Even if founders commit themselves to doing things "differently" than other companies by seeking B-Corp status, a designation to indicate that the company plans to pursue a social or environmental goal in addition to profit, once the company is public, new investors can force the company to abandon B-Corp status and put profits over people.[8]

If you're a middle-class or upper-middle-class reader without any credit card debt, you might read this list and think, "Well, I'm not a banker, I'm not a politician, I don't work for Visa. I am not implicated in this system."

But you are! Or, more specifically, you are if you're a "convenience user" of a credit cards who pays their bill in full each month, and you are if you've got any savings in the bank or in a retirement account. I don't bring this up to make you feel guilty, but rather to show how all the pieces of the machine are connected. The credit card rewards earned by Americans with good credit scores and no debt are paid for by the higher prices all Americans must pay for their gas, groceries, clothing, and medicine to finance the system. And it is important to understand how the debt machine is funded. The money lent out in the form of credit card debt comes from many places. It comes from the money Americans put in their checking accounts, savings accounts, and money market accounts. According to a careful study conducted by economists Atif Mian, Ludwig Straub, and Amir Sufi, as the rich have gotten richer in the United States, their extra money hasn't gone to start new companies or to conduct research into new technologies: it has been lent out to America's poor and middle class. Although the top 1 percent has vastly more wealth than middle-class savers, the same phenomenon is true for them as well—their savings are used to fuel the indebtedness of the poor. As a result, the more affluent Americans are able to save, the more aggressive banks will be in tempting poor Americans to borrow: history shows that the banks won't let this money sit idle and would rather lend it at a high price to consumers than at a low price to other businesses.

Too many politicians falsely believe that credit card debt and consumer borrowing are needed to keep the economy humming. But what Mian, Straub, and Sufi's research shows is that the rise of the debt machine is strangling innovation and growth: lending to the poor creates predictably higher returns than nearly any other investment, including the investments in research, technology, and infrastructure that would be most likely to create new jobs and grow the economy. The debt machine is a critical piece of the puzzle of inequality: as the rich get richer from lending to the poor, the poor get poorer by turning over their paychecks as interest and fees. Part of the problem that Mian, Straub, and Sufi identify is the fact that non-bank companies hold an increasingly high percentage of *their* balance sheets in the form of bank assets that are turned into consumer debt. In other words, if you own *any* stock, even if it's in a business that appears to have nothing to do with credit card debt, the odds are good that your investment is fueling the debt machine.[9]

Part of the problem is that ordinary Americans have no *choice* but to fuel the debt machine if they ever want to retire. All the standard advice about the percentage of paychecks that Americans should save for retirement assumes that Americans invest all of their retirement savings. The debt machine pits neighbors against one another: millions of Americans have the chance to retire with dignity *specifically because* other Americans are stripped of their last pennies. It's not only the super-rich who are implicated: it's also the ordinary teachers, firefighters, and other public employees lucky enough to receive pensions, which are often invested in predatory lending schemes.[10]

I also wrote this book for the consumers and workers who are in debt: the people trapped in the debt machine's gears. The current system was not designed by workers and consumers, nor was it designed to benefit workers and consumers. I wrote this book for the millions of Americans around the country who uplift their communities in ways big and small but who nevertheless get ground down, by employers who underpay them, by banks that keep jacking up prices, and by a government that doesn't have their back. I wish I could offer magic words every American could use to ensure they would never need to rely on high-priced credit, and that they would always get a fair deal: the truth is that many people struggle, and would have struggled regardless of any individual choices they made. If you're in debt or are wondering how to build credit, you might find Appendix B helpful, where I have tried to compile my most useful tips, although their value is limited in the context of our broken system.

As Chrystin Ondersma, professor of law at Rutgers writes, "Black and other marginalized individuals and communities are being dispossessed of wealth and income, and debt is the mechanism of this dispossession. Those in power, even if not actively in favor of this result, are in fact accepting an economic system that is wholly dependent on keeping much of its population, particularly the most marginalized, trapped in inescapable indebtedness."[11]

For decades, banks have run tens of thousands of experiments on the American public, without our consent and without our awareness, tinkering with hundreds of variables to figure out what induces the greatest amount of borrowing. Undoubtedly, there will always be some people who want or need to borrow money. The more salient question is how much debt Americans could avoid if every American understood the true and total cost of credit cards at the time they made purchases, if credit cards were stripped of their unnecessary and confusing (though superficially attractive) bells and whistles, and if banks were banned from raising customers' credit limits without their consent. My educated guess is that these three changes would reduce the amount of credit card debt in the United States by more than half.

The technologies and algorithms of the debt machine are not neutral: they are conceptualized and built by specific people, at specific organizations, with specific goals. We can't evaluate the choices Americans make as if they are acting in a vacuum. We must evaluate the choices with an awareness that the financial sector has spent billions of dollars to influence and alter their course.

Sometimes, I imagine myself, and every other human, exploring a beautiful mountain range. Even if we are free to walk anywhere on the mountain range, many of us will be inclined to walk where we see signposts and established paths. The debt machine has built our existing paths—for many Americans, these paths lead to a lifetime of instability, with the final years of one's life spent working thanklessly at a low-wage job while their health deteriorates, or confronting poverty. We must build new paths.

I have written about the credit card industry because that is what I know. It is a world I have immersed myself in for the last eight years, picking it apart and thinking about every component. And I have written about the credit card industry because, despite the relative lack of media and political attention that it has received over the last ten years, it is a major part of the economic lives of many Americans.

But I hope my own experience working at Capital One might provide some insight into how capitalism, more generally, is conducted in our era of acute inequality. In the decades after Capital One was founded, the two pillars of its strategy—mass experimentation on human subjects, and optimization through machine learning—would come to define many other industries. Perhaps the only thing that makes the consumer financial sector truly different from other parts of the economy, like retail, food service and delivery, or transportation, is that those sectors have mostly used the tools of Capitalism 2.0 to squeeze their workers, to the benefit of shareholders and customers. By contrast, the consumer financial sector, operating in a market where Americans find comparison shopping nearly impossible, has learned to mostly squeeze their customers, to the benefit of their shareholders and managers.

I have read a lot of "business books," the types written by current or former executives of "hot" companies, and for the most part, the only significant ethical quandary they describe is the question of whether or not to lay off employees when a business is struggling or pivoting in a different direction. None seemed to describe the confusion I often felt. I grew up in a middle-class home, where I was taught to seek stability in a job, not the chance to make a difference. My parents, whom I love dearly, and who I also think are extremely smart, didn't exactly encourage me to find a career I enjoyed, and, in fact, my dad often emphasized that nobody *really* likes their jobs. After all, the things that people really *enjoy* doing they will usually do for free. Jobs were places where you would do something that somebody else needed you to do, get paid, and leave. If you were lucky enough to have access to a good education, and wise enough to take advantage of it, the daily tasks at least wouldn't be demeaning or physically demanding. When I got to college, many of my classmates had wild ambitions, some selfish, and some altruistic. At a college like Duke, you were told you would and could change the world. There *were* plenty of opportunities to change the world at Capital One, tinkering with the rules that touched millions of customers. We had too much power and not enough wisdom. I felt ashamed and disoriented but also grateful— grateful to have won the lottery, grateful to have been chosen, grateful that my coworkers were nice to me, grateful for all the free lunches I ate, and for the free personal training sessions at the gym, grateful to be one of the people tinkering with the levers.

Part of my ambivalence came from the fact that nearly every component of Capital One's credit card business practices that felt wrong to me appeared to be in use by every other large credit card issuer (or, I assumed, for practices that were a bit more buried beneath the surface, that the other banks would be happy to employ the practices if they were clever enough to figure them out). And I could always point to a few very bad things that other credit card issuers did that Capital One didn't do. Namely, we did not cheat customers out of their credit card rewards through an impossible array of gotchas, nor did we engage in the practice called retroactive interest, described in chapter 4, except in a credit card portfolio that Capital One bought from HSBC and then sold to Citi almost immediately. Capital One, of course, did much more subprime lending than the other banks, but internally this was always framed in a positive light: Capital One was the only major bank willing to give so many Americans a chance with credit. The fact that all the questionable practices we engaged in were done by every other bank, and were legal, provided some of my coworkers a seemingly infinite amount of ethical comfort.

Should we have felt guilty? Should I feel guilty? In a sense, yes, but I have also found some clarity and comfort in reading Marx, who writes, "I do not by any means depict the capitalist and the landowner in rosy colors. But individuals are dealt with here only insofar as they are the personifications of economic categories, the bearers of class relations and interests. My standpoint, from which the development of the economic formation of the society is viewed as a process of natural history, can less than any other make the individual responsible for the relations whose creature he remains, socially speaking, however much he may subjectively raise himself above them."[12] In other words, the problems of debt are systemic. When I left Capital One, somebody else took my place. We may make individual decisions, but the system can always replace us. As of 2019, nearly 2 million people work for banks, many in low-paying customer jobs, and that number is expected to keep growing. What makes the debt machine a bit different though from other systems of oppression is that much of it was built during my lifetime, by people who are still around.

Competition and innovation cannot solve the basic problems of consumer debt. Companies engaging in predatory business practices earn the outsized profits needed to have a dominant advantage in marketing, something particularly important for maintaining market share in the segment where consumers need to hear they've been preapproved before they're willing to apply. Expensive products with rewards and hidden fees very frequently appear to be a better value than substantially less expensive, simpler products, particularly because consumers are poorly equipped to understand and compare true and total borrowing costs. When Americans can't effectively comparison shop on price, none of the lenders have a reason to bother competing on price, and the most typical byproduct of innovation is just to increase the returns for investors. Congress and the CFPB should focus less on encouraging "innovation," and focus more on reining in predatory practices and establishing a marketplace where the true and total costs of borrowing become obvious to Americans before they get into debt.

I have tried to imagine a system of credit in which every loan granted made the borrower's life better. As described herein, a high proportion of all credit card debt is accrued through credit limit increases, and I think banks and credit unions who wish to behave ethically need to start by examining their credit limit increase programs. It is a clear abrogation of ethical responsibility to offer more credit to people if any close examination of their circumstances would reveal that they are already deeply struggling with their level of debt. If banks were to look at their role in America's debt crisis honestly, they would frankly assess how often they raise the credit limits of Americans who very clearly find available credit to be an irresistible temptation—the high proportion of their customers who use, nearly immediately, the majority of credit they've been granted, every time they're granted more. It would not be paternalistic to, for example, *ask* those deeply in debt if they actually want more credit.

As I finish writing the conclusion to this book, I have little idea what I'll do next. My need to explain the rottenness at the core of the credit card industry and the pathway to building a more equitable financial system has organized my every choice over the last several years, and now I have said my bit. And so, I am faced with the same dilemma as so many other young people: nearly every company where I could work seems more than a little bit evil, even those companies that deliver important goods and services.

I think I have reached some important answers about the nature of consumer debt in the twenty-first century. I don't feel like I have reached a satisfactory answer about how an American can earn a living and, simultaneously, feel at peace with the consequences of one's actions upon the world. We each have some degree of responsibility for the choices we make, but when we live in a system based on greed, opportunism, and exploitation, rather than a system rooted in solidarity and compassion, there are no easy answers for any given individual in isolation. I am sure more than a few people will read this book (or, at least, read a summary of this book) and conclude that I am an enormous hypocrite for having profited for five years from the system of exploitation described herein. And let me just say, those critiques are absolutely correct: I am, ethically, *delinquent,* too.

Acknowledgments

This book would not have been possible without the intellectual, emotional, and practical assistance I receive daily from my girlfriend, Deborah Shapiro, who I love very dearly. Not many writers are lucky enough to live with an archivist cum former copy editor, especially not an archivist cum former copy editor who is so dazzling and delightful to be around.

The regular encouragement and substantive feedback of my friend Carrie Mills was, likewise, essential. I'd also like to thank my friend Sam for helping me recognize that my particular attachments and sense of obligation to my colleagues were not good reasons to continue to work in the credit card industry.

I owe a huge debt of gratitude to Ashwin Vasan and Rachel Schneider for their generosity in providing early feedback on this project. Rachel Schneider and Cathy O'Neil also deserve words of thanks for giving me advice on how to write a book, and, critically, for warning me that it would be very difficult. Thank you to Terri Friedline for incisive feedback at a critical stage in the project.

Thank you to those who helped to bring this book to life: Naomi Schneider, Summer Farah, Lynda Crawford, and Francisco Reinking. Thank you to those who provided anonymous reviews of the manuscript.

I had very little exposure to the craft or business of writing two years ago, and accordingly, I'd like to thank two other editors in particular, Torie Bosch from *Slate* and s.e. smith from *TalkPoverty,* for encouragement, thoughtful edits, and guidance as I transitioned out of banking into journalism.

Thank you to Moritz Schularick and Alina Bartscher for their assistance using the "SCF+" dataset. The Schularick team did tremendous work to clarify the picture of consumer debt over time, by reconciling disjoint surveys and datasets. I benefited immensely from their efforts, and from Alina Bartscher's generosity in guiding me through the data. Thank you to Serdark Ozkan, Zachary Bethune, Mary Zaki, and Scott Schuh for the helpful clarifications they provided on their research.

I'd like to thank my many former colleagues at Capital One who shared their wisdom and treated me every day with kindness, especially those colleagues who use their positions of influence to improve outcomes for consumers. Some people will no doubt read *Delinquent* as an indictment of the corporation and its employees, which is not and has never been my intent. Although we must all be accountable for the choices we make, my sharpest critiques are meant for the broader economic system in which we all participate. While I have my own suspicions and biases on the matter, I cannot say with any certainty whether it is better to challenge flawed institutions from the outside or improve them from the inside. I do believe either can be done to the benefit of the world at large. I won't list the individual colleagues to whom I am most grateful by name, but I hope they read this paragraph knowing that I continue to humbly appreciate them and value their friendship and keen intellects.

Thank you to the many people I interviewed for this book, particularly to Kathleen, Peggy, Kathryn R., Kathryn G., Tasha, Michael, Rachel, Joe, Naomi, Alisha, and Doreen Traylor, for being so generous with their time and for sharing their perspectives. I'd also like to thank my cousin Stephanie, and my friends Elise, Chelsea, and Katie F. for connecting me with interviewees, travel companions Kat Zhang and Katie Kuzin, along with the many friends and family who hosted me while I traveled to do research for this book.

Finally, to my parents: thank you for all your love and support.

APPENDIX A About My Research Process

During my time working in the credit card industry, I came to understand a lot about how credit cards impacted their borrowers, predominantly through looking at data and learning about industry practices. I nevertheless understood that I didn't have a full picture. Although the recommendations found in this book are my own (the political opinions of my interviewees varied, including their opinions about financial regulation), it was nevertheless important to me that my recommended path forward be shaped *in dialogue* with American debtors.

I have included this section so that readers can assess for themselves how much trust to place in the conclusions I have drawn from interviewing Americans about their credit card debt. I believe there are strengths and weaknesses to the approach I took to conducting interviews, but, of course, these interviews are not the sole source of information I used to draw the conclusions you've read. This discussion pertains only to the interviews I conducted of people related to their experiences as borrowers and consumers, not interviews I conducted of current or former employees of the financial sector.

I considered three approaches to conducting the interviews found in this book: the approach of a "market researcher" or "user researcher"; the approach of a journalist; or the approach of an academic. Each of these three approaches comes with a unique set of norms, procedures, and attitudes. For example, in journalism, it is generally considered inappropriate to offer compensation to one's subjects, while offering compensation to interview subjects is commonplace in academic research and in market research. Qualitative academic research often makes use of a set interview protocol (e.g., using a fixed list of questions in one's interviews), takes care to collect key pieces of demographic data about interviewees, and often considers methods for how to standardize and compile responses to draw conclusions. This approach can aid in assessing whether the interviewees were representative of a target population and ease the process of drawing specific conclusions about key subgroups. Journalists rarely stick to a strict script with their interview subjects and focus more on what can be learned through a narrative process. I ultimately chose to approach the work through the lens of a journalist, in part because when I began this project, before having a signed book contract, I thought I might create one or more magazine-style articles based on my findings rather than a book. Accordingly, I did not pay any of my interview subjects, although after conducting the interview with Doreen Traylor, who is mentioned in chapter 3, I chose to subscribe to her Patreon.

My goal in conducting my interviews was to make sure I heard from a wide cross-section of American debtors. I did not expect that I could achieve a fully representative sample, but I did believe I could reach my goal of making sure no common debt experiences were missing from my sample. Accordingly, I identified a list of subgroups from which I wanted to conduct interviews. I achieved my goal of interviewing two or more people with credit card debt or who had past credit card debt from the following groups: Americans with and without a college education, Black Americans, White Americans, Latinx Americans, low-wage workers (those earning under $15 per hour), middle-income Americans, and high-income Americans (those with a household income above $100,000), those credit card debtors who had also had payday loans, those who had charged off on a debt without declaring bankruptcy, those who had declared bankruptcy, parents, Americans with disabilities, those who had experienced homelessness, those with relatively low-peak credit card balances (under $5,000), and those with high-peak credit card balances (over $25,000). I did not succeed at my goal of interviewing multiple people who attributed their debt specifically to medical emergencies.

Every interviewee was told that I was asking them questions in order to do research for a book about debt, although the bulk of interviews were conducted before reaching a publication agreement with the University of California Press. Some interviewees agreed that I could use their first and last names, and, in other cases, they asked me to only use their first name, so for consistency, I have only used first names or, when needed, first name and last initial.

I found interview subjects in four ways: through "person on the street" interviews, through my personal network, through other reporting projects, and online. I'll discuss the strengths and weaknesses of each approach.

I conducted "person on the street" interviews in Hamtramck, Michigan (an enclave of Detroit); Chicago, Illinois; St. Paul, Minnesota; Council Bluffs, Iowa; Seattle, Washington; Scottsdale, Arizona; Albuquerque, New Mexico; Houston, Texas; New Orleans, Louisiana; and Meridian, Mississippi. For these interviews,

I approached passersby and identified myself as a journalist working on a book about Americans experiences with debt. For those willing to talk, I always started with the same first question: "If you could change one thing about banks, lenders, or credit card companies, what would it be?" My second question, if the person was open to talking more, but the first question didn't generate natural follow-up questions was, "Do you think banks make it too easy to get into debt, or too hard for people to get credit?" Many conversations were relatively brief, under five minutes, but still informative in the sense that the interviewee provided basic information about their experiences borrowing money, and a high-level of assessment of whether or not they were glad they had borrowed the money, along with their opinions of lenders. A few of these conversations were much longer. In most cities, I targeted urban or peri-urban areas with foot traffic, although in Houston (not a particularly walkable city!) I also conducted these interviews on the campus of Houston Community College. One concern I had at the outset of the project was that I would talk disproportionately to people who had extreme experiences with debt, leading them to have very positive or negative attitudes towards lenders—my "person on the street" interviews were an important corrective to this risk. Forty of my sixty-two total interviews were "person on the street" interviews. One disadvantage of these interviews was that I did not always collect a full suite of demographic information from these interviewees (although I was struck by the generosity of spirit of so many people I talked to, but there are limits to how much people want to share with a stranger on the street with an audio recorder who is not affiliated with a specific publication or academic institution).

Some of my interviewees were friends or were introduced to me by friends or family members. These interviewees included Joe in Washington, DC; Kathryn R. in Washington DC; Kathryn G. in Sacramento, California; Peggy in St. Charles, Missouri; Tasha in Milwaukee; and Rachel in Orange County, California. These interviewees were generous enough to allow me to ask questions about all their debt experiences over the course of their lives, and these subjects provided the richest social and psychological insights about their own stories. These interviews were all conducted in person, with the exception of my interview with Rachel who I interviewed by phone. Michael, Tasha's husband, wrote me a letter explaining his own experiences with debt and credit, focusing on credit events prior to marrying Tasha. This group was socioeconomically and geographically diverse, with household incomes ranging from under $40,000 to over $100,000, but all these interviewees were White, and the majority were female. This group also tended to have more extreme experiences with debt (three subjects had more than $20,000 in credit card debt; one had a credit card chargeoff; and one had a bankruptcy). When you tell people in your social network that you'd like to interview folks about their experiences with credit card debt, you will disproportionately be introduced to those with large amounts of debt, rather than small amounts.

Since 2018, I have also conducted interviews about economic issues more generally, writing articles for various online publications about matters like childcare subsidies in Iowa, Hurricane Harvey recovery, and the economic experiences of first-generation college graduates. I always asked these interview subjects about their credit card debt and other types of consumer debt because it was always relevant to whatever other topic I was reporting on. These interviews gave me a deeper understanding of specific experiences—for example, surviving and rebuilding after a natural disaster.

Finally, I found four additional research subjects online: Doreen, Alisha, Rick, and Naomi. I regularly searched on Twitter for people who had written recent tweets about their own credit card debt (people often turn to social media to commemorate that they have paid off their credit card debt). I only contacted those whose online identity included a first name, last name, and US-based location. I did not take any steps to independently verify the identities of the people I interviewed in this fashion other than a basic online search, but I had no reason to believe any of those I contacted were trolls, bots, or had otherwise falsified their identities. I interviewed Doreen Traylor because she had written a comment on HackerNews (a Web forum affiliated with Y Combinator) responding to an article I had written about working at Capital One published in the *New Republic*. Her comment mentioned her past experiences borrowing money while homeless. I was particularly interested in hearing her perspective because her comment suggested that she disagreed with some of the conclusions I had drawn about the nature of debt. This was the only interview I conducted where I had a specific idea before conducting the interview of what the person's opinions about credit access might be.

In total, I conducted sixty-two interviews of consumers between 2018 and 2021. About 15 percent of the interviews were primarily related to being unbanked, not getting credit (e.g., being declined for credit or having the perception that they would be declined for credit), or about people's decisions to avoid debt or credit.

In what follows, I have included the list of questions I most often asked people (during some interviews, I had a printout of this list or a similar list of questions), although as I have mentioned, I did not strictly stick to a particular interview protocol. When I knew I would be able to have a long conversation with a particular person, I focused instead on going through their debt experiences chronologically before asking these questions, and in some of my "person on the street" interviews, I asked only three or four questions total.

INTERVIEW PROTOCOL:

- If you could change one thing about banks, lenders, or credit card companies, what would it be?
- Do you think banks make it too hard to get credit, or too easy to get into debt?

[Based on responses, ask follow-up questions to establish if they have firsthand experience with credit card debt or other forms of short-term loans, or learn about why they have avoided using credit.]

For those with first-hand experience with credit card debt:

- Do you remember when and why you got your first credit card?
- How many credit cards do you have?
- Where does most of your credit card debt come from? What was going on in your life when you accrued the debt?
- (For those who still have credit card debt): Do you have any goals or plans for paying off credit card debt? How much debt did you have at the max, and how much do you have now?
- When you think about credit cards, would you say that for you personally, over the course of your whole life, they have caused more stress or helped reduce stress?
- Is there anything you know now about credit that you wish you had learned earlier?
- Have you ever borrowed money outside of credit cards? What were the circumstances?
- How would your life be different if credit cards didn't exist at all?
- Have you ever struggled to make the minimum payments on your credit card?
- What has been your most memorable experience related to your credit card debt?
- What do you hope your usage of credit cards will look like in one year?

APPENDIX B **Advice for Consumers**

Although many of these tips are scattered around the book, I wanted to pull together my advice about navigating the credit card system. I should emphasize that the credit card system is not designed for you to win, and navigating it, especially if your job doesn't pay very well, or if you don't have a job, is extremely tricky. I've included these tips for educational purposes, but some of this information may become outdated or may not apply in your situation. You will need to supplement these tips with your own research.

There are three main reasons Americans get credit cards: to borrow money, to build their credit scores, and to earn rewards. I'll start by talking about how to build your credit score.

HOW TO BUILD YOUR CREDIT SCORE

You may have heard that having *no* credit score is just as bad as having a *low* credit score. That's not entirely true. Your credit score or your credit report can be used for many different purposes—potential landlords can check your credit reports with your permission, as can car insurance companies, lenders, some cell phone providers and utility companies, along with employers in some states. People with minimal or no information on their credit reports look like strangers: banks don't have enough information to assess whether the given consumer is relatively high risk or relatively low risk. Whether this will result in especially high prices depends a lot on the circumstances and on whether the entity can otherwise verify your identity. But after just six months to a year of on-time payments, the credit score of someone without much credit history can go up by a lot. By comparison, a single negative piece of information on a credit report can last for seven years. So, if you are not in a position to make bill payments on time, you shouldn't open up any new loans to build credit: if you miss a single payment, you will have shot yourself in the foot. For many purposes, especially insurance and employment, consumers who don't have credit scores or credit reports are protected by state laws that say that these consumers need to be treated as if they have average credit scores, instead of being punished for the lack of information.

It's helpful to check your own credit reports. There are three especially important credit reports—those made by Transunion, Equifax, and Experian. You can do so for free at AnnualCreditReport.com. The version of your credit report you see at AnnualCreditReport.com will not contain any credit scores like FICO or Vantage. If you want to see a credit score, which can also be helpful, you'll have to sign up for a credit monitoring service: Credit Karma, Credit Sesame, and Credit Wise by Capital One are free, among others. It doesn't really matter if the website you're using shows you your Vantage or FICO score: their formulas aren't different enough to make a big difference for most people. Moreover, banks make their own credit scores on top of FICO and Vantage. If you've heard that FICO is a "real score," and Vantage is a "fake score," that's simply not true.

The reality is that the banks' own custom-built risk models matter much more than *either* FICO or Vantage. There's also multiple versions of FICO and multiple versions of Vantage with different formulas. I'm not saying this to freak you out; these risk scores will, in most cases, be highly correlated with one another. If you see anything wrong on your credit report, you will want to let the credit bureau know about the mistake. All the credit monitoring services will help you interpret your credit score and know if it is low, medium, or high. As mentioned elsewhere in the book, the credit monitoring services make their money from trying to get you to open credit cards, receiving payments from credit card companies in exchange. If you're prepared to ignore all the ads and recommendations, using a free service like Credit Karma, Credit Sesame, or Credit Wise is probably better than using a paid service (and some paid services also have advertisements!).

If your credit score is under 650, you're normally going to pay high interest rates on car loans and credit cards. You either won't be able to refinance your student loan debt, or you won't get a good interest rate. You might get turned down for apartments. Your car insurance rates will likely be much higher— possibly even twice as high as those with good credit scores. The lower your score, the more expensive everything will be. A credit score above 700 is good enough for most purposes. You may get the lowest interest rate offered at a car dealership for an auto loan and shouldn't have to pay extra for car insurance.

It's important to know that you can achieve a good credit score—a credit score above 700—even if you only have one loan. Just one credit card, just one student loan, or just one auto loan open at a given time is enough to build a relatively high credit score if you never miss any payments. So if you already have one of these loans open, and your credit score is low, or if you don't have a credit score yet because you're new to credit, just keep making on-time payments on this loan, and eventually your credit score will improve (this process will only take a few months if you don't have any negative credit history on your report). If you have a lot of negative information on your credit report, it will not necessarily speed up the process to have many loans; what makes a bigger difference is just waiting for negative information to become older and eventually disappear from your credit report.

If you want to buy a house, you'll want to take a few more steps to get the lowest rate. Specifically, you will want to have at least two loans, probably three loans, open for at least a year before you apply for a mortgage. When you're buying a house, you want a "thick file"—for mortgage lenders to have a lot of information about you. Mortgage lenders generally don't like it if you have applied for credit shortly before applying for a mortgage, so unless you really need to, don't apply for new credit cards or loans in the six months before you try to buy a house. You may be able to find a lender who will manually underwrite a mortgage for you if you have never used credit cards before. One such company, Churchill Mortgage, heavily advertises on the Dave Ramsey Show, but I am not able to specifically endorse Churchill Mortgage as I have no firsthand experience. People without credit scores can also qualify for FHA mortgages, which generally have higher interest rates than conventional mortgages. The most typical route to get a good interest rate on a mortgage though, is to have a good credit score. You will know that you will likely qualify for the lowest rate on a mortgage (or close to the lowest rate) if your credit score is above 700, if you have more than two years of credit history, and you have records of payments on at least two or three separate loans, (assuming your income and down payment are also in order).

If you don't have any credit cards right now, what's a good credit card to build credit with? Ideally, something without an annual fee, because you will want to keep this credit card open for as long as possible. If you are completely new to credit and get declined for the first credit card you apply for, don't get discouraged. Wait a few weeks and then try again with a different credit card company. It is often easier to be approved for credit cards when you have one piece of information—an indication that you were declined for a credit card (e.g., an inquiry on your credit report)—than literally no pieces of information. The odds are relatively high that you will get the highest credit limit if you apply for a credit card in person at whatever bank or credit union you have a checking account with. No matter what, don't pick a card as your first card that says Mastercard World Elite or Visa Signature on the bottom (Visa Platinum, for example, would be fine, as would Discover), because if you choose a card that has a high minimum credit limit, you will likely be declined. Whether or not the card has rewards is actually not a big factor in your approval odds.

YOU DO NOT NEED TO PAY ANY INTEREST ON YOUR CREDIT CARD TO GET A GOOD CREDIT SCORE

Your credit score will not increase any more quickly by paying credit card interest. So if your only goal is to improve your credit score and you don't have any need to borrow money, you can just buy one thing a month on your credit card (or put a recurring payment on your credit card like Netflix), and pay your bill in full. I would consider signing up for automatic payments, even if you want to check out your bill every month before making a payment, and even if you want to double check that you have enough money in your checking account before the bill gets paid. Most credit card companies make it relatively easy to alter your automatic payment amount if you log into your account online.

NEVER BUY ANYTHING ON A CARD THAT USES "RETROACTIVE INTEREST" OR "DEFERRED INTEREST"

Retroactive interest, also known as deferred interest (explained in chapter 5), is one of the easiest ways to financially ruin yourself. Literally the only exception here would be in the case of a medical emergency. If a card with retroactive interest is the only way you can buy furniture, sleep on a blanket until you can buy furniture from Craigslist.

If you are new to credit and don't have any negative information on your credit report, the odds are very high that you can qualify for a run-of-the-mill credit card, with no security deposit. The only circumstance in which it advisable to consider getting a secured card or a credit building loan is when, (1) you do not have *any* open loans that you can make payments toward; and (2) there is a lot of negative information on your credit report—for example, a repossession or a chargeoff; or (3) your main goal for having a secured card is specifically for the purpose of renting cars. If you get a secured card, the same advice as previously stated applies: you don't need to pay any interest to have your credit score go up. As discussed in the book, my skepticism of secured cards comes from the fact that most account holders do end up borrowing money on the card, and it winds up being very expensive for them. I would advise not getting a secured card until you're sure you *won't* need it to borrow money—it is going to be hard to raise your credit score when you are really struggling from month to month. In that circumstance, you are better off holding onto your security deposit and spending it if you have an emergency.

HOW TO BORROW MONEY

If you need to borrow money, you should try to compare at least five loan or credit card options; I'd strongly suggest including at least one credit union in your list of comparisons. Depending on the situation, I would also recommend including at least one personal loan, which will often have a much lower interest rate, but may not make sense in every situation. Personal loan companies you may want to consider include LendingClub, LightStream, and Payoff, although there are many other similar companies: as of 2021, the companies I've mentioned let you check online to see if you were preapproved, and find out your interest rate without submitting an application or having an "inquiry" on your credit report. If your current score is not very good, you could also consider OneMain Financial; their interest rates are very high, but are lower than a typical payday loan. No matter what type of loan you get, you should be wary of any add-on insurance products, which are often so full of loopholes that the coverage is useless. Most personal loan companies will allow you to pay off loans early without a penalty, so if you need to borrow money but you're not exactly sure how much, you could err on the high side and then repay what you don't need. (The only downside is that there is often a one-time origination fee that is based on the amount you borrow originally.)

How do you find the loans and credit cards to compare? You're going to want to see what you're qualified for—what loans you are likely to be approved for, and at what interest rate. In the comparison-shopping phase, you want to do this ideally without submitting a formal application, so your credit score isn't dinged by too many "inquiries." Almost every major credit card company has a tool on their website for checking what cards they'll approve you for, and these generally will also tell you what interest rate you will receive. Unfortunately, a lot of credit unions don't let you check online to see if you're prequalified online. As of April 2021, Navy Federal Credit Union does: they're the largest federally chartered credit union in the United States and their field of membership covers mostly military families. With many other credit unions, you might have to make an educated guess about whether or not your odds of approval are high, based on your credit score. Because the *highest* interest rate offered by many credit unions is lower than the *lowest* interest rate offered by some credit card companies, it's still worth keeping them in your list.

If you need to borrow money, the APR will usually be the most important characteristic of the credit card to look at. An annual fee is more of a tiebreaker between credit cards, unless you are pretty confident that you are going to borrow less than $1,000: the more debt you have, the more the APR will matter relative to the annual fee. Most big banks charge the same dollar amount of late fee, which is the maximum they're allowed to charge by law (an amount that increases with inflation). I would not even pay attention to the rewards. If you really want to earn card rewards, and occasionally need to borrow money, you're better off having two cards, and making sure the reward-earning card is always paid off in full every month.

Remember that as of 2021, banks and credit unions must ask for your income and assess whether, based on your income, you can repay the loan. So if your income is zero dollars, do not even try to apply for a loan, although you can include unemployment insurance, SSI/SSDI, child support, and alimony in your income, and if you are over twenty-one you may use any household income that you have access to. I should also state that many credit card companies don't verify income for the majority of their applicants, although I cannot advise you to commit fraud (and you should know that if you commit fraud, you may lose the ability to have your debt forgiven in bankruptcy).

Before you borrow money, you should remember that if you borrow money this month, you're going to have even *less money* next month. If you're not unemployed and looking for work, and you're facing a recurring gap between how much you earn and how much you need to spend every month, you should spend five minutes brainstorming all the possible strategies you could use. The reason I say to spend five minutes brainstorming is because when we're feeling anxious or overwhelmed, our minds tend to hone in on only one or two possibilities, instead of our full range of options. Some possibilities could be identifying any government programs you might be eligible for, including ones run by your city or state, looking for ways to get prescriptions for less money, selling your car or house if you own either of those, finding a less expensive place to live or getting roommates, or going to a food bank. I mention these things because taking one of these steps today could prevent you from needing to take two or more of these steps tomorrow if you use a credit card.

IF YOU ALREADY HAVE CREDIT CARD DEBT

Your first move should be to figure out how much money you can dedicate each month to debt repayment—for example, by making a budget. I know it is not easy to budget if your income is not the same every month, but as a starting point, something approximate is better than nothing. If you can't dedicate any money to debt repayment, or not enough to make your minimum payments, I'll explain what to do in the section "If You Can't Pay Your Bills." When you're making a budget, you should take a look backward at your last few months' worth of spending—doing so is more accurate than guessing what your expenses will be, because most of us tend to forget things otherwise. Some people will encourage you to treat your debt like it is an emergency, and live on lentils and rice and stay indoors until it is fully paid off; that may or may not be worth the sacrifices it would take, but if you are savvy with math, I would attempt to figure out how much money you could ultimately save on credit card or loan interest by doing so, and decide whether it would be worth it. If you want to save the most money on interest and fees, make sure to always make your minimum payments on every loan, and then pay off your debts in order from the highest-interest to lowest-interest rates. There's one other approach you could try instead: some people find it psychologically rewarding to use a "snowball" method instead, where they pay off their smallest debts first instead of paying off their highest interest rate loans first. If you think this strategy will motivate you to pay down your debt more quickly, it might be worth it.

Your next move should be to see if you can get some or all your debt onto a lower interest rate. You can follow the same steps that I explained in "how to borrow money" for finding lower cost loans and credit cards.

Nearly all credit cards let you transfer your balance from other credit cards. If you are getting a special rate offer, like a 0 percent interest rate teaser, there will usually be a one-time fee to initiate the balance transfer, often 2 percent or 3 percent of the balance. Paying this fee would normally be worth it unless you were on track to pay off that debt in the next two or three months anyways. But even without a promotional rate, if you have two credit cards, and let's say one has a 27 percent interest rate, and the other one has a 19 percent interest rate, you could still transfer the balance from the 27 percent interest rate card to the 19 percent interest rate card and save money. Usually when you do so on your standard interest rate (e.g., the "purchase rate"), as opposed to a promotional low interest rate, you don't pay a balance transfer fee. (Double-check with your credit card company to be sure.) So moving your balance between your credit cards is a really easy way to save money if you have available credit on your lowest interest credit card. If your lowest interest rate credit card doesn't have any available credit, consider asking for a credit limit increase.

EARNING REWARDS

Only think about credit card rewards if you are confident that you can pay your bill in full every month. I am not going to offer much advice about credit card rewards, because I don't think that they're a particularly good system and I know many people end up borrowing money when they didn't originally plan to. I will say that you should be warned that most bloggers who hype credit card points earn money from getting you to open credit cards, earning a "bounty" each time, so they tend to overstate the value of credit card rewards.

IF YOU CAN'T PAY YOUR BILLS

If you fall far behind on a credit card bill, it will eventually "charge off." The credit card company might continue trying to collect on the debt, or they might sell your account to a debt collection company. If you come into a little extra cash, for example, when you get your annual tax refund, it's a good time to see if any of your lenders will take a lump sum payment in exchange for forgiving your debt. There is good advice available on this topic online that you should read if you are pursuing a settlement, but the most important point is that if you are trying to get the bank or debt collection company to settle your debt, make sure to get the deal in writing.

If either the bank or the debt collection company sues you to try to get you to pay them back, always show up to court, even if you can't afford a lawyer. Ask for proof that you owe all the money shown, and ask for proof that the interest rate is valid. Frequently, debt collection companies will have lost the paperwork showing the sum total of how your balance accrued (for example, how much is principal, how much is interest, and how much are fees), and they're counting on you not to show up in court. When your original lender is the one suing you, it's less likely that they'll come totally unprepared, so if they're the one suing you, and you're not totally broke, be prepared to have to pay some or all of the debt. Let the judge know if you can't afford to pay the debt. If you don't show up, normally the bank automatically wins what's called a "default judgment," and they can go after the money in your checking account or try to garnish your paycheck (depending on which state you live in, they can also pursue your spouse). In some states, if you fail to appear in court, you can be arrested and held in contempt of court.

If you're struggling to make payments on your credit card bills, and you have a lot of credit card debt (especially if you have $10,000 or more), you should absolutely research bankruptcy, but I can't say whether it will definitely be the right answer for you. It's important to know that as of April 2021, student loan debt will not go away in bankruptcy. Bankruptcy is especially helpful if you can qualify for a Chapter 7 bankruptcy: in a Chapter 7 bankruptcy you have to forfeit certain assets (most working-class people don't have any assets that would qualify), but then your debt is forgiven. A Chapter 13 bankruptcy doesn't forgive your debt: it puts you on a payment plan instead, but should stop your existing debtors from harassing you. If you are worried about hurting your credit score, you should keep in mind that the credit score drop from declaring bankruptcy isn't necessarily worse than the credit score drop from missing a lot of payments on your debt. If you feel bad about getting your debt forgiven, remember that big corporations declare bankruptcy all the time! There are some filing fees with bankruptcy, which is why it doesn't make sense to declare bankruptcy if you only have $500 or $1,000 worth of debt.

Under some situations, if you are eligible for Chapter 7 bankruptcy, it can be strategic to declare bankruptcy even if you *can* afford to repay your bills, but you will have to heavily weigh the pros and cons. If you are feeling overwhelmed by debt collections or the possibility of bankruptcy, consider checking out the website of the national nonprofit Upsolve, which helps Americans declare bankruptcy, and search online to find the legal services organizations in your county or state. (Disclosure: I have done a small amount of paid editorial work for Upsolve.) Legal services organizations are nonprofit organizations (usually federally funded) that offer free help with civil legal problems that Americans face, for example, eviction, foreclosure, wage theft, and debt collection; usually, you must have a very low income to qualify for their help.

WHEN A BANK IS TREATING YOU UNFAIRLY

File a complaint online with the Consumer Financial Protection Bureau. This creates a written record of the problem, and banks must respond to your complaint within fifteen days. While your problem won't be fixed on the same day, the odds become very high that your problem gets fixed eventually, assuming that the bank was violating either their own written policies or the law. If you're making your second or third phone call to your bank to try to resolve a problem, go ahead and tell them that you plan to file a complaint with the CFPB if the problem isn't resolved promptly. You can file complaints against banks, lenders, debt collection companies, credit bureaus, and some other types of financial services companies.

If your bank wasn't violating their own written policies or the law, but you think what they did *should* be illegal, write a letter to your member of Congress and to your senators.

As a last reminder, I wrote this book because millions of Americans do everything right, or make a few honest mistakes, and wind up in terrible situations. It's not your fault.

Notes

PREFACE

1. Nuala Sawyer Bishari, "Keeping the Homeless Out of Sight Makes Their Lives More Dangerous," *SF Weekly*, August 21, 2019, https://www.sfweekly.com/topstories/keeping-the-homeless-out-of-sight-makes-their-lives-more-dangerous/.

2. The total number of borrowers reported across the listed loan types is from "Survey of Household Economics and Decisionmaking," ed. Board of Governors of the Federal Reserve System (2018). The data shown reflects responses to questions BK2_c, BK2_d, C4A, and C3. Approximately $143 billion in interest reflects the sum of credit card interest, credit card late fees, credit card cash advance fees, payday loan interest, title loan interest, and pawn shop interest. Total credit card interest in 2018 totaled $113 billion; see "Americans Will Pay $122 Billion in Credit Card Interest This Year—50% More Than 5 Years Ago," Money, April 1, 2019, https://money.com/credit-card-interest-2019/. Total 2018 credit card late fees and cash advance fees totaled $14 billion; see Bureau of Consumer Financial Protection, *The Consumer Credit Card Market* (2019), 67–111, https://files.consumerfinance.gov/f/documents/cfpb_consumer-credit-card-market-report_2019.pdf. Annual fees were excluded because those fees accrued both to cardholders who paid their monthly bills in full, as well as those who did not, and therefore aren't always accurately labeled as borrowing costs. The non–credit card fees and interest reported totaled $16 billion, collected from

Karen Graham and Elaine Golden, *2019 Financially Underserved Market Size Study,* Financial Health Network (Chicago), December 20, 2019, https://finhealthnetwork.org/research/2019-financially-underserved-market-size-study/.

CHAPTER 1

1. Louis Hyman, *Borrow: The American Way of Debt* (New York: Vintage Books, 2012), 118.

2. Florence Griffith Naomi Sizemore Trammel, Unidentified Speaker, "Oral History Interview with Naomi Sizemore Trammel, March 25, 1980. Interview H-0258. Southern Oral History Program Collection (#4007)," interview by Allen Tullos, 1980, https://docsouth.unc.edu/sohp/H-0258/H-0258.html. Sizemore Trammel's year of birth is derived from her obituary in the *Greenville News*; based on her age at death, her birth year was either 1886 or 1887.

3. Rowena Olegario, *The Engine of Enterprise: Credit in America* (Cambridge, MA: Harvard University Press, 2016), 118.

4. Hyman, *Borrow,* 8–10; Benjamin Davidson, "Super City: Los Angeles and the Birth of the Supermarket, 1914–1941," *California History* 93, no. 3 (2016): 9–27, https://doi.org/10.1525/ch.2016.93.3.9; Lendol Calder, *Financing the American Dream: A Cultural History of Consumer Credit* (Princeton, NJ: Princeton University Press, 1999), 69–71.

5. Calder, *Financing the American Dream,* 96.

6. Calder, *Financing the American Dream,* 23, 171–173.

7. For the 2019 credit card interest rate, see Board of Governors of the Federal Reserve System (US), Commercial Bank Interest Rate on Credit Card Plans, Accounts Assessed Interest [TERMCBCCINTNS], retrieved from FRED, Federal Reserve Bank of St. Louis, April 29, 2021, https://fred.stlouisfed.org/series/TERMCBCCINTNS. For discussion on costs of lending, see chapter 6 in this book.

8. Olegario, *The Engine of Enterprise,* 88.

9. Olegario, *The Engine of Enterprise,* 107; Mark R. Wilson. "Household Finance Corp," in Electronic Encyclopedia of Chicago, Chicago Historical Society, 2005, http://www.encyclopedia.chicagohistory.org/pages/2708.html; Robert Barba, "Fortress Bulks Up in Consumer Finance with HSBC Deal," *American Banker* (New York), March 6, 2013, ProQuest.

10. Olegario, *The Engine of Enterprise,* 98–104.

11. Hyman, *Borrow,* 115.

12. Here and throughout the text, "working class" is used as shorthand for households whose income is at or below the 50th percentile unless otherwise stated, while "middle class" is used as shorthand for households whose income is between the 50th and 90th percentile. For descriptions of working-class and middle-class borrowing behaviors in the twentieth century, see Hyman, *Borrow;* and

Gunnar Trumbull, *Consumer Lending in France and America: Credit and Welfare* (New York: Cambridge University Press, 2014). The proportion of working-class families without non-mortgage debt is drawn from the SCF+ dataset, as is the ratio of debt to income for working class families in 1950 and 2016. This dataset, assembled by Moritz Kuhn, Moritz Schularick, Ulrike I. Steins, Alina Bartscher, and Lukas Gehring, combines the Survey of Consumer Finances, conducted by Economic Behavior Program of the Survey Research Center at the University of Michigan from 1947 to 1977, with the Survey of Consumer Finances, conducted by the Federal Reserve since 1983. A description of the methodology used by the investigators can be found in Moritz Kuhn, Moritz Schularick, and Ulrike I. Steins, "Income and Wealth Inequality in America, 1949–2016," *Journal of Political Economy* 128, no. 9 (2020). The author obtained the dataset from Schularick and Bartchser on April 14, 2020. This dataset is subsequently cited as SCF+.

13. U.S. Census Bureau, "Recapitulation on the Tables of Population, Nativity and Occupation" in *1860 Census: Population of the United States,* 1864, 66–90, https://www2.census.gov/library/publications/decennial/1860/population/1860a-46.pdf.

14. U.S. Census Bureau, Introduction to *1860 Census: Population of the United States,* 1864, 7, https://www2.census.gov/library/publications/decennial/1860/population/1860a-02.pdf.

15. U.S. Census Bureau, "Recapitulation," 3.

16. Felipe González, Guillermo Marshall, and Suresh Naidu, "Start-up Nation? Slave Wealth and Entrepreneurship in Civil War Maryland," *Journal of Economic History* 77, no. 2 (2017): 373–405. https://doi.org/10.1017/S0022050717000493.

17. Katie Benner, "Wachovia Apologizes for Slavery Ties," *CNN Money,* June 2, 2005, https://money.cnn.com/2005/06/02/news/fortune500/wachovia_slavery/; Bank Admits It Owned Slaves," *The Guardian,* January 21, 2005, https://www.theguardian.com/world/2005/jan/22/usa.davidteather; Bank of America, "Slavery Era Disclosure Affidavit," San Francisco Office of the City Administrator, https://sfgov.org/ccsfgsa/sites/default/files/Slavery%20Era%20Disclosure%20Ordinance/SE_Bofa__4584.pdf; U.S. Bancorp, "Slavery Era Disclosure Affidavit," San Francisco Office of the City Administrator, https://sfgov.org/ccsfgsa/sites/default/files/Slavery%20Era%20Disclosure%20Ordinance/Institutional%20History%20US%20Bancorp%2095%20pages.pdf.

18. David A. Skeel Jr., "The Genius of the 1898 Bankruptcy Act," *Bankruptcy Development Journal* 15: 321–341, Faculty Scholarship at Penn Law, 720.

19. Olegario, *The Engine of Enterprise,* 110–111; Philipp Ager, Leah Platt Boustan, and Katherine Eriksson, "The Intergenerational Effects of a Large Wealth Shock: White Southerners after the Civil War," NBER Working Paper 25700, September 2019, https://www.nber.org/papers/w25700?.

20. Kenneth A. Snowden, "Mortgage Rate and American Capital Market Development in the Late Nineteenth Century," *Journal of Economic History* 47, no. 3 (September 1987): 675.

21. Mehrsa Baradaran, *The Color of Money: Black Banks and the Racial Wealth Gap,* First Harvard University Press paperback edition (Cambridge, MA: Harvard University Press, 2017), 33.

22. Baradaran, *The Color of Money,* 18–21.

23. Baradaran, *The Color of Money,* 35.

24. For a comprehensive treatment of this history, see Richard Rothstein, *The Color of Law: A Forgotten History of How Our Government Segregated America,* (New York: Liveright, 2017).

25. Rothstein, *The Color of* Law, 182–183.

26. For historic loan shark interest rates, see Rolf Nugent, "The Loan Shark Problem," *Law and Contemporary Problems* 8, no. 1 (Winter 1941): 5, https:// scholarship.law.duke.edu/lcp/vol8/iss1/2/; Olegario, *The Engine of Enterprise,* 107. For contemporary payday loan interest rates, see "What is a payday loan?," updated June 2, 2017, https://www.consumerfinance.gov/ask-cfpb/what-is-a-payday-loan-en-1567/; for the changing meaning of the term "loan shark" across time, see Robert Mayer, "Loan Sharks, Interest-Rate Caps, and Deregulation," Washington and Lee Law Review 69, no. 2 (2012), https://scholarlycommons .law.wlu.edu/wlulr/vol69/iss2/10.

27. Calder, *Financing the American Dream,* 118; Mayer, "Loan Sharks," 813; Charles R. Geisst, *Loan Sharks: The Birth of Predatory Lending* (Washington, DC: Brookings Institution Press, 2016), 208–212; Mark H. Haller and John V. Alviti, "Loansharking in American Cities: Historical Analysis of a Marginal Enterprise," *American Journal of Legal History* 21, no. 2 (1977): 128–134, https://doi.org /10.2307/845211.

28. Baradaran, *The Color of Money,* 194

29. Haller and Alviti, "Loansharking," 128–134; Geisst, *Loan Sharks,* 51.

30. William Osborne Stoddard, "Pawnbrokers and Loan-Officers," *Harper's Magazine,* June 1869, https://harpers.org/archive/1869/06/pawnbrokers-and-loan-offices/.

31. Geisst, *Loan Sharks,* 73–75.

32. Nugent, "The Loan Shark Problem," 8.; Theresa Schmall and Eva Wolkowitz, *2016 Financially Underserved Market Size Study* (Center for Financial Services Innovation, 2016), 42, https://finhealthnetwork.org/research/2016-financially-underserved-market-size-study/.

33. "Ticket Shows Grant Pawned Watch," *New York Times,* January 22, 1933, https://www.nytimes.com/1933/01/22/archives/ticket-shows-grant-pawned-watch.html?searchResultPosition = 13; "His $1,000 Teeth in Pawn, Negro Cheers Rise in Cotton," *New York Times,* September 11, 1932, https://www

.nytimes.com/1932/09/11/archives/his-1000-teeth-in-pawn-negro-cheers-rise-in-cotton.html?searchResultPosition = 40.

34. Calder, *Financing the American Dream*, 44.

35. Calder, *Financing the American Dream*, 43–52.

36. Stoddard, "Pawnbrokers and Loan-Officers," 126.

37. Dollar figures reported in 2016 dollars from SCF+.

38. An overall view of debt servicing ratios (e.g., the percent of post-tax income directed to lenders) does not show a positive upward trend, largely because of the high amount of income growth among the top 1 percent. However, debt servicing ratios, when broken out by income group, have increased substantially for the bottom 90 percent of American households by income. See Alina K. Bartscher et al., "Modigliani Meets Minsky: Inequality, Debt, and Financial Fragility in America, 1950–2016," Staff Report No. 924, Federal Reserve Bank of New York Staff Reports, May 2020, https://www.newyorkfed.org/medialibrary/media/research/staff_reports/sr924.pdf, 43.

39. Atif Mian, Ludwig Straub, and Amir Sufi, "The Saving Glut of the Rich," working paper, February 2021, 19, https://scholar.harvard.edu/files/straub/files/mss_richsavingglut.pdf; U.S. Bureau of Economic Analysis, Personal Saving Rate [PSAVERT], retrieved from FRED, Federal Reserve Bank of St. Louis, April 29, 2021, https://fred.stlouisfed.org/series/PSAVERT.

40. "Inequality in America: A National Town Hall," Bernie Sanders, 2018, https://www.youtube.com/watch?v=-EV8XfM9CZo.

41. Price J. Fishback and Andrew J. Seltzer, "The Rise of American Minimum Wages, 1912–1968," IZA DP No. 12793, IZA Institute of Labor Economics Discussion Paper Series, February 2020, 10, http://ftp.iza.org/dp12973.pdf.

42. Michael Harrington, *The Other America: Poverty in the United States*, First Collier Books Edition 1994 (New York: Macmillian Publishing Company, 1962), 21–175.

43. Richard V. Burkhauser et al., "Evaluating the Success of President Johnson's War on Poverty: Revisiting the Historical Record Using a Full-Income Poverty Measure," NBER Working Paper 26532, December 2019, http://www.nber.org/papers/w26532.

44. "Inflation: Changing Farm Policy to Cut Food Prices," *TIME*, April 9, 1973, http://content.time.com/time/magazine/article/0,9171,903930,00.html; Sharon Boswell and Lorraine McConaghy, "Lights out, Seattle," *Seattle Times*, November 3,1996, https://special.seattletimes.com/o/special/centennial/november/lights_out.html.

45. Jimmy Carter, *July 15, 1979: Crisis of Confidence Speech*, Miller Center, https://millercenter.org/the-presidency/presidential-speeches/july-15–1979-crisis-confidence-speech.

46. The federal government's perspective on income growth over time is drawn from Ellen Steele, *The Distribution of Household Income, 2017*, Congressional Budget Office, October 2, 2020, https://www.cbo.gov/publication/56575. Compare with Oren Cass, *The Cost-of-Thriving Index: Reevaluating the Prosperity of the American Family*, Manhattan Institute, February 20, 2020, https://www.manhattan-institute.org/reevaluating-prosperity-of-american-family.

47. See volumes of cash advance fees, annual fees, and late fees in 2018 from Bureau of Consumer Financial Protection, *The Consumer Credit Card Market* (2019), 67–111, https://files.consumerfinance.gov/f/documents/cfpb_consumer-credit-card-market-report_2019.pdf. See credit card interest collected in 2018 from "Americans Will Pay $122 Billion in Credit Card Interest This Year—50% More Than 5 Years Ago," Money, April 1, 2019, https://money.com/credit-card-interest-2019/. The US census bureau reported 128 million households in 2018.

CHAPTER 2

1. Gunnar Trumbull, *Consumer Lending in France and America: Credit and Welfare* (New York: Cambridge University Press, 2014), 88.

2. Leonie Barrie, "Online Tracker Lists Apparel Brands' Response to Covid-19," April 17, 2020, just-style, https://www.just-style.com/news/online-tracker-lists-apparel-brands-response-to-covid-19_id138557.aspx.

3. *Merriam-Webster.com Dictionary*, "Machine," https://www.merriam-webster.com/dictionary/machine.

4. The first reference reflects the proportion of US adults achieving a Level 1 on the numeracy scale according to the international PIAAC system. The second reference reflects the proportion of US adults achieving a Level 2. See Madeline Goodman et al., *Literacy, Numeracy, and Problem Solving in Technology-Rich Environments among U.S. Adults: Results from the Program for the International Assessment of Adult Competencies 2012: First Look*, U.S. Department of Education (Washington, DC: National Center for Education Statistics, October 2013), https://nces.ed.gov/pubs2014/2014008.pdf.

5. The only major difference between the minimum payment formulas used by Citi and Capital One is that, for customers with lower credit card balances, Citi uses a minimum payment floor of $20 while Capital One uses a floor of $25.

6. Mary Zaki, "Heterogenous Responses to Interest Rate Price Disclosures," University of Maryland, http://www.terpconnect.umd.edu/~mzaki/papers/Interestrate_heterogeneous.pdf.

7. Trumbull, *Consumer Lending*, 77–79.

8. "Non-Housing Debt Balance," ed. Equifax Federal Reserve Bank of New York Consumer Credit Panel, Household Debt and Credit Report (Federal

Reserve Bank of New York), November 2021, https://www.newyorkfed.org/microeconomics/hhdc.html.

9. Bureau of Consumer Financial Protection, The Consumer Credit Card Market (2019), 35, https://files.consumerfinance.gov/f/documents/cfpb_consumer-credit-card-market-report_2019.pdf

10. Zaki, "Heterogenous Responses to Interest Rate Price Disclosures," 5.

11. Nilas Möllenkamp, "Determinants of Loan Performance in P2P Lending" (bachelor's thesis, University of Twente, 2017), 13, http://essay.utwente.nl/72876/1/M%C3%B6llenkamp_BA_BMS.pdf.

12. Sophia Kunthara, "Affirm's IPO Filing Reveals Nearly a Third of Its Revenue Comes from a Single Customer," crunchbase news, November 18, 2020, https://news.crunchbase.com/news/affirm-s1-ipo/.

13. Mary Zaki, "Revolving Credit: Shrouded by Construction," University of Maryland, 22, https://terpconnect.umd.edu/~mzaki/papers/revolving_shrouding_3_10_2018.pdf.

14. Paul S. Calem and Loretta J. Mester, "Consumer Behavior and the Stickiness of Credit-Card Interest Rates," *American Economic Review* 85, no. 5 (1995), http://www.jstor.org/stable/2950992.

15. These percentages refer to Sears and JCPenney card ownership in 1979. See Louis Hyman, *Borrow: The American Way of Debt* (New York: Vintage Books, 2012), 145.

16. David Caplovitz, "Consumer Problems of the Low-Income" (ACCI 1964 Annual Conference, Madison, WI, American Council on Consumer Interests).

17. Joint Economic Committee, *Economic Problems of Women: Hearings, Ninety-Third Congress, First Session,* 79 United States Congress, 548 (1973).

18. Committee on Banking, Housing and Urban Affairs, *Hearings on S. 1281 to Improve Public Understanding of the Role of Depository Institutions in Home Financing,* 1, 94, United States Senate 564 (1975).

19. Trumbull, *Consumer Lending,* 179.

20. *See* Norman I. Silber, "Discovering That the Poor Pay More: Race Riots, Poverty, and the Rise of Consumer Law," *Fordham Urban Law Journal* 44, no. 5 (2017): 1325–1326, https://ir.lawnet.fordham.edu/ulj/vol44/iss5/1/; and Trumbull, *Consumer Lending,* 169.

21. Trumbull, *Consumer Lending,* 189.

22. Beryl Satter, *Family Properties: How the Struggle Over Race and Real Estate Transformed Chicago and Urban America* (New York: Picador, 2009), 370–71.

23. Portions of this chapter first appeared on Forbes.com. See Elena Botella, "Under New Rules, Banks Will No Longer Earn Civil Rights 'Brownie Points' for Pushing Families into Credit Card Debt," *Forbes.com,* May 20, 2020, https://www.forbes.com/sites/elenabotella/2020/05/20/cra-occ-credit-card-debt/.

24. Nick Bourke, *Safe Credit Card Standards: Policy Recommendations for Protecting Credit Cardholders and Promoting a Functional Marketplace,* Pew Charitable Trusts, March 31, 2009, https://www.pewtrusts.org/-/media/assets /2009/03/31/final8247_pct_creditcard_v3.pdf.

25. "Testimony of Nick Bourke, Manager of the Safe Credit Cards Project at the Pew Charitable Trusts, Regarding HR 3639," Pew Charitable Trusts, https:// web.archive.org/web/20110505230324/http://www.pewtrusts.org/uploadedFiles /wwwpewtrustsorg/Speeches/Bourke_PCT_Testimony_HR3639_FINAL.pdf.

26. There are eight total standards, one of which is broadly defined—for example, "Cardholder relationships will be based on simple and easily understood rules. All key information about the account will be provided in short, plain language statements highlighting important information and possible actions to be taken." See Bourke, *Safe Credit Card Standards.*

27. Consumer Financial Protection Bureau, "Card Act Report," October 1, 2013, https://files.consumerfinance.gov/f/201309_cfpb_card-act-report.pdf. Although the original statute creating a federal consumer financial protection agency, the Dodd-Frank Wall Street Reform and Consumer Protection Act, referred to the new agency as the "Bureau of Consumer Financial Protection," it is more commonly known as the Consumer Financial Protection Bureau (CFPB), and the agency has referred to itself as the Consumer Financial Protection Bureau or CFPB on most documents, except under the agency's acting director Mick Mulvaney, who served from 2017 until 2018, and on some documents under director Kathy Kraninger, who served from 2018 until 2021. The convention we follow in this book's notes is to match the agency name (either Consumer Financial Protection Bureau or Bureau of Consumer Financial Protection) as printed on each document.

28. Elena Botella, "Why Credit Card Debt Is at an All-Time High, While Unemployment Is at a 50-Year Low," *Forbes.com,* February 13, 2020, https:// www.forbes.com/sites/elenabotella/2020/02/13/credit-card-debt-all-time-high-inflation-recession/.

29. Consumer Financial Protection Bureau, "CARD Act Report."

30. Matty Simmons, *The Credit Card Catastrophe: The 20th Century Phenomenon That Changed The World* (New York: Barricade Books, 1995), 22–26.

31. Simmons, *The Credit Card Catastrophe,* 22.

32. Simmons, *The Credit Card Catastrophe,* 40.

33. Hillel Black, *Buy Now, Pay Later,* Giant Cardinal Edition (New York: Giant Cardinal, June, 1962), 16.

34. For the income cutoffs associated with credit card issuers, see Black, *Buy Now, Pay Later,* 19. For the definition of the "big three" credit card companies, see Trumbull, *Consumer Lending,* 40.

35. David S. Evans and Richard Schmalensee, *Paying with Plastic: The Digital Revolution In Buying and Borrowing,* 2nd ed. (Cambridge, MA: MIT Press, 2005), 56.

36. American Express, "Our Story," accessed March 3, 2016, https://web
.archive.org/web/20160303203130/https://secure.cmax.americanexpress.com
/Internet/GlobalCareers/Staffing/Shared/Files/our_story_3.pdf.

37. Evans and Schmalensee, *Paying with Plastic*, 57.

38. Debt levels reported in 2016 dollars, "SCF+" (see chap. 1, n. 12).

39. For the percent of adults with a credit card in 1989, see Sandra E. Black
and Donald P. Morgan, "Meet the New Borrowers," *Current Issues in Economics
and Finance* 5, no. 3 (1999), https://www.newyorkfed.org/medialibrary/media
/research/current_issues/ci5–3.pdf.

40. *Nigel Morris (Capital One) at Startup Grind Washington DC*, Startup
Grind, May 16, 2013. https://www.startupgrind.com/events/details/startup-grind-
washington-dc-hosted-nigel-morris-cofounder-of-capital-one/.

41. *Nigel Morris (Capital One) at Startup Grind Washington DC*.

42. House Financial Services Committee, *Report Together with Dissenting
Views to Accompany H.R. 627*, U.S. House of Representatives (April 27, 2009),
10, https://www.congress.gov/111/crpt/hrpt88/CRPT-111hrpt88.pdf.

43. Eric K. Clemons and Matt E. Thatcher, "Capital One: Exploiting an Information-Based Strategy" (paper presented at the Thirty-First Annual Hawaii
International Conference on System Sciences, Kohala Coast, HI, 1998).

44. Banking, Housing and Urban Affairs, *Regulatory Requirements and
Industry Practices of Credit Card Issuers*, 109 United States Senate, 124 (2005).

45. Black and Morgan, "Meet the New Borrowers. "

46. Stephen Kleege, "Signet Coming on Strong in Card Wars Series: 4," *American Banker* (New York), April 26, 1993, ProQuest.

47. Saul Hansell, "Spending It; Merchants of Debt," *New York Times*, July 2,
1995, 3, https://www.nytimes.com/1995/07/02/business/spending-it-mechants-
of-debt.html.

48. Sam Zuckerman, "How Providian Misled Card Holders," *San Francisco
Chronicle*, July 25, 2002, ProQuest.

49. Suzanne Koudsi, "Sleazy Credit," *Fortune*, March 4, 2002, https://money
.cnn.com/magazines/fortune/fortune_archive/2002/03/04/319134/index.htm.

50. In 2000, Capital One reported a year-end US managed consumer loan
outstanding balance of $29.5 billion. See Capital One, 2000 Annual Report,
p. 10, from Capital One investor relations website, https://ir-capitalone.gcs-web
.com/static-files/064d6d57-be20–4e40–a850–454ed90ec551. Part of this balance reflects their auto lending business, whose financial results were not separately reported. However, they separately cite (p. 18) that their auto-lending business had tripled in size since they acquired Summit Finance in 1998. At the time
of acquisition, Summit Finance had $260 million in serviced loans; see Bloomb-
erg News, "Company News; Capital One Plans Purchase of Auto Financing Company," *New York Times*, July 17, 1998, National edition, D. This suggests that as
of 2000, the auto lending business had an outstanding loan balance of under

$1 billion, implying that the credit card outstanding balance was at least $27 billion. Capital One reported their end-of-year number of accounts as 33,774,000 (see 2000 Annual Report, p. 10). Providian reported a year-end credit card outstanding balance of $27.1 billion and reported their number of accounts across all lines of business to be 16,270,000. See Providian Financial, Annual Report, p. 39–68, from Mergent Online.

51. Black and Morgan, "Meet the New Borrowers " 1–2.

52. *Nigel Morris (Capital One) at Startup Grind Washington DC.*

53. Thomas Kirchoff (thomas-kirchoff), LinkedIn, https://www.linkedin.com/in/thomas-kirchoff/.

54. Consumer Financial Protection Bureau, *The Consumer Credit Card Market* (December 2017), 200, https://files.consumerfinance.gov/f/documents/cfpb_consumer-credit-card-market-report_2017.pdf.

55. *Nigel Morris (Capital One) at Startup Grind Washington DC.*

56. Charles Fishman, "This Is a Marketing Revolution," *Fast Company,* April 30, 1999, https://www.fastcompany.com/36975/marketing-revolution.

57. Per public earnings statements, Capital One 2017 noninterest expense was $14.19 billion, while 2018 noninterest expense was $14.90 billion. Capital One 2018 net interest income was $22.46 billion, while 2018 net interest income was $22.88 billion.

58. Ellen Cannon, "Getting a New Credit Card? Six Questions to Ask Your Issuer," *Christian Science Monitor,* August 25, 2016, https://www.csmonitor.com/Business/Saving-Money/2016/0825/Getting-a-new-credit-card-Six-questions-to-ask-your-issuer.

59. Bruce Kennedy, "Why Many Millennials Don't Have Credit Cards," *CBS News,* September 8, 2014, https://www.cbsnews.com/news/most-millennials-dont-have-credit-cards-and-prefer-it-that-way/.

CHAPTER 3

1. As of 2018, 44.7 million Americans have student loan debt. See Nigel Chiwaya, "These Five Charts Show How Bad the Student Loan Debt Situation Is," *NBC News,* April 24, 2019, https://www.nbcnews.com/news/us-news/student-loan-statistics-2019-n997836.

2. For data on the total interest and fees collected in the overdraft, short-term installment loan, payday loan, and title loan markets, see Eric Wilson and Eva Wolkowitz, *2017 Financially Underserved Market Size Study,* Center for Financial Services Innovation, December 2017, https://s3.amazonaws.com/cfsi-innovation-files-2018/wp-content/uploads/2017/04/27001546/2017-Market-Size-Report_FINAL_4.pdf.

3. Most news stories describing the total amount of credit card debt reference the Federal Reserve Household Debt and Credit Report, which counts all "outstanding balances" on credit cards, including the balances from customers who pay their credit card bills in full every month. Of the total amount of credit card outstanding balances ($930 billion), 82 percent is estimated to be debt that is revolved month-to-month. See Daniel Grodzicki and Sergei Koulayev, "Sustained Credit Card Borrowing," October 6, 2019, https://doi.org/http://dx.doi .org/10.2139/ssrn.3403045.

4. Megan DeMatteo, "My First Unsecured Credit Card Came With a $20,000 Limit—Here's Why That Is Rare Today," *CNBC Select*, November 25, 2020, https://www.cnbc.com/select/card-act-protections-for-young-people/.

5. "Survey of Household Economics and Decisionmaking," ed. Board of Governors of the Federal Reserve System (2018), https://www.federalreserve.gov /consumerscommunities/shed_data.htm. Responses cited are from question C3 ["Do you currently have any outstanding unpaid credit card debt?"]. There is strong reason to believe that those who responded "yes" are actually carrying an interest-bearing credit card balance, based on cross-referencing responses to a similar question, C4A ["In the past 12 months, how frequently have you carried an unpaid balance on one or more of your credit cards?"] Of those whose response to question C4A was "Never carried an unpaid balance (always pay in full)," only 9 percent answered in response to question C3 that they currently had outstanding unpaid credit card debt.

6. For an analysis of how earnings vary for American workers over their lifespans, see Fatih Guvenen et al., "What Do Data on Millions of U.S. Workers Reveal about Lifecycle Earnings Dynamics?," (working paper, October 15, 2020). https:// nbviewer.jupyter.org/github/serdarozkan/papers/blob/master/GKOS_2020.pdf. One of the paper's authors, Serdar Ozkan, confirmed to me by email that the peak of income for the median worker occurred at forty-eight years of age.

7. "Survey of Household Economics and Decisionmaking," responses to question C3A.

8. Grodzicki and Koulayev, "Sustained Credit Card Borrowing," 8.

9. Tamara Draut and Javier Silva, *Borrowing to Make Ends Meet: The Growth of Credit Card Debt in the '90s*, Demos (2003): 5, https://www.demos.org/sites /default/files/publications/borrowing_to_make_ends_meet.pdf.

10. Minimum payments for credit cards are often calculated as 1 percent of the credit card's balance, plus any fees and finances charged assessed over that period. A minimum payment at that level will always be just high enough to make sure the debt is being "amortized"—for example, if the customer makes payments and no new purchases, their debt amount will go down over time, albeit slowly. For a credit card with a 24 percent APR, the minimum payment then could be 3 percent of the total balance (1%+24%/12 = 1%+2% = 3%). Our

hypothetical person is considered to have $1,283 in disposable income per month, and you would expect a balance of $42,778 to have a minimum payment of $1,283 ($42,778*.03 = $1,283).

11. Richard A. Feinberg, "Credit Cards as Spending Facilitating Stimuli: A Conditioning Interpretation," *Journal of Consumer Research* 13 (December 1986), 348–356. See also Elizabeth C. Hirschman, "Differences in Consumer Purchase Behavior by Credit Card Payment System," *Journal of Consumer Research* 6 (June 1979), 58–66.

12. Scott Schuh, Oz Shy, and Joanna Stavins, "Who Gains and Who Loses from Credit Card Payments? Theory and Calibrations," Research Department Public Policy Discussion Papers, 2010 No. 10–3, Federal Reserve Bank of Boston, August 2010, https://www.bostonfed.org/publications/public-policy-discussion-paper/2010/who-gains-and-who-loses-from-credit-card-payments-theory-and-calibrations.aspx.

13. Jud Linville, Credit Suisse Financial Services Forum, February 12, 2014, https://www.citigroup.com/citi/investor/quarterly/2014/tr140212a.pdf?ieNocache = 271.

14. Jennifer Brozic, "5 Best Same Day Loans of 2021," *Credit Karma,* updated March 5, 2021, https://www.creditkarma.com/personal-loans/i/same-day-loans.

15. Megan Leonhardt, "Nearly 25% of Americans Are Going into Debt Trying to Pay for Necessities Like Food," *CNBC.com,* May 24, 2019, https://www.cnbc.com/2019/05/23/nearly-25-percent-of-americans-are-going-into-debt-trying-to-pay-for-necessities.html.

16. "Poll: Few Americans with Credit Card Debt Willing to cut Back Luxury Spending," creditcards.com, updated July 11, 2019, https://www.creditcards.com/credit-card-news/luxury-spending-poll/.

17. Bloomberg, "Why Millennials Are Ditching Credit Cards," *Fortune,* February 27, 2018, https://fortune.com/2018/02/27/why-millennials-are-ditching-credit-cards/.

18. For information about Capital One's "low and grow" strategy see "Review: Journey Student Rewards from Capital One," Magnify Money, updated June 5, 2017,https://web.archive.org/web/20200804111915/https://www.magnifymoney.com/blog/reviews/capital-one-journey-student-review743336894/. Lending tree review does not discuss the "low and grow" strategy as referenced in the text. For information about Capital One credit limits starting at $300 or $500, see customer user reviews published by WalletHub and Credit Karma: "Capital One® Platinum Credit Card," *WalletHub,* https://wallethub.com/d/capital-one-platinum-83c/; "Overall Card Rating," *Credit Karma,* https://www.creditkarma.com/reviews/credit-card/single/id/CCCapitalOne1009.

19. "Capital One Financial (COF) Q2 2020 Earnings Call Transcript," Motley Fool, updated July 21, 2020, https://www.fool.com/earnings/call-transcripts/2020/07/22/capital-one-financial-cof-q2-2020-earnings-call-tr.aspx.

20. Shoshanna Zuboff, *The Age of Surveillance Capitalism: The Fight for a Human Future at the New Frontier of Power* (New York: PublicAffairs, 2019), 302–303.

21. Scott Fulford and Scott Schuh, "Consumer Revolving Credit and Debt over the Life Cycle and Business Cycle," Working Paper, no. 15–17 (2015): 3, https://www.bostonfed.org/publications/research-department-working-paper/2015/consumer-revolving-credit-and-debt-over-the-life-cycle-and-business-cycle.aspx.

22. Fulford and Schuh, "Consumer Revolving Credit and Debt over the Life Cycle and Business Cycle," 4.

23. M. M. Hetherington and P. Blundell-Birtill, "The Portion Size Effect and Overconsumption—Towards Downsizing Solutions for Children and Adolescents," *Nutrition Bulletin* 43, no. 1 (March 2018), https://onlinelibrary.wiley.com/doi/full/10.1111/nbu.12307.

24. "The High Cost of Descending into Drug-Related Debt," creditcards.com, 2012, https://web.archive.org/web/20201018072847/https://www.creditcards.com/credit-card-news/addiction-substance-abuse-financial-disaster-1264/.

25. Fulford and Schuh, "Consumer Revolving Credit and Debt over the Life Cycle and Business Cycle," 48.

26. "SCF+" (see chap. 1, n. 12). In 2016, those with a household income at or below the 50th percentile held 26 percent of all revolving credit card debt.

27. Hooman Estelami and Donald R. Lehmann, "The Impact of Research Design on Consumer Price Recall Accuracy: An Integrative Review," *Journal of the Academy of Marketing Science* 29, no. 1 (2001): 36–49.

28. Claire Kramer-Mills, Rebecca Landau, Joelle Scally, *The State of Low Income America: Credit Access and Debt Payments* (New York: New York Federal Reserve, November 2020), https://www.newyorkfed.org/medialibrary/media/outreach-and-education/community-development/the-state-of-low-income-america-credit-access-debt-payment.

29. For context on the credit card segments targeted by various credit card issuers see Andrew R. Johnson, "Card Issuers Circling Subprime Borrowers Again," *MarketWatch*, October 11, 2011, https://www.marketwatch.com/story/card-issuers-circling-subprime-borrowers-again-2011-10-11; and Elena Botella, "Why Ally Bank Is Paying $2.6 Billion to Buy a Bank You've Never Heard Of," *Forbes.com*, February 24, 2020, https://www.forbes.com/sites/elenabotella/2020/02/24/ally-bank-merrick-cardworks-subprime/. Another indication of the consumer segments targeted by various companies shows up in who they are marketing credit cards to on various affiliate advertising sites. As of April 2021, credit card companies advertising on Credit Karma in the "fair credit" or "bad credit" category included Credit One, Celtic Bank and Merrick Bank (among others), while credit card companies advertising only in the "excellent credit" or "good credit" categories included Bank of America, Chase, Citi, and Wells Fargo. Capital One did not advertise on Credit Karma on April 9, 2021. As of December

2019, credit card companies advertising on Credit Karma in the "fair credit" or "bad credit" category included Merrick Bank, Capital One, Citi, and Celtic Bank (among others). Most credit card issuers do not publish the percentage of their loan balances or customers with subprime credit scores, but the percent of subprime customers is strongly related to the percent of customers who are "delinquent" or past due in any month, which most issuers publish to investors. By this measure, as of 2018, Capital One skewed the most subprime of major credit card issuers, followed by Bank of America, Citi, and Discover, who had similar delinquency rates. Delinquency rates at JPMorgan Chase were lower still, followed by American Express, whose delinquency rate was roughly half of the level of Capital One's. See Ventakesh Iyer, "Delinquencies Show Rising Trend at Major Card Issuers in September," *S&P Global Market Intelligence,* October 26, 2018, https://www.spglobal.com/marketintelligence/en/news-insights/trending/jkzpci1hrwxgjbn_hpydkg2.

30. Song Han, Benjamin J. Keys, and Geng Li, "Credit Supply to Personal Bankruptcy Filers: Evidence from Credit Card Mailings," Finance and Economics Discussion Series 2011–29, Federal Reserve Board, Washington, DC, May 2011, https://www.federalreserve.gov/pubs/feds/2011/201129/index.html.

31. Malcolm Gay, "White Flight and White Power in St. Louis," *TIME,* August 13, 2014, https://time.com/3107729/michael-brown-shooting-ferguson-missouri-white-flight/.

32. Joseph Shapiro, "In Ferguson, Court Fines and Fees Fuel Anger," *NPR,* August 25, 2014, https://www.npr.org/2014/08/25/343143937/in-ferguson-court-fines-and-fees-fuel-anger.

33. Abbye Atkinson, "Consumer Bankruptcy, Nondischargeability, and Penal Debt," *Vanderbilt Law Review* 70, no. 3 (April 2017): 920, https://scholarship.law.vanderbilt.edu/vlr/vol70/iss3/3.

34. Alanna McCargo and Jung Hyun Choi, *Closing the Gaps: Building Black Wealth through Homeownership,* (New York: Urban Institute, updated December 2020): 7, https://www.urban.org/sites/default/files/publication/103267/closing-the-gaps-building-black-wealth-through-homeownership_1.pdf.

35. William H. Frey, *Even as Metropolitan Areas Diversify, White Americans Still Live in Mostly White Neighborhoods* (Washington, DC: Brookings, March 23, 2020), https://www.brookings.edu/research/even-as-metropolitan-areas-diversify-white-americans-still-live-in-mostly-white-neighborhoods/.

36. Simon Firestone, "Race, Ethnicity, and Credit Card Marketing," *Journal of Money, Credit and Banking* 46, no. 6 (September 2014): 1205–1224, https://onlinelibrary.wiley.com/doi/abs/10.1111/jmcb.12138.

37. Catherine Ruetschlin and Dedrick Asante-Muhammad, *The Challenge of Credit Card Debt for the African American Middle Class,* (Demos; NAACP, December 2013): 9, https://www.demos.org/sites/default/files/publications/CreditCardDebt-Demos_NAACP_0.pdf.

38. The Center Square, "By the Numbers: Hamtramck Ranks the Poorest of Michigan Towns," *The Center Square,* July 6, 2019, https://www.thecentersquare .com/michigan/by-the-numbers-hamtramck-ranks-the-poorest-of-michigan-towns/article_8386dab4–9f45–11e9–9202–470d958e07e7.html.

39. Sheila D. Ards et al., "Bad Credit and Intergroup Differences in Loan Denial Rates," *Review of Black Political Economy* 24 no. 1–2 (2015); Monica Garcia-Perez, Sarah Elizabeth Gaither, and William Darity Jr., *Baltimore Study: Credit Scores,* (Washington, DC: Washington Center for Economic Growth, March 4, 2020): 8, https://equitablegrowth.org/wp-content/uploads/2020/03/030420-WP-Credit-Scores-Garci%CC%81a-Pe%CC%81rez-Gaither-and-Darity.pdf.

40. "Survey of Household Economics and Decisionmaking," ed. Board of Governors of the Federal Reserve System (2018).

41. "SCF+." Those with no credit card debt are included in the mean—for example, the mean is the average of zero and nonzero values, reflecting those with and without debt. Respondents to the Survey of Consumer Finances survey appear to underreport their levels of debt, however, the relative differences between groups are informative.

42. "Survey of Household Economics and Decisionmaking," ed. Board of Governors of the Federal Reserve System (2018).

43. For an example of where this argument was made, see Ryan M. Goodstein et al., "What Accounts for Racial and Ethnic Differences in Credit Use?" FDIC Division of Depositor & Consumer Protection Working Paper No. 2018–01, Federal Deposit Insurance Corporation, Washington, DC, July 2018. http://dx.doi .org/10.2139/ssrn.3220050; percent of adults with credit card debt from "Survey of Household Economics and Decisionmaking," ed. Board of Governors of the Federal Reserve System (2018).

44. Bruce Bartlett, "The Whiners Who Earn $200,000 and Complain They're Broke," *New Republic,* July 20, 2020, https://newrepublic.com/article/158555 /whiners-earn-200000-complain-theyre-broke.

45. See Mischel, Walter, Yuichi Shoda, and Philip K. Peake, "The Nature of Adolescent Competencies Predicted by Preschool Delay of Gratification," *Journal of Personality and Social Psychology* 54, no. 4 (1988): 687–696, https://doi .org/10.1037/0022–3514.54.4.687. There are other, earlier studies using a similar experimental design, reaching similar conclusions, using other rewards like cookies, pretzels, or candy.

46. Scott Fulford and Scott Schuh, "Credit Card Utilization and Consumption over the Life Cycle and Business Cycle," Federal Reserve Bank of Boston Research Department Working Paper 2017 Series, 17: 4, September 2011, https://www .bostonfed.org/publications/research-department-working-paper/2017/credit-card-utilization-and-consumption-over-the-life-cycle-and-business-cycle.aspx.

47. Theresa Kuchler, "Sticking to Your Plan: Hyperbolic Discounting and Credit Card Debt Paydown," SIEPR Discussion Paper No. 12–025, Stanford

Institute for Economic Policy Research, Stanford, CA, March 14, 2013, https://web.archive.org/web/20200709194000/https://siepr.stanford.edu/sites/default/files/publications/TKuchler_Sticking_to_Your_Plan_3.pdf.

48. David Brooks, "Marshmallows and Public Policy," *New York Times*, May 7, 2006, https://www.nytimes.com/2006/05/07/opinion/07brooks.html.

49. Sam Stein, "The Scientist Who Taught Cookie Monster Self-Control Has a Warning for Congress," *HuffPost*, updated September 18, 2015, https://www.huffpost.com/entry/marshmallow-test-science-funding_n_55fc2a1ee4b00310edf6b4d3.

50. Tyler W. Watts, Greg J. Duncan, and Haonan Quan, "Revisiting the Marshmallow Test: A Conceptual Replication Investigating Links between Early Delay of Gratification and Later Outcomes," *Psychological Science* 29, no. 7 (May 25, 2018), https://doi.org/10.1177/0956797618761661.

51. *Consumer Reports* and *Parents* magazine both indicate that the use of a second-hand crib or car seat may create a safety hazard. See Are Secondhand Car Seats Safe?," *Consumer Reports*, January 28, 2017, https://www.consumerreports.org/car-seats/are-secondhand-car-seats-safe/; and Andrea Cooley, "Baby Essentials That Are OK to Buy Used," *Parents*, https://www.parents.com/baby/gear/registries-buying-guides/buying-baby-gear-used/.

52. WealthSimple, "Debt: A Love Story," WealthSimple Magazine, November 5, 2018, https://www.wealthsimple.com/en-us/magazine/couple-debt.

53. AnnaMaria Andriotis, "Banks Left to Guess on Credit Decisions," *Wall Street Journal*, June 30, 2020, Eastern Edition.

54. Erica Sandberg, "Loan Forbearance: How to Know If It's Right for You," Experian, October 29, 2019, https://www.experian.com/blogs/ask-experian/what-is-loan-forbearance/.

55. Paul Kiel, "Unseen Toll: Wages of Millions Seized to Pay Past Debts," *ProPublica*, September 15, 2014, https://www.propublica.org/article/unseen-toll-wages-of-millions-seized-to-pay-past-debts.

56. Jonathan Morduch and Rachel Schneider, *The Financial Diaries: How American Families Cope in a World of Uncertainty*, (Princeton, NJ: Princeton University Press, 2017).

57. "Non-Housing Debt Balance," ed. Equifax Federal Reserve Bank of New York Consumer Credit Panel, Household Debt and Credit Report (Federal Reserve Bank of New York), https://www.newyorkfed.org/microeconomics/hhdc.html.

58. Jeff Larrimore, "Holiday Spending and Financing Decisions in the 2015 Survey of Household Economics and Decisionmaking," FEDS Notes, Federal Reserve Board of Governors, Washington, DC, December 1, 2019, https://doi.org/10.17016/2380-7172.1866.

59. Louis DeNicola, "More Than 50% of Parents Go into Unnecessary Debt for Their Kids," Credit Karma, August 21, 2018, https://www.creditkarma.com/insights/i/more-than-50-percent-parents-unnecessary-debt-for-kids.

60. Angelia Littwin, "Beyond Usury: A Study of Credit-Card Use and Preference among Low-Income Consumers," *Texas Law Review* 86, no. 3 (February 2008).

61. Anuj K. Shah and Jens Ludwig, "Option Awareness: The Psychology of What We Consider," *American Economic Review* 106, no. 5 (2016), https://doi .org/10.1257/aer.p20161098.

62. Fran R. Schumer, "Downward Mobility: You Thought You'd Live Better Than Your Parents Did. Wrong.," *New York*, August 16, 1982, https://nymag .com/news/features/48652/.

63. "Media Kit," Ramsey Solutions, https://www.ramseysolutions.com/company /newsroom/media-kit.

64. Dave Ramsey, *The Money Answer Book: Quick Answers to Everyday Financial Questions* (Nashville: Thomas Nelson, 2010), loc. 57 of 1559, Kindle.

65. See Lisa Fu, "Debt-Conscious Millennials Are a Threat to Credit Cards," *Bloomberg*, February 27, 2018, https://www.bloomberg.com/news/articles /2018–02–27/debt-conscious-millennials-ditch-credit-cards-threaten-industry. See also Sarah Whitten, "Debt-Averse Millennials Steer Clear of Credit Cards," *CNBC.com*, September 8, 2014, https://www.cnbc.com/2014/09/05/debt-averse-millennials-steer-clear-of-credit-cards.html.

66. H. E. Hershfield, "The Self over Time," *Current Opinion in Psychology* 26 (Apr 2019), https://doi.org/10.1016/j.copsyc.2018.06.004.

67. Stanford University, "The Vividness of Your Future Self: Using Immersive Virtual Reality to Increase Retirement Saving," https://healthpolicy.fsi.stanford .edu/research/the_vividness_of_your_future_self_using_immersive_virtual_ reality_to_increase_retirement_saving.

68. Paul Kiel and Annie Waldman, "The Burden of Debt on Black America," *The Atlantic*, October 9, 2015, https://www.theatlantic.com/business/archive /2015/10/debt-black-families/409756/.

CHAPTER 4

1. See Mark R. Rank and Thomas A. Hirschl, "The Likelihood of Experiencing Relative Poverty over the Life Course," *PLoS ONE* (2015), https://doi.org /https://doi.org/10.1371/journal.pone.0133513. See also Melissa Kollar, Jessica Semega, John Creamer, Abinash Mohanty, *Income and Poverty in the United States: 2018*, United States Census Bureau (2019), https://www.census.gov/content /dam/Census/library/publications/2019/demo/p60–266.pdf.

2. Lauren Bauer, "The COVID-19 Crisis Has Already Left Too Many Children Hungry in America," *Brookings Institution*, May 6, 2020, https://www .brookings.edu/blog/up-front/2020/05/06/the-covid-19-crisis-has-already-left-too-many-children-hungry-in-america/.

3. "Capital One Financial Corp (COF) Q1 2020 Earnings Call Transcript," Motley Fool, 2020, https://www.fool.com/earnings/call-transcripts/2020/04/23/capital-one-financial-corp-cof-q1-2020-earnings-ca.aspx.

4. Capital One, 2020 Q2 Earnings Release Presentation, p. 10, Capital One Investor Relations, https://ir-capitalone.gcs-web.com/static-files/90f1a42b-0a37-4507-8557-c0b98caeda70.

5. JPMorgan Chase, 2Q20 Earnings Presentation, p. 10, JPMorgan Chase & Co. Investor Relations, July 14, 2020, https://www.jpmorganchase.com/content/dam/jpmc/jpmorgan-chase-and-co/investor-relations/documents/quarterly-earnings/2020/2nd-quarter/2q20-earnings-presentation.pdf; Bank of America, 2Q20 Financial Results Presentation, p. 3, Bank of America Investor Relations, https://d1io3yog0oux5.cloudfront.net/_87667ddf946046aafb55746bac852609/bankofamerica/db/806/7018/earnings_release/2Q20+Earnings.pdf.

6. "Capital One Financial (COF) Q2 2020 Earnings Call Transcript," Motley Fool, updated July 21, 2020, https://www.fool.com/earnings/call-transcripts/2020/07/22/capital-one-financial-cof-q2-2020-earnings-call-tr.aspx.

7. Matthew Dalton and AnnaMaria Andriotis, "Debt on Credit Cards Falls Amid Pandemic," *Wall Street Journal* (New York), August 3, 2020, Eastern edition.

8. Meta Brown et al., "The Financial Crisis at the Kitchen Table: Trends in Household Debt and Credit," *Current Issues in Economics and Finance* 19, no. 2 (2013), https://www.newyorkfed.org/medialibrary/media/research/current_issues/ci19-2.pdf.

9. Peter Ganong and Pascal Noel, "Consumer Spending during Unemployment: Positive and Normative Implications," *American Economic Review* 109, no. 7 (2019), https://doi.org/10.1257/aer.20170537.

10. For a discussion on the range of estimates for what percentage of unemployed Americans borrow, see Kyle Herkenhoff, Gordon Phillips, and Ethan Cohen-Cole, "How Credit Constraints Impact Job Finding Rates, Sorting & Aggregate Output" (January 20, 2019), 4, http://faculty.tuck.dartmouth.edu/images/uploads/faculty/gordon-phillips/credit_access_job_finding.pdf. For the percentage of Americans who can cover an unexpected expense, see Board of Governors of the Federal Reserve System, *Report on the Economic Well-Being of U.S. Households in 2018* (Washington, DC, May 2019), https://www.federalreserve.gov/publications/files/2018-report-economic-well-being-us-households-201905.pdf.

11. See Scott Fulford and Scott Schuh, "Credit Card Utilization and Consumption over the Life Cycle and Business Cycle," Federal Reserve Bank of Boston Research Department Working Paper 2017 Series, 17: 4, September 2011, https://www.bostonfed.org/publications/research-department-working-paper/2017/credit-card-utilization-and-consumption-over-the-life-cycle-and-business-cycle.aspx. Additional research makes it clear that the de-leveraging wasn't primarily due to

non-performing debts being written off by issuers. See Brown et al., "The Financial Crisis at the Kitchen Table."

12. Allison Cole, "Do Consumers Rely More Heavily on Credit Cards While Unemployed?" Research Data Reports No. 16–06, Federal Reserve Bank of Boston, December 20, 2016, https://www.frbatlanta.org/-/media/documents/banking/consumer-payments/research-data-reports/2016/do-consumers-rely-more-heavily-on-credit-cards-while-unemployed/rdr1606.pdf.

13. Zachary Bethune, "Consumer Credit, Unemployment, and Aggregate Labor Market Dynamics" (working paper, December 2017), https://drive.google.com/file/d/1Tvn5i3v22TL8U6p1kCI6z-Jw4nCLP9au/view.

14. Email from Zachary Bethune to Elena Botella, July 24, 2020.

15. Tami Luhby, "More Than 50% of US Adults Live in Households That Lost Income in Pandemic," *CNN*, updated July 30, 2020, https://www.cnn.com/2020/07/30/politics/lost-income-jobs-covid-congress/index.html.

16. Atif Mian and Amir Sufi, *House of Debt: How They (and You) Caused the Great Recession, and How We Can Prevent It from Happening Again* (Chicago: The University of Chicago Press, 2014), 6.

17. Mian and Sufi, *House of Debt*, 9.

18. "Capital One Financial Corp (COF) Q1 2020 Earnings Call Transcript."

19. Fatih Guvenen et al., "What Do Data on Millions of U.S. Workers Reveal about Lifecycle Earnings Dynamics?," (working paper, October 15, 2020), https://nbviewer.jupyter.org/github/serdarozkan/papers/blob/master/GKOS_2020.pdf.

20. Consumer Financial Protection Bureau, *The Consumer Credit Card Market* (December 2015), 13–14, https://files.consumerfinance.gov/f/201512_cfpb_report-the-consumer-credit-card-market.pdf.

21. Joe Leydon, "Maxed Out," *Variety*, March 21, 2006, https://variety.com/2006/film/reviews/maxed-out-1200517549/.

22. "Do Credit Card Laws Not Value Homemakers?," *NPR*, May 22, 2012, https://www.npr.org/2012/05/22/153283424/do-credit-card-laws-not-value-homemakers; Herb Weisbaum, "Credit-Card Rules Get Easier for Stay-Home Partners," *NBC News*, May 8, 2013, https://www.cnbc.com/id/100720709; Blake Ellis, "Stay-at-Home Mom Fights New Credit Card Rule," *CNN Money*, May 16, 2012, https://money.cnn.com/2012/05/16/pf/credit-cards-stay-at-home-moms/index.htm.

23. Loren Berlin, "Holly McCall, Stay-at-Home Mom, Challenges Credit Card Rules, But Questions Persist," *HuffPost*, May 21, 2012, https://www.huffpost.com/entry/holly-mccall-credit-card-rules_n_1528395.

24. "Technology: New Power for the People," *Roll Call*, updated June 7, 2012, https://www.rollcall.com/2012/06/07/technology-new-power-for-the-people/.

25. Berlin, "Holly McCall."

26. Richard Cordray, *Watchdog: How Protecting Consumers Can Save Our Families, Our Economy, and Our Democracy* (New York: Oxford University Press, 2020), 49.

CHAPTER 5

1. Rick Brooks, "Post Office Plan Could Produce More Junk Mail," *Wall Street Journal*, April 3, 2003, Eastern edition, ProQuest.

2. For data on the number of credit card solicitations sent across time, see "Direct Mail Is Far from Dead for Most Issuers," Acxiom, updated March 1, 2019, https://www.acxiom.com/blog/direct-mail-is-far-from-dead-for-most-credit-card-issuers/.

3. Bureau of Consumer Financial Protection, *The Consumer Credit Card Market* (2019), 80, https://files.consumerfinance.gov/f/documents/cfpb_consumer-credit-card-market-report_2019.pdf.

4. Credit One Bank, "Credit One Bank Launches New Cash Back Rewards Card Backed by the American Express Network," News Release, October 2, 2019, https://newsroom.creditonebank.com/2019-10-02-Credit-One-Bank-Launches-New-Cash-Back-Rewards-Card-Backed-by-the-American-Express-Network; "Charles Schwab," https://www.aboutschwab.com/charles-schwab.

5. Bureau of Consumer Financial Protection, *The Consumer Credit Card Market* (December 2015), 103, https://files.consumerfinance.gov/f/201512_cfpb_report-the-consumer-credit-card-market.pdf.

6. Bureau of Consumer Financial Protection, The Consumer Credit Card Market (2019), 84.

7. Kenneth P. Breevort, Robert B. Avery, and Glenn B. Canner, "Credit Where None Is Due? Authorized-User Account Status and Piggybacking Credit," *Journal of Consumer Affairs* 47, no. 3 (Fall 2013):518–547, https://doi.org/10.1111/joca.12020.

8. For a reference point for subprime first-payment default rates, see Elevate, 2018 Annual Report, pp. 88–110, Elevate Investor Relations, https://s23.q4cdn.com/490591927/files/doc_financials/2019/ar/Annual-Report-2018.pdf. See also Sijia Wang, "Default Risks in Marketplace Lending" (PhD diss., Kent State University, 2020), 84, http://rave.ohiolink.edu/etdc/view?acc_num=kent1583508817334501; Allen Taylor, "Using AI to Improve Underwriting," Lending Times, March 13, 2017, https://lending-times.com/2017/03/13/using-ai-to-improve-underwriting/.

9. Stefania Albanesi and Domonkos F. Vamossy, "Predicting Consumer Default: A Deep Learning Approach," National Bureau of Economic Research Working Paper Series No. 26165, August 2019, https://doi.org/10.3386/w26165.

10. "Capital One Financial (COF) Q2 2020 Earnings Call Transcript," Motley Fool, July 21, 2020, https://www.fool.com/earnings/call-transcripts/2020/07/22/capital-one-financial-cof-q2-2020-earnings-call-tr.aspx.

11. "Opioid Overdose Crisis," National Institute on Drug Abuse, updated May 27, 2020, https://www.drugabuse.gov/drug-topics/opioids/opioid-overdose-crisis.

12. Owen Amos, "Why Opioids Are Such an American Problem," *BBC News*, October 25, 2017, https://www.bbc.com/news/world-us-canada-41701718.

13. Brian Goldstone, "The Pain Refugees," *Harper's Magazine*, April 2018, https://harpers.org/archive/2018/04/the-pain-refugees/.

14. Bureau of Consumer Financial Protection, The Consumer Credit Card Market (2019), 67–68.

15. The late fee wasn't literally the only fee our credit cards had. There was, for example, still a fee for taking out cash advances, and a fee if you made a payment that was subsequently returned. I did understand why, for the sake of implication, these less common fees might have been glossed over.

16. Mike Munger and Russ Roberts, *Munger on Milk*, podcast audio, EconTalk2013, https://www.econtalk.org/munger-on-milk/.

17. Excerpt from a complaint to the CFPB by a borrower in Virginia on April 12, 2020. The CFPB redacts certain identifying information, in this case the name of the retailer where the consumer purchased the ring, which was referenced several times in her comment. The author has made very minor edits to the comment for readability. The full text of the complaint can be queried from the CFPB Consumer Complaint Database, https://www.consumerfinance.gov /data-research/consumer-complaints/.

18. "Best Buy Credit Card," WalletHub, https://wallethub.com/d/best-buy-credit-card-1449c/; Claire Tsosie and Paul Soucy, "Lowe's Advantage Card Review: A Must-Have for Diehard DIYers," *NerdWallet*, January 31, 2021, https://www.nerdwallet.com/reviews/credit-cards/lowes-advantage; Kimberly Palmer and Paul Soucy, "5 Things to Know about the Home Depot Credit Card," NerdWallet, April 29, 2021, https://www.nerdwallet.com/article/credit-cards /home-depot-credit-card; John S Kiernan, "2021 Amazon Store Card Review," *WalletHub*, June 26, 2020, https://wallethub.com/edu/cc/amazon-store-card-review/25962.

19. Sumit Agarwal et al., "Regulating Consumer Financial Products: Evidence from Credit Cards," *Quarterly Journal of Economics* 130, no. 1 (February 2015): 111–164, https://doi.org/10.1093/qje/qju037.

20. Nathaniel Popper, Michael J. de la Merced, and Ron Lieber, "Intuit Is Expected to Buy Credit Karma in $7 Billion Deal," *New York Times*, updated February 26, 2020, https://www.nytimes.com/2020/02/23/business/credit-karma-intuit-deal.html.

21. Joshua M. Frank, *Predatory Credit Card Lending: Unsafe, Unsound for Consumers and Companies*, Center for Responsible Lending (May 2012), https:// www.responsiblelending.org/credit-cards/research-analysis/Unsafe-Unsound-Report-May-2012.pdf.

22. Andrea Long Chu, *Females* (Brooklyn, NY: Verso, 2019), 25.

23. Hillel Black, *Buy Now, Pay Later* (New York: Giant Cardinal, 1962), 7.

24. James D. Scurlock, *Maxed Out: Hard Times in the Age of Easy Credit* (New York: Scribner, 2007), 98.

25. CompareCards, "Nearly 50 Million Cardholders Had Credit Limits Reduced, Card Closed Involuntarily in Last Month Due to COVID-19 Impact," News Release, May 4, 2020, https://www.prnewswire.com/news-releases /nearly-50-million-cardholders-had-credit-limits-reduced-card-closed-involuntarily-in-last-month-due-to-covid-19-impact-301051973.html.

26. While some purchases can't be made on a credit card, nearly all credit cards allow for cash advances, admittedly, often with a higher interest rate and /or additional fees.

27. Kevin Connor and Matthew Skomarovsky, *The Predators' Creditors*, Public Accountability Initiative (2010), https://public-accountability.org/report /the-predators-creditors/.

28. Stephen Burd, "Which College Will Replace Wash U. as the Least Socioeconomically Diverse in the Country?," *Hechinger Report*, April 8, 2015, https:// hechingerreport.org/which-college-will-replace-wash-u-as-the-least-socioeconomically-diverse-in-the-country/.

29. Jake Meth, "The Tragic Side of Tide Pods," *Fortune*, February 19, 2020, https://fortune.com/longform/tide-pod-poisoning-injuries-epidemic/.

30. Consumer Financial Protection, *The Consumer Credit Card Market* (December 2015), 218.

31. Consumer Financial Protection Bureau, The Consumer Credit Card Market (2019), 236.

32. Lisa Rowan, "Should You Get Amazon's New Credit Card for People with Bad Credit?" *Lifehacker*, June 10, 2019, https://twocents.lifehacker.com /should-you-get-amazons-new-card-for-people-with-bad-cre-1835376164.

33. Consumer Financial Protection Bureau, *Card Act Report* (October 1, 2013), 82, https://files.consumerfinance.gov/f/201309_cfpb_card-act-report.pdf.

34. Jud Linville, Credit Suisse Financial Services Forum, February 12, 2014, https://www.citigroup.com/citi/investor/quarterly/2014/tr140212a.pdf?ieNocache = 271.

35. My description simplifies how revenue and liabilities are recognized for the lay reader who may not be familiar with accounting. See "Revenue Changes for Rewards Programs," BKD CPAs & Advisors, https://www.bkd.com/sites /default/files/2020–03/Revenue-Changes-for-Rewards-Programs.pdf.

36. Alexandria White, "Chase Freedom Flex vs. Chase Freedom Unlimited: Which Is the Best Card?," *CNBC Select*, Updated January 14, 2021, https://www .cnbc.com/select/chase-freedom-flex-vs-chase-freedom-unlimited/; Kelly Dilworth, "Discover 5% Cash Back Calendar," *The Balance*, Updated November 2, 2020, https://www.thebalance.com/discover-5-cash-back-calendar-4776088.

37. Bureau of Consumer Financial Protection, *The Consumer Credit Card Market* (December 2015), 227–236.

38. Paul J. Davies, "Cash Cow Credit Cards May Get Hit by U.K. Bank Regulators; High Cost of Debt Has Led to a Proposal to Curb Credit-Card Charges," *Wall Street Journal*, April 3, 2017, https://www.wsj.com/articles/cash-cow-credit-cards-may-get-hit-by-u-k-bank-regulators-1491223450.

39. James Andrews, "Teacher Told to Pay Half His Wages a Month or His Credit Card Will Be Suspended," *Mirror Money*, January 8, 2020, https://www.mirror.co.uk/money/teacher-told-pay-half-wages-21225739.

40. StepChange, "Record Number of People Contacting Us in 2018," News Release, April 3, 2019, 2019, https://www.stepchange.org/media-centre/press-releases/debt-statistics-2018.aspx; Sue Anderson, "A Year On from New rules, Is Credit Card 'Persistent Debt' Becoming any Less Persistent?," *StepChange Debt Charity, Medium*, August 30, 2019, https://medium.com/@StepChange/a-year-on-from-new-rules-is-credit-card-persistent-debt-becoming-any-less-persistent-6eec8c73c274.

41. Anderson, "A Year on from New Rules."

42. Derin Clark, "FCA Suspends Credit Card Persistent Debt Rules Eue to Concerns of Covid-19 on Finances," *Moneyfacts*, March 19, 2020, https://moneyfacts.co.uk/news/credit-cards/fca-suspends-credit-card-persistent-debt-rules-due-to-concerns-of-covid-19-on-finances/.

43. This example illustrates one of the most common patterns of behavior among United States credit card borrowers. It uses 24 percent as the interest rate, and assumes the borrower *is not* anchored to making the minimum payment, which typically would be closer to $75.

44. Nicole Pedersen-McKinnon, "Your Unused, Emergency Card Limit Now Risks Your Credit Rating," *Sydeny Morning Herald*, February 8, 2018, https://www.smh.com.au/money/borrowing/your-unused-emergency-card-limit-now-risks-your-credit-rating-20180207-h0v8uo.html.

45. Caleb Triscari, "New Laws Will Prevent Banks from Inviting Credit Card Users to Increase Limits," *SmartCompany*, February 16, 2018, https://www.smartcompany.com.au/finance/new-laws-to-prevent-banks-from-inviting-consumers-to-increase-credit-card-limits/.

46. "CG-5 Consent for Increases in Credit Limits," Government of Canada, updated October 2, 2018, https://www.canada.ca/en/financial-consumer-agency/services/industry/commissioner-guidance/guidance-5.html; Financial Conduct Authority, "New Credit Card Rules Introduced by the FCA," News Release, February 27, 2018, https://www.fca.org.uk/news/press-releases/new-credit-card-rules-introduced-fca.

47. Board of Governors of the Federal Reserve System, *Report to the Congress on Reductions of Consumer Credit Limits Based on Certain Information as to Experience or Transactions of the Consumer* (May 2010), 1–3, https://www.federalreserve.gov/boarddocs/rptcongress/creditcard/2009/consumercredit reductions.pdf.

48. Steven Pressman and Robert H. Scott III, "Consumer Debt and Poverty Measurement," *Focus* 27, no. 1 (Summer 2010): 12, https://www.irp.wisc.edu /publications/focus/pdfs/foc271b.pdf.

49. Michelle J. White, "Bankruptcy Reform and Credit Cards," *Journal of Economic Perspectives* 21, no. 4 (Fall 2007): 175, https://pubs.aeaweb.org/doi /pdfplus/10.1257/jep.21.4.175.

50. Lyle Daly, "Personal Bankruptcy Statistics for 2020," *The Ascent* (March 24, 2020), https://www.fool.com/the-ascent/research/personal-bankruptcy-statistics/.

51. Stefania Albanesi and Jaromir Nosal, "Insolvency after the 2005 Bankruptcy Reform," presented at "Household Finance," November 21, 2014, *National Bureau of Economic Research Working Paper Series* No. 24934 (2018): 16, https://doi.org/10.3386/w24934.

52. Albanesi and Nosal, "Insolvency after the 2005 Bankruptcy Reform."

53. Erin El Issa, "Americans' Relationship with Credit Cards: It's Complicated, Survey Reveals," *NerdWallet*, September 16, 2020, https://www .nerdwallet.com/article/credit-cards/americans-relationship-with-credit-cards-its-complicated.

54. Erin El Issa, "Survey: Credit Card Debt and Regret Go Hand in Hand," *NerdWallet*, February 13, 2018, https://www.nerdwallet.com/article/credit-cards /credit-card-debt-psychology-2018.

55. Scott Fulford and Scott Schuh, "Credit Card Utilization and Consumption over the Life Cycle and Business Cycle," Federal Reserve Bank of Boston Research Department Working Paper 2017 Series, 17:4, September 2011, https://www .bostonfed.org/publications/research-department-working-paper/2017/credit-card-utilization-and-consumption-over-the-life-cycle-and-business-cycle.aspx.

56. Scott Schuh, Oz Shy, and Joanna Stavins, "Who Gains and Who Loses from Credit Card Payments? Theory and Calibrations," Research Department Public Policy Discussion Papers, 2010 No. 10–3, Federal Reserve Bank of Boston, August 2010, https://www.bostonfed.org/publications/public-policy-discussion-paper/2010/who-gains-and-who-loses-from-credit-card-payments-theory-and-calibrations.aspx.

57. Jackson Lewis, "Lawmakers Push Back on Swipe Fee Increase," *CSP*, March 9, 2021, https://www.cspdailynews.com/technologyservices/lawmakers-push-back-swipe-fee-increase.

58. Andrew Martin, "Card Fees Pit Retailers against Banks," *New York Times*, July 15, 2009, https://www.nytimes.com/2009/07/16/business/16fees.html; Keith Bradsher, "U.S. Looks to Australia on Credit Card Fees," *New York Times*, November 24, 2009, https://www.nytimes.com/2009/11/25/your-money/credit-and-debit-cards/25card.html.

59. Richard Hunt et al., "Durbin Amendment Is a Failure for Customers: Repeal the Merchant Markup," *The Hill*, October 6, 2016, https://thehill.com

/blogs/congress-blog/economy-budget/283612-durbin-amendment-is-a-failure-for-customers-repeal-the; "Interchange," Consumer Bankers Association, https://www.consumerbankers.com/cba-issues/interchange; Paul Gackle, "The Fight over Interchange Fees," *Frontline*: "The Card Game," *PBS*, November 24, 2009, https://www.pbs.org/wgbh/pages/frontline/creditcards/themes/interchange.html.

60. PR Newswire, "2019 Study on Credit Card Profitability in the United States—Interest Spreads and Credit Quality Set the Course for 2020," January 7, 2020, https://www.prnewswire.com/news-releases/2019-study-on-credit-card-profitability-in-the-united-states---interest-spreads-and-credit-quality-set-the-course-for-2020-300982496.html; Sageworks, "Why Gas Station Profits Are Drying Up," *Inc.*, November 10, 2014, https://www.inc.com/sageworks/running-on-empty-why-private-gas-stations-cant-squeeze-out-a-profit.html; Barbara Bean-Mellinger, "What Is the Profit Margin for a Supermarket?" *Houston Chronicle*, updated November 14, 2018, https://smallbusiness.chron.com/profit-margin-supermarket-22467.html.

61. Lynne Marek, "Mastercard, Visa, Fiserv and Others Band Together as Renewed Battles over Swipe Fees Brew," *Payments Dive*, March 5, 2021, https://www.paymentsdive.com/news/payments-leadership-council-mastercard-visa-american-express-discover-FIS-Fiserv-Global-Payments/596229/.

62. Marek, "Mastercard, Visa, Fiserv and Others"; Brian Riley, "Payment Industry Leadership Council: Tied in at the Top," *Payments Journal*, March 11, 2011, https://www.paymentsjournal.com/payment-industry-leadership-council-tied-in-at-the-top/.

63. Maya Jackson-Randall, "Consumer Bureau's No. 2 to Leave Agency," *Wall Street Journal*, November 13, 2012, https://www.wsj.com/articles/SB100014241278873235510045781169015 65158098.

64. U.S. Department of the Treasury, "Readout: Treasury Deputy Secretary Wally Adeyemo Met with the Payments Leadership Council," April 6, 2021, https://home.treasury.gov/news/press-releases/jy0107.

65. Shoshanna Zuboff, *The Age of Surveillance Capitalism: The Fight for a Human Future at the New Frontier of Power* (New York: PublicAffairs, 2019), 302–303.

66. Mary Zaki, "Heterogenous Responses to Interest Rate Price Disclosures." http://www.terpconnect.umd.edu/~mzaki/papers/Interestrate_heterogeneous.pdf.

67. Marc Hochstein, "Capital One Makes Candid Recruitment Pitch to SxSW Techies," *American Banker* (New York), Mar 17, 2015, ProQuest.

68. Francisca Moreno Schwerter, "Piñera por La Polar: 'Un millón de chilenos fueron abusados, no fueron respetados,'" La Tercera, August 17, 2011, https://www.latercera.com/noticia/pinera-por-la-polar-un-millon-de-chilenos-fueron-abusados-no-fueron-respetados/; Alexei Barrionuevo, "Rise of Consumer Credit

in Chile and Brazil Leads to Big Debts and Lender Abuses," *New York Times*, July 24, 2011, https://www.nytimes.com/2011/07/24/business/global/abuses-by-credit-issuers-in-chile-and-brazil-snare-consumers.html.

69. "Perez (UDI) aboga por 'Sernac' para bancos y financieras: 'hay un abuso al que hay que poner freno,'" Artículo breve, *UPI Chile*, April 7, 2010, Gale.

70. Sheisha Kulkarni, Santiago Truffa, and Gonzalo Iberti, "Removing the Fine Print: Standardization, Disclosure, and Consumer Loan Outcomes" (working paper, 2020): 8–47. https://static1.squarespace.com/static/58b5e6e15016e1efa 0bfd0a5/t/5f2c82053c536a4fed8566a7/1596752397307/DisclosureandDefault+ August.pdf.

71. Kulkarni, Truffa, and Iberti, "Removing the Fine Print," 1–33.

72. Consumer Financial Protection Bureau, *The Consumer Credit Card Market* (December 2017), 200, https://files.consumerfinance.gov/f/documents/cfpb_ consumer-credit-card-market-report_2017.pdf.

CHAPTER 6

1. Information on the changes in prices of TVs, computers, vehicles, and clothing gathered from the following sources: "Have Cars Actually Gotten More Expensive Over Time?," *Washington Post*, updated March 13, 2017, https://www .washingtonpost.com/cars/have-cars-actually-gotten-more-expensive-over-time /2017/03/13/5c5b9d30–081b-11e7-bd19-fd3afa0f7e2a_story.html; "Are TVs Really Cheaper Than Ever? We go Back a few Decades to See," CNET, updated November 23, 2017, https://www.cnet.com/news/are-tvs-really-cheaper-than-ever-we-go-back-a-few-decades-to-see/; Evan Comen, "Check Out How Much a Computer Cost the Year You Were Born," *USA Today*, October 3, 2018, https:// www.usatoday.com/story/tech/2018/06/22/cost-of-a-computer-the-year-you-were-born/36156373/; "Consumer Price Index for All Urban Consumers: Apparel in U.S. City Average," ed. U.S. Bureau of Labor Statistics, Federal Reserve Bank of St. Louis (FRED), October 23, 2020, https://fred.stlouisfed.org/series /CPIAPPSL.

2. According to the Social Security Administration, median net compensation was $16,118 in 1994, and $34,248 in 2019. According to the FDIC, total net operating income for all FDIC insured banks was $52 billion in 1994, and $230 billion in 2019. See "Measures of Central Tendency for Wage Data," Social Security Administration, https://www.ssa.gov/oact/cola/central.html; "Net operating income," ed. FDIC, QBP Time Series Spreadsheets.

3. Bureau of Consumer Financial Protection, *The Consumer Credit Card Market* (2019), 56, https://files.consumerfinance.gov/f/documents/cfpb_consumer-credit-card-market-report_2019.pdf.

4. "Delinquency Rate on Credit Card Loans, All Commercial Banks," ed. Board of Governors of the Federal Reserve System (US) (FRED, https://fred .stlouisfed.org/series/DRCCLACBS.

5. Shailesh Mehta, PBS *Frontline: "The Card Game,"* July 7, 2009, https:// www.pbs.org/wgbh/pages/frontline/creditcards/interviews/mehta.html.

6. FS Card, "FS Card Inc. to Launch Build Card in 2015," news release, October 30, 2014, https://www.globenewswire.com/news-release/2014/10/30/1146686/0 /en/FS-Card-Inc-to-Launch-Build-Card-in-2015.html.

7. Sumit Agarwal et al., "Regulating Consumer Financial Products: Evidence from Credit Cards," *Quarterly Journal of Economics* 130, no. 1 (February 2015): 111–164. https://doi.org/10.1093/qje/qju037.

8. Agarwal et al., "Regulating Consumer Financial Products."

9. Bureau of Transportation Statistics, "First Quarter 2020 U.S. Airline Financial Data," news release, June 15, 2020, https://www.bts.gov/newsroom /first-quarter-2020-us-airline-financial-data.

10. For a reference point on the cost of funds for non-bank credit card lenders, see Business Wire, "Fair Square Financial Completes $300 Million Credit Card Securitization," news release, February 19, 2020, https://www.businesswire .com/news/home/20200219006028/en/CORRECTING-and-REPLACING%C2% A0Fair-Square-Financial-Completes-300-Million-Credit-Card-Securitization.

11. Erin El Issa, "2019 Consumer Credit Card Report," *NerdWallet,* July 31, 2019,https://www.nerdwallet.com/blog/credit-card-data/2019-consumer-credit-card-report/.

12. Daniel Grodzicki and Sergei Koulayev, "Sustained Credit Card Borrowing," October 6, 2019, https://doi.org/http://dx.doi.org/10.2139/ssrn.3403045.

13. Marco Di Maggio and Vincent W. Yao, "FinTech Borrowers: Lax-Screening or Cream-Skimming?" Paper presented at the First New York Fed Research Conference on FinTech, New York, March 22, 2019, https://www.newyorkfed .org/medialibrary/media/research/conference/2019/fintech/Yao_fintech.

14. Michael Moeser, "Why Fintechs—and Snoop Dogg—Are in the $160 Billion Installment Lending Market," *PaymentsSource,* February 19, 2020, https:// www.paymentssource.com/list/why-fintechs-and-snoop-dogg-are-in-the-160-billion-installment-lending-market.

15. The author used Prosper's investor platform to review loans available to be funded on October 14, 2020, whose credit score was between 700 and 719. According to a 2019 report by the CFPB, 53 percent of all adults with a credit score have a score above 720. Bureau of Consumer Financial Protection, *The Consumer Credit Card Market* (2019).

16. Sudheer Chava, Nikhil Paradkar, and Yafei Zhang, "Winners and Losers of Marketplace Lending: Evidence from Borrower Credit Dynamics." Paper presented at the 18th annual Bank Research Conference, FDIC Center for Financial Research, September 7, 2018, https://www.fdic.gov/analysis/cfr/bank-research-

conference/annual-18th/24-paradkar.pdf; Di Maggio and Yao, "FinTech Borrowers," 23–24.

CHAPTER 7

1. Of the $930 billion in outstanding credit card balances, Grodzicki and Koulayev estimate that 82 percent (e.g., $762 billion) is debt revolved month-over-month. See Daniel Grodzicki and Sergei Koulayev, "Sustained Credit Card Borrowing," October 6, 2019, https://doi.org/http://dx.doi.org/10.2139/ssrn.3403045.

2. For an analysis of the level of competition, intensive marketing, and profitability of the credit card industry in the 1990s, see Board of Governors of the Federal Reserve System, *The Profitability of Credit Card Operations of Depository Institutions* (August 1997), https://www.federalreserve.gov/boarddocs/rptcongress/creditcard/1997/default.htm.

3. Kyle F. Herkenhoff and Gajendran Raveendranathan, "Who Bears the Welfare Cost of Monopoly? The Case of the Credit Card Industry," NBER Working Paper 26604, Boston, January 2020, 2, https://www.nber.org/system/files/working_papers/w26604/w26604.pdf.

4. Charles R. Geisst, *Loan Sharks: The Birthday of Predatory Lending* (Washington, DC: Brookings Institution Press, 2016), 119–159.

5. The Consumer Financial Protection Bureau's Office of Research, "Data Point: Credit Card Revolvers," (July 2019), https://files.consumerfinance.gov/f/documents/bcfp_data-point_credit-card-revolvers.pdf.

6. Nick Bourke et al., *Fraud and Abuse Online: Harmful Practices in Internet Payday Lending,* Pew Charitable Trusts (October 2014), 3, https://www.pewtrusts.org/~/media/assets/2014/10/payday-lending-report/fraud_and_abuse_online_harmful_practices_in_internet_payday_lending.pdf.

7. Advance America, at the time, the nation's largest payday lender, was publicly traded until its purchase by Grupo Elektra in 2012. In 2011, Advance America reported $295 million in store-level, non-advertising expenses, a figure which does not include credit losses. They reported 1.3 million distinct customers in 2011, which means the per-customer store level operating expenses total nearly $220 per customer. By comparison, Advance America reported $108 million in "provisions for doubtful accounts." These figures effectively reverse the profit model for credit card lending, where loan losses far exceed operating expenses.

8. Dalié Jiménez and Jonathan Glater, "Student Debt Is a Civil Rights Issue: The Case for Debt Relief and Higher Education Reform," *Harvard Civil Rights—Civil Liberties Law Review* 55, no. 1 (February 4, 2020), https://papers.ssrn.com/sol3/papers.cfm?abstract_id=3475224. Although credit card companies have also offered payment insurance to protect borrowers facing a loss in income, these payment protection programs have often been offered on fraudulent or

predatory terms: see Richard Cordray, *Watchdog: How Protecting Consumers Can Save Our Families, Our Economy, and Our Democracy* (New York: Oxford University Press, 2020), 47–48.

9. After Hurricane Harvey, 90 percent of SBA loan dollars were directed to households, rather than small businesses. See U.S. Small Business Administration, "TX 15274–20 SBA Tops $3 Billion in Disaster Assistance Loans to Businesses and Residents Impacted by Hurricane Harvey," news release, January 3, 2018, https://www.sba.gov/content/tx-15274–20-sba-tops-3-billion-disaster-assistance-loans-businesses-and-residents-impacted.

10. "Physical Damage Loans," Small Business Administration, https://www.sba.gov/funding-programs/disaster-assistance/physical-damage-loans.

11. For the ratio of grants to SBA loans, see *Texas Hurricane Harvey Recovery Guide*, FEMA (August 2018), 2, https://web.archive.org/web/20200726122309/https://www.fema.gov/media-library-data/1535741330175-f46e9a841bb61e-25547685f69bbeccda/1_Year_Texas_Harvey_Recovery_Guide.pdf.

12. U.S. Small Business Administration, *Fact Sheet—Disaster Loans* (May 1, 2020), https://www.sba.gov/sites/default/files/news/SC_16435_Fact_Sheet.pdf.

13. U.S. Small Business Administration, *Fact Sheet—Disaster Loans*.

14. Zach Goldstein, "New Data: Why 800,000 Applicants Were Denied Federal Disaster Assistance Loans," *Center for Public Integrity*, August 27, 2019, https://publicintegrity.org/environment/new-data-reveals-why-800000-applicants-were-denied-federal-disaster-assistance-loans/.

15. Mehrsa Baradaran, "A Short History of Postal Banking," *Slate*, August 8, 2014, https://slate.com/news-and-politics/2014/08/postal-banking-already-worked-in-the-usa-and-it-will-work-again.html.

16. "Public," Bank of North Dakota, https://bnd.nd.gov/public/; Will Peischel, "How a Brief Socialist Takeover in North Dakota Gave residents a Public Bank," The Highlight, *Vox*, October 1, 2019, https://www.vox.com/the-highlight/2019/9/24/20872558/california-north-dakota-public-bank.

17. Committee for a Responsible Budget, "Cory Booker's 'Baby Bonds' Plan," US Budget Watch, December 19, 2019, http://www.crfb.org/blogs/cory-bookers-baby-bonds-plan; Hilary W. Hoynes and Jesse Rothstein, "Universal Basic Income in the US and Advanced Countries," *National Bureau of Economic Research Working Paper Series* No. 25538 (2019), https://doi.org/10.3386/w25538.

18. National Credit Union Administration, *Quarterly Credit Union Data Summary*(2020Q2),https://www.ncua.gov/files/publications/analysis/quarterly-data-summary-2020-Q2.pdf.

19. Nick Bourke and Ardie Hollifield, *Still Waiting: "Unfair or Deceptive" Credit Card Practices Continue as Americans Wait for New Reforms to Take Effect*, Pew Health Group, Pew Charitable Trusts (October 2009), https://www.pewtrusts.org/-/media/legacy/uploadedfiles/wwwpewtrustsorg/reports/credit_cards/pewcreditcardsoct09finalpdf.pdf.

20. Kelly Dilworth, "Low Interest, Plain Vanilla Cards Rare from Major Issuers," creditcards.com, December 15, 2017, https://web.archive.org/web/20210305200632/https://www.creditcards.com/credit-card-news/low-interest-plain-vanilla-cards-rare-major-issuers/.

21. CompareCards, "CompareCards Releases 2018 Credit Card Fee Report," news release, May 28, 2018, https://www.prnewswire.com/news-releases/comparecards-releases-2018-credit-card-fee-report-300655746.html.

22. Experian, *The State of Credit Unions* (2017), 5, https://www.experian.com/assets/credit-unions/reports/cu-state-of-credit-report.pdf.

23. Experian, *The State of Credit Unions*, 3–6.

24. Elena Botella, "Can a Pagan Credit Union Break the Spell of Big Banking?," *The Outline*, September 30, 2019, https://theoutline.com/post/8021/can-a-pagan-credit-union-break-the-spell-of-big-banking.

CHAPTER 8

1. For the number of adults without a checking account or a credit card, see Board of Governors of the Federal Reserve System, *Report on the Economic Well-Being of U.S. Households in 2018* (Washington, DC, January 30, 2020), https://www.federalreserve.gov/publications/files/2018-report-economic-well-being-us-households-201905.pdf. For the number of adults without a credit score, see Kenneth P. Brevoort, Philipp Grimm, and Michelle Kambara, "Data Point: Credit Invisibles," Consumer Financial Protection Bureau, (May 2015), https://files.consumerfinance.gov/f/201505_cfpb_data-point-credit-invisibles.pdf.

2. Nick Bourke et al., *Fraud and Abuse Online: Harmful Practices in Internet Payday Lending,* Pew Charitable Trusts (October 2014), 3, https://www.pewtrusts.org/~/media/assets/2014/10/payday-lending-report/fraud_and_abuse_online_harmful_practices_in_internet_payday_lending.pdf.

3. Brevoort, Grimm, and Kambara, "Data Point: Credit Invisibles," 12.

4. Richard Cordray, *Watchdog: How Protecting Consumers Can Save Our Families, Our Economy, and Our Democracy* (New York: Oxford University Press, 2020), 145.

5. Colin Wilhem, "Big Data vs. the Credit Gap," *Politico*, February 7, 2018, https://www.politico.com/agenda/story/2018/02/07/big-data-credit-gap-000630/.

6. James C. Scott, *Seeing Like a State : How Certain Schemes to Improve the Human Condition Have Failed,* (New Haven: Yale University Press, 1998).

7. Angelia Littwin, "Beyond Usury: A Study of Credit-Card Use and Preference among Low-Income Consumers," *Texas Law Review* 86, no. 3 (February 2008).

8. Tullio Jappelli and Marco Pagano, "Public Credit Information: A European Perspective," in *Credit Reporting Systems and the International Economy,* ed. Margaret J. Miller (Cambridge, MA: MIT Press, 2003), 95–96.

9. Kenneth P. Brevoort and Michelle Kambara, "CFPB Data Point: Becoming Credit Visible," Consumer Financial Protection Bureau, (June 2017), https://files .consumerfinance.gov/f/documents/BecomingCreditVisible_Data_Point_Final .pdf.

10. Tom Parrent and George Haman, *Updated Credit Scoring and the Mortgage Market*, Quantilytic, LLC (Progressive Policy Institute, December 2017), 41, https://www.progressivepolicy.org/wp-content/uploads/2017/12/UpdatedCredit Scoring_2017.pdf.

11. Larry Santucci, "Moving into the Mainstream: Who Graduates from Secured Credit Card Programs?," Federal Reserve Bank of Philadelphia Payment Cards Center Discussion Paper No. 19–2, May 2019, 27, https://doi.org/http:// dx.doi.org/10.21799/frbp.dp.2019.02.

12. Larry Santucci, "The Secured Credit Card Market," Federal Reserve Bank of Philadelphia Payment Cards Center Discussion Paper No. 16–3, November 1, 2016, https://ssrn.com/abstract = 2862961.

13. Santucci, "The Secured Credit Card Market," 20.

14. Santucci, "The Secured Credit Card Market," 25.

15. Consumer Financial Protection Bureau, "Targeting Credit Builder Loans: Insights from a Credit Builder Loan Evaluation," (July 2020), https://files .consumerfinance.gov/f/documents/cfpb_targeting-credit-builder-loans_report_ 2020–07.pdf.

16. Based on offers advertised online on Self.inc on October 28, 2020.

17. National Consumers Law Center et al., "Re: Comments in Response to Request for Information Regarding Use of Alternative Data and Modeling Techniques in the Credit Process, Docket No. CFPB-2017–0005," letter to Monica Jackson, Office of the Executive Secretary of Consumer Financial Protection Bureau, May 19, 2017, https://www.nclc.org/images/pdf/credit_reports/comments-alt-data-may2017.pdf.

18. Brady Porche, "Poll: Women More Prone Than Men to Miss Card Payments," creditcards.com, July 2, 2018, https://www.creditcards.com/credit-card-news /late-payment-survey/.

19. "Message From PD&R Senior Leadership," U.S. Department of Housing and Urban Development, June 11, 2018, https://www.huduser.gov/portal /pdredge/pdr-edge-frm-asst-sec-061118.html.

20. Michael Turner and Patrick Walker, *Potential Impacts of Credit Reporting Public Housing Rental Payment Data*, Office of Policy Development and Research, U.S. Department of Urban Development (October 2019), https://www .huduser.gov/portal/sites/default/files/pdf/Potential-Impacts-of-Credit-Reporting.pdf.

21. Committee on Financial Services, *Examining the Use of Alternative Data in Underwriting and Credit Scoring to Expand Access to Credit*, U.S. House of Representatives, 3 (2019).

CHAPTER 9

1. "Capital One Financial (COF) Q1 2021 Earnings Call Transcript," *Motley Fool*, April 27, 2021, https://www.fool.com/earnings/call-transcripts/2021/04/27/capital-one-financial-cof-q1-2021-earnings-call-tr/.

2. "Synchrony Financial (SYF) Q1 2021 Earnings Call Transcript," *Motley Fool*, April 27, 2021, https://www.fool.com/earnings/call-transcripts/2021/04/27/synchrony-financial-syf-q1-2021-earnings-call-tran/.

3. "Discover Financial Services (DFS) Q4 2020 Earnings Call Transcript," *Motley Fool*, January 21, 2021, https://www.fool.com/earnings/call-transcripts/2021/01/21/discover-financial-services-dfs-q4-2020-earnings-c/.

4. Credit Karma, "Credit Karma Tax Now Helps to Put Your Refund to Work," press release, February 4, 2020, https://www.creditkarma.com/pressreleases#:~:text = in%20the%20U.S.-,About%20Credit%20Karma,half%20of%20all%20U.S.%20millennials.

5. Stacy Wakefield, "A New Business Model in Credit Score—With Stacy Wakefield," interview by Michael Cyger, Domain Sherpa, September 3, 2012, https://www.domainsherpa.com/stacy-wakefield-creditkarma-interview/.

6. "Rates and Notices," LendUp, https://www.lendup.com/rates-and-notices.

7. Sasha Orloff, "Google Is Right to Ban Short-Term Loan Ads, But I Won't Stop Offering Short-Term Loans. Here's Why." GV Library (blog,), p. 34, *Medium*, May 19, 2016, https://library.gv.com/google-is-right-to-ban-short-term-loan-ads-but-i-wont-stop-offering-short-term-loans-here-s-why-3f386e6fbeba#.6q3odrqpi. To calculate a rough percentage of those generally excluded from bank credit available at interest rates below 36 percent, I took the percentage of US consumers with credit scores between under 579, as well those with a thin or stale credit file, although as discussed in the previous chapter, those with thin or stale credit files are treated very differently by lenders depending on whether or not negative information like past bankruptcies appear on their credit files. Roughly one in three of those with thin or stale credit files would have relatively easy access to credit. For distribution of US adults by credit scores, see Bureau of Consumer Financial Protection, The Consumer Credit Card Market (2019), 35, https://files.consumerfinance.gov/f/documents/cfpb_consumer-credit-card-market-report_2019.pdf.

8. Dennis R. Shaughnessy, "The Public Capital Markets and Etsy and Warby Parker," SEI at Northeastern (blog), Northeastern University, October 10, 2018, https://www.northeastern.edu/sei/2018/10/the-public-capital-markets-and-etsy-and-warby-parker/.

9. Atif Mian, Ludwig Straub, and Amir Sufi, "The Saving Glut of the Rich," (working paper, February 2021), https://scholar.harvard.edu/files/straub/files/mss_richsavingglut.pdf.

10. Abbye Atkinson, "Commodifying Marginalization," *Duke Law Journal* 71, no. 4 (January 2022): 773–844, https://scholarship.law.duke.edu/dlj/vol71 /iss4/1.

11. Chrystin Ondersma, "Borrowing Equality: Dispossession and the Need for an Abolitionist Approach to Survival Debt," *Columbia Law Review* 120 no. 8 (December 2020): 299–320.

12. Karl Marx, *Capital Volume I,* trans. Ben Fowkes (New York: Penguin Books, 1990), 92.

Index

Founded in 1893,
UNIVERSITY OF CALIFORNIA PRESS
publishes bold, progressive books and journals
on topics in the arts, humanities, social sciences,
and natural sciences—with a focus on social
justice issues—that inspire thought and action
among readers worldwide.

The UC PRESS FOUNDATION
raises funds to uphold the press's vital role
as an independent, nonprofit publisher, and
receives philanthropic support from a wide
range of individuals and institutions—and from
committed readers like you. To learn more, visit
ucpress.edu/supportus.